D0105382

York County
Community College

In Memory of
Clara E. Merrifield

☰ TALKING

PICTURES ☰

≡ TALKING

PICTURES ≡

WITH THE
PEOPLE WHO
MADE THEM

**Sylvia Shorris and
Marion Abbott Bundy**

**With a Foreword by
Robert Altman**

The New Press   New York

For Earl Shorris

and Stephen Bundy

Photo of Lester Cole on p. 84 courtesy of Jo Dee Hutchason.
Photo of Frank McCarthy on p. 58 courtesy of Rupert Allan.
All other photographs courtesy of the subject of the interview.

Copyright © 1994 by Sylvia Shorris and Marion Abbott Bundy

Published in the United States by The New Press, New York
Distributed by W. W. Norton & Company, Inc.,
500 Fifth Avenue, New York, NY 10110

Library of Congress Cataloging-in-Publication Data

Talking pictures : with the people who made them /
   Sylvia Shorris and Marion Abbott Bundy.
         p. cm.
      Includes bibliographical references.
      ISBN 1-56584-175-1
      1. Motion pictures—California—Los Angeles—Biography.
   2. Motion picture industry—California—Los Angeles—History.
   I. Shorris, Sylvia. II. Bundy, Marion Abbott.
   PN1993.5.U65T26   1994
   791.43'09794'94—dc20   94-1487
                                                                 CIP

Book design by Acme Art, Inc.

Established in 1990 as a major alternative to the large, commercial publishing houses, The New Press is the first full-scale nonprofit American book
publisher outside of the university presses. The Press is operated editorially
in the public interest, rather than for private gain; it is committed to publishing in innovative ways works of educational, cultural, and community value
that, despite their intellectual merits, might not normally be "commercially"
viable. The New Press's editorial offices are located at the City University of
New York.

Printed in the United States of America
94 95 96 97   9 8 7 6 5 4 3 2 1

*Although the motion picture may not live forever as a work of art,
except in a few instances, it will be the most efficient way of showing posterity how we live now.*

                                        —IRVING THALBERG

*I enjoy working. People ask me why I'm not retired. It's because I
get bored to death doing nothing. I have a charming house up in
the Hollywood hills, and I look down on Hollywood and spit!*

                                        —ARTHUR LUBIN
                                        Comedy Director
                                        (at eighty-five)

CONTENTS

Contents

Foreword

For me, making films has always been about collaboration and surprise. The opinion of a grip, the eye of the editor, the experiment of the cameraman, and all the spontaneous things that happen within the filmmaking family add to the final artistic whole. I always say that after the casting is completed, ninety percent of my job is done—then I depend on the talent and inspiration of those around me to find a vision.

Talking Pictures presents a fascinating portrait of the "Golden Age" of Hollywood from the perspective of people who may be unfamiliar to us but whose stories are no less fascinating than those of the moguls and stars.

I came into film before the advent of film school, learning as I went, working my way up in industrial films and television, learning every aspect of the business. It is interesting to see how the studio system—despite its many flaws and abuses—provided a kind of training ground. As compared to the freelance existence of many contemporary professionals, the studio system provided a kind of security hard for editors, technicians, and craftsmen to find today.

This book answers the questions I think many people ask themselves when they see the credits at the end of a film: Who are these people and what do they do? What are *their* stories? Moviemaking owes as much to these people—not to mention those whose names may not even appear in the credits, the studio representatives and story editors—as it does to those of us whose names appear above the title.

Robert Altman

Acknowledgments

Finding people was the hard part. It was like a treasure hunt. One of the first "kind strangers" who helped us was David Shepard, director of special projects at the Directors Guild of America. He not only gave us a comprehensive list of directors and assistant directors but also made the guild offices available for several interviews.

Georgia Marcher of the American Cinema Editors Guild found Rudi Fehr; Eleanor Grand ran an ad for us in the Editors Guild newspaper, which yielded Bert Wrench.

Ed Murphy, who died shortly after we began this project, found Florence Haley and Maxine Marx.

The Motion Picture and Television Fund in Woodland Hills, California, was a gold mine. The Fund is a model retirement home (with an adjacent hospital) that is open to any industry member with twenty years of service. On numerous visits there we were aided by Bill Campbell, Stephanie Rose Dean, Maris Fick, Addie Hamilton, and Kim Sauber.

University of California at Berkeley's Pacific Film Archive was a friendly haven with knowledgeable staff and an excellent reference library.

Anne Tofflemire arranged a meeting with Sammy Cahn; Susan Ehrlich found Arthur Lonergan and William Fadiman; Carol Peckham remembered a newspaper article about Hubert Voight. When we were in Los Angeles, Jay Shanker called daily with helpful leads and urged us to contact Sam Jaffe.

Jerry Walsh kindly put us in touch with the Altmans. Kathryn was helpful in suggesting people to interview, and Bob generously took time from his hectic shooting schedule to write the foreword to this book.

We are deeply grateful to André Schiffrin, Matthew Weiland, Akiko Takano, Don McMahon, and the rest of the intelligent and good-natured crew at The New Press, and to our agent, Roberta Pryor, for believing in the value of our endeavor and helping it come to fruition.

Sadly, seventeen of our subjects—John Bright, Ralph Butler, Sammy Cahn, Lester Cole, Jack Cummings, Bob Flatley, George Folsey, Nancy Green, Anna Hill Johnstone, Al Keller, Arthur Lonergan, Florence Mack, Frank McCarthy, Jim Noblitt, Ed Rike, Hubert Voight, and Eleanor Wolquitt—died before this book was completed. To their families and friends, our deep sympathy. Thanks to Blanche Cole, Michael Cole, and Jo Dee Hutchason for helping us track down a wonderful photograph of Lester Cole; and to Rupert Allan for the picture of Frank McCarthy.

Earl Shorris gave birth to the idea of this book, urged us to stay with it, and offered continuing words of encouragement over the seven years it took to complete. James and Anthony Shorris went right to the heart of the matter, providing a reliable and user-friendly tape recorder.

We shall always be grateful to Greta Herman, without whose encouragement and optimism this book could never have been started or completed.

Stephen Bundy contributed his usual sage advice along the way, coupled with the example of his own very high standards. Jody Fung, Gaye Walworth, and Gardner Smith entertained Emma and William Bundy, making it possible for us to work.

Special thanks to Susanne Tilney Peyton and Bernard Peyton for technical support.

Betsy Houghteling, our mutual friend, may have started it all by introducing us in New York in 1981. Many other friends and family members helped in ways too numerous to recount here. To all of you, our real gratitude.

To our subjects, including those whom for reasons of space we were not able to include: In sharing your unique memories, you have taught us something about one of our national treasures, the American movie. You have also taught us about the enormous satisfaction of work well done, the lasting benefits of doing what you love, and the beauty of old age. Thank you.

Marion Abbott Bundy
Sylvia Shorris

Introduction

Every Friday afternoon during the school year, when I was growing up in the Bronx, my mother would pick me up at three o'clock for our weekly trip to the movies. This ritual was strictly observed from the time I was six until the year I turned twelve, when my widowed mother remarried and I was sent to live with an aunt and uncle.

We went to the movies as equals. She never took me to children's films or films considered appropriate for children. We went to see what my mother enjoyed: love stories, musicals, screwball comedies. We often sat through two showings of our favorites. In the thirties this was possible because there was no such thing as a two o'clock show or a four o'clock show. The show began when you got there (usually in the middle of the picture), and you could stay as long as you liked.

We were avid consumers of fan magazines such as *Modern Screen* and *Photoplay,* so we thought we knew everything about the private lives of the stars. Our walks home were full of what we thought of as "insider" gossip: how Fred and Ginger were not really friends off screen, why Cary Grant's latest girlfriend wasn't good enough for him (he was our favorite so nobody was *ever* good enough), how we disapproved of Jean Harlow's platinum hair.

My mother was a movie fan of world-class proportions. She had gone to Rudolph Valentino's funeral! What's more, she had persuaded her sister, who was six months' pregnant, to go with her. Valentino had been the idol of millions of women, so there was a tremendous outpouring of grief at the Frank E. Campbell Funeral Home on that hot August day of 1926. Overcome by emotion, many fainted, a few were trampled, and the police had to be called out to restore order. My mother and aunt stayed on until the coffin was brought out. Then they, too, succumbed to their anguish and burst into tears. They arrived home red-eyed and exhausted. Their husbands thought they were crazy. The men didn't understand the pull of the movies, but I did.

My mother and I had a special way of experiencing the movies. We liked to sit up front, with as many empty seats around us as possible. Then we "entered" into whatever was happening up there on the screen. We danced with Fred Astaire, exchanged wisecracks with Cary Grant, shared a bus seat with Clark Gable. If one of them had spoken to us from the screen, we wouldn't have been surprised in the least.

We were so immersed in the pictures we saw that when we left the theater, blinking after hours in the dark, we were always surprised to find ourselves in the Bronx. How did we get here? we wondered. We had just been in Paris, in Rio, in San Francisco. That was our reality, not what awaited us outside the theater.

I was to observe over those years (which held some of the happiest memories of my childhood) what a powerful effect the movies had, especially on my mother. She was a young widow, living with her mother and daughter, controlled by their needs and demands. She knew her prospects were limited—at least until the next trip to the movies. Then, seated in front of the screen, anything was possible. Even a happy ending.

As for me, the movies showed what the world outside our Bronx apartment was like, or more accurately, what it might be like in the best of all possible worlds. My own world was fatherless, grandmother-ridden, lonely. Through the movies I could experience warm family life. (I loved the Andy Hardy films because of Lewis Stone, who played Judge Hardy. Now *that* was a father.) I could have exciting adventures and limitless aspirations. The movies gave me my dreams.

=

The early fifties found me in Mexico City, doing public relations and translating for a movie exhibitor, Luis Montes. He was the most powerful theater owner in Mexico—rich, well educated, and highly civilized. I owed him a lot because he got me my working papers (no small accomplishment) and because he was always protective of me in a difficult climate for a young woman alone.

This bottom-line, nitty-gritty, where-the-public-plunks-down-its-money part of the business was a side never covered in *Modern Screen,* and it was an education for me. I observed that Montes was treated exceedingly well by Hollywood producers and directors who happened to pass through. He and other exhibitors were the bread and butter of the business. It was clear that his choice of films to show in his theaters influenced the decisions made back in Hollywood and New York. A film's profit or loss then, as now, often was not decided until the receipts from the foreign exhibitors were in.

My deeper connection to the film business came through the friendships I developed with some of the blacklisted Hollywood screenwriters who had fled to Mexico. Though they were chronically short of money, they were clearly the stars of the American colony in those days. Everyone wanted to be in their company and hear their stories. They were much admired for their principles by most, if not all, of us. They could have continued their lucrative careers had they been willing to testify before the House Un-American Activities Committee in Washington, selling out their friends and their souls. They chose not to.

John Bright and his wife, Mura, were my closest friends and became my family while I was in Mexico. They lived with their two young sons in a large rented house in one of the best residential neighborhoods, but the house was nearly empty of furnishings (which was ironic because Mura worked as a decorator). Their lights and telephone were often cut off. They had a maid who was really a nanny for the boys (that amenity was always the last to go), but she frequently went unpaid, staying on because she adored Johnny and Casey. (Juan O'Casey was John's *nom de plume* when he wrote for *Esquire* during that period.)

Through the Brights I met Robert Rossen, who was in Mexico shooting *The Brave Bulls*. Bright had written the script, but his name could not appear in the credits. Rossen had just been subpoenaed to testify in Washington and was staying on in Mexico while trying to decide what to do. He hated the thought of naming names, but he didn't want to stop working in Hollywood.

One night I went with Rossen to see the first rough cut of *The Brave Bulls*. It was a special night, for several people in the room, including Rossen himself, didn't know if they would ever work again. They didn't seem so much film industry workers concerned for their professional futures as lovers saddened at the prospect of parting. I had never seen such concentration and involvement. They were all, literally and figuratively, up there on the screen. Afterward there was the usual post mortem, but the mood was tense and poignant. I remember how I envied them, even at this difficult moment in their lives, their luck in doing work that meant so much to them, even though several were to pay a heavy price.

Rossen continued to agonize over going to Washington. One night he decided to leave Mexico and go to El Paso to visit Tom Lea, the author of the novel *The Brave Bulls*. Rossen was trying to postpone a decision as long as possible. He made his plane reservation in the name of Robert Rosen, his idea of an alias and maybe his unconscious wish to be discovered.

In the end, of course, he did testify, thinking it would save his career. It didn't. He didn't work for years—not until the sixties. Then he made several movies, one of which, *The Hustler,* was a fine achievement that should have redeemed him but somehow didn't. The picture garnered several Academy Awards, but none for the director. He died at fifty-seven, a bitter and angry man. He had been torn between his politics and his need to do the work he loved. His work won, but he lost.

Men like Rossen were creatures of the movies. It never occurred to them that they could do anything else. They were artists, people who must frequently sacrifice in order to practice their art. John Bright, while in Mexico, wrote screenplays in English; they were then translated into Spanish, and someone else got the screen credit. While they were politically acceptable in Mexico, these films weren't even shown in the United States, where they were considered inflammatory. Bright continued to do his work, though he was underpaid and unappreciated.

Dalton Trumbo was another writer who had to work under assumed names for years (even winning an Academy Award in 1956 for *The Brave One* under the name of Robert Rich). Kirk Douglas finally broke the blacklist by hiring Trumbo to write the screenplay for *Spartacus* under his own name. I remember Trumbo's coming-out-of-jail party in Mexico City. With his innate sense of the dramatic, he caused everyone to gasp when they saw him. His red hair had turned white in jail.

When I returned to the United States in 1954, I got a job in the New York office of Twentieth Century–Fox as one of many assistants to Spyros P. Skouras, the president of the company. He was a rough-edged, inarticulate man, who had started out in life as the son of a shepherd in the mountains of Greece and emigrated to America, where he became a pilot in World War I. After the war, he and his two brothers Charlie and George opened a nickelodeon in St. Louis. This modest beginning led to their ownership of a huge chain of movie theaters. Charlie and George remained on the exhibition side of the industry, but Spyros became interested in production. He was basically a money man, but the former pilot had fallen in love with technology during World War I. In the fifties, when many feared that television was destroying the movie industry, Skouras turned to technology. Twentieth Century–Fox developed the wide-screen process known as Cinemascope, which was expected to bring the crowds back to the theaters. Eventually, all the studios developed their own versions of wide-screen projection, but the crowds never really returned.

My first day on the job, Skouras asked me to send a letter to Winston Churchill (causing me much panic because I didn't know how to address him), offering to install one of the first Cinemascope screens at Chartwell, the Churchill country home. Churchill declined the honor.

Skouras's enthusiasm for Cinemascope was not diminished, however. He persisted in his belief that technology could save the movies, part of his painfully imperfect understanding of the medium. He continued to put technology, or form, ahead of content. He overlooked the importance of making good movies. I regularly attended screenings of new films with him. Other studio executives were always in attendance, and the comment most often made was, "You did it again, Spyros." Often, about halfway through the picture, I would hear gentle snoring sounds, indicating that Skouras was perhaps more of a critic than he knew.

Darryl Zanuck, who was head of production at this time, had a better understanding of the medium. He had been producing films all his life and had had many successes, but they were all behind him. Zanuck and Skouras were always at odds. Skouras, in Zanuck's view, was an ignorant know-nothing whose only interest was in pacifying the stockholders. Skouras thought that Zanuck too often forgot that business was business. He wanted him to stop putting his girlfriends into expensive productions. Eventually, both Skouras and Zanuck were forced out. Fox's films were losing money steadily, and the stockholders felt it was time for a changing of the guard.

These were the waning years of the studio system, a system that had worked in spite of its constraints. Some actors may not have always been happy at being forced to accept binding seven-year contracts, but many felt cherished and protected by their studios. They were brought along slowly and carefully, given acting lessons, singing and dancing lessons. They were told who to be seen with, and their reputations were zealously guarded. These actors felt deeply connected to their studios.

For the most part, the system worked for the rest of the industry as well. With studios each turning out between sixty and one hundred films a year there was always work for the technical people. They went from one picture to another with scarcely a day's lapse. After the unions were formed, they were well paid, had good working conditions, and had the protection of insurance. Most of them were tremendously loyal to their studios, and some worked all of their lives at the same studio. Many did not even receive screen credits, which were the life-blood of the business, but they had a sense of participation in a collaborative effort that was new to the world of art.

Each studio had its own identity. MGM, with its king-of-the-jungle image, was the acknowledged leader of the pack. They had "more stars than there are in the heavens." This was proven on the occasion of the twenty-fifth anniversary of the studio, when a photograph was taken of all their stars, seated in alphabetical order, and published in all the major magazines. Among them were June Allyson, Joan Crawford, Clark Gable, Greta Garbo, Greer Garson, Katharine Hepburn, Gene Kelly, Peter Lawford, Myrna Loy, Ricardo Montalban, Walter Pidgeon, Jane Powell, William Powell, Elizabeth Taylor, Robert Taylor, Spencer Tracy, and Esther Williams. No small constellation. MGM films also had the finest production values because money was no object. They went for the best.

Louis B. Mayer was the most patriarchal of all the studio heads. He considered his employees his family, and, like many real fathers, he was not above manipulating his children with the weapons at hand: his ability to cry on cue and, with the universally acknowledged "best feet in the business," to walk his victims into the ground until they gave in to his demands.

Other studios had their own strengths. Twentieth Century–Fox was run with great efficiency for many years by Darryl Zanuck. Producer Frank McCarthy recalled that his boss kept a master chart under the glass top of his desk, which enabled him to draw up a budget, crew, and cast for a film even before they had a title for it. According to McCarthy, Zanuck could tell at a glance which actors and directors were available at any given time, how much they were paid, what films were nearing completion, and even the status of the crews and who among them worked well together. He was a hands-on executive who made many of the studio's films his personal projects, meaning he was involved in every aspect of filmmaking.

Jack Warner kept his studio solvent during the worst years of the Depression, using a combination of thrift (no more than one take of any scene), poor-mouthing ("We're losing money . . ."), and a genuine feel for what the public wanted to see (upbeat musicals and gangster films). He never took his finger off the pulse, and the pulse was his own.

Columbia's Harry Cohn was reviled by one and all, but he knew enough to let Frank Capra make the kind of films he wanted to make: heartwarming, happy-ending stories that sent the audience out of the theater feeling good.

The difference between Skouras and the moguls who had built the industry was that he could understand finance and technology but lacked their instinct for content. The studio system, sometimes clumsy, often heartless in the hands of Mayer, Warner, or Cohn, nurtured artistic endeavor in spite of itself. It recognized and encouraged the sense of collaboration among all of its employees. It was essentially a company of moviemakers such as has not been seen since nor may ever be seen again.

How the studio system came about, what effect it had on the people behind the camera, and how some of the film industry's technological creators affected the content of the movies was a subject yet to be explored in the history of filmmaking.

When Marion Abbott Bundy and I decided to do this book, we hoped to find answers, or at least clues, to some of the questions about the great flowering of the movies. Why were the twenties, thirties, and forties the golden age of the industry? In one year, 1939, there were so many fine films produced that the Academy of Motion Picture Arts and Sciences had great difficulty deciding which film should win the award for best picture. *Gone with the Wind* was finally selected, but one could understand how any of the others (*Dark Victory, Goodbye, Mr. Chips, Love Affair, Mr. Smith Goes to Washington, Ninotchka, Of Mice and Men, Stagecoach, The Wizard of Oz, Wuthering Heights*) could just as easily have been chosen. What factors led to this one glorious year? Was it the achievement of the studio system? Advancements in technology? Or the public's great receptivity in a time of continuing economic depression and the looming threat of war? Maybe it was the confluence of all these elements.

As we got deeper into our interviews, we made a great discovery. The people who worked in the industry in those years, even the humblest of them, were not merely laborers without interest or understanding. They were not worker bees following imprinted orders. They were a proud cadre of master builders, men and women who knew they were in at the creation of a new art form. The movies would never be invented again, not the way they were in those early years. These people were creating the form as they went along. Some of their success was due to improved technology, some of it was attributable to simple yet brilliant improvisation. These people were a key factor in the creation of Hollywood's Golden Age.

We interviewed all kinds of people who had worked behind the scenes, from producers and directors to grips and gaffers. Theoretically if not actually, most of them had nothing to do with the content of the film, but they had everything to do with its form and technology. By assimilating their stories we began to realize how technology, form, and content are perhaps less separated and more deeply integrated in film than in any other art form.

Stanley Kauffmann, in *A World of Film* (1966), writes: "In an age imbued with technological interest, the film art flowers out of technology. Excepting architecture, film is the one art that can capitalize directly and extensively on this century's luxuriance in applied science."

This complex "form" of film calls for both specialization and collaboration. Our subjects, each in his or her own way, contributed not only to the technology of moviemaking but, in a spirit of cooperation and teamwork, however large or small their contributions, to the form and even the content. And it was all for the good of the film. This was the genius and the beauty of the studio system.

Going as far back as the early twenties and even before, technology was being invented and improvised. On one of D. W. Griffith's early silent films, the prop man couldn't find any checked tablecloths for lunch one day. As the cast ate at a white-clothed table, Billy Bitzer, Griffith's legendary camera operator (they weren't yet called "cinematographers"), noticed how the white cloth reflected light onto the actors' faces, and he realized how useful reflectors could be.

One day a member of George Folsey's camera crew took a plain piece of plywood and cut holes in it in order to cast flattering shadows on Joan Crawford's face. Until then, they had been using large leaves, causing one of the actors to dub Folsey

"George Foliage." The invention even had an improvised name; it was called a "cokuloris," a word Folsey said came from a book of fairy tales. Later the word was shortened to "kook." Kooks are still used today.

Artie Jacobson, an assistant director, recalled the difficulties of shooting inside Macy's while filming *Miracle on 34th Street,* until one of the crew thought to mount a camera on an escalator. Jacobson was still amazed, forty years later, at "how those guys could improvise."

Directors felt the same way. Edward Bernds, a soundman for Frank Capra during the thirties, told us with misty eyes that Mr. Capra had said to him after they finished shooting *Mr. Smith Goes to Washington:* "I want you to know that you've been more help to me than anybody. I mean that."

The men and women interviewed here were both participants and witnesses to an immensely exciting time in history, and when they are gone there will be no one else to tell us what it was like. Several of them have died since the beginning of this project, but they have left us their invaluable testimony. Among them were some personal friends: John Bright, Eleanor Wolquitt, and Nancy Green. All are missed, but we are comforted by the resonance of their remembrances.

We thought readers would want to hear the stories of these remarkable people—and they were all remarkable—who were present at the birth of a new art about which Erich von Stroheim said: "Everything could be done with film, the only medium in which you could reproduce life as it really was."

At the American Film Institute tribute in his honor in 1985, Gene Kelly acknowledged the crucial contributions of the many unknown and unsung of the industry when he said: "Nobody knows the names of all those people who worked so hard to make us look good. . . . Without them we would have fallen on our faces."

Those who live on remain active and involved. Some volunteer their time, others work for their guilds, nearly all keep up with the industry, reading about new developments and staying in touch with their old comrades. Though age has affected them in different ways, they are still passionate, still opinionated, still vitally connected.

We hope that this book is not an elegy but a celebration—of lives dedicated to work and art.

Sylvia Shorris
September 1993

≡ FALLING
IN LOVE
WITH THE
MOVIES ≡

Assistant director Arthur Jacobson (kneeling, sixth from left), with cast and crew of *The Wild Party* (Paramount, 1929).

ARTHUR JACOBSON

Assistant Director

In David Stenn's 1988 biography of Clara Bow, Arthur Jacobson is described as her strapping six-foot boyfriend. It is hard to reconcile that image with the frail old man who greets us when we arrive at his Culver City apartment to begin our first interview.

Artie (as he immediately insists we call him) is sitting on a couch, wrapped in a blanket although it is a warm September day. He apologizes for not getting up, explaining that his hips bother him. He hastens to add that he has just renewed his driver's license and gets around quite well.

He is a legendary raconteur, and the years fall away as he regales us with story after story of picture-making under such directors as William Wellman, Leo McCarey, Wesley Ruggles, George Seaton, Lewis Seiler, Irving Brecher, and Joshua Logan.

I was born on 100th Street and Madison Avenue. I'm eighty-four. I had been in the picture business in New York for five years before I ever came out here. That's going back pretty far.

There was not a breath of theatrical background in my family—in any way, shape or form. I was just a guy looking for a job; I hated school. I went to two high schools for a total of six months.

Before high school I went to P.S. 44, which is on 175th Street, where there was one of the first motion picture studios, the

Biograph Studio. They had just built it about two years before I discovered what it was all about. We're talking about 1916, a long time ago.

In those days a studio had two parts: it had a lower and an upper stage. The upper stage was covered with glass. They used Cooper-Hewitt lights—long, tubular lights, something like neons now, but these were blue. Every night when the Biograph people worked (and they worked all the time) this whole glass dome was blue. I got curious, and being a typical New York punk, snuck in one night without asking anybody.

I took a look at what was going on, and I saw these beautiful dames. They wore that thick, yellow makeup, but they were beautiful and I thought, "This is for me."

So the first thing I tried to do was get a job there. But no matter who I talked to, when they heard how old I was they said to forget it. So I went and got what they called working papers. I was still going to school.

"What experience do you have?" they'd ask. Who knows from experience? I didn't even know what the hell the word meant.

I said, "I've got two hands and I'm willing. I want to work. How much you pay me is not important, but I want to work in this place. I like it." I went to the movies, but I knew nothing about the way they were made.

Came a day when I was standing on a corner with some friends, at Southern Boulevard and 174th Street. In the winter we used to go into a German bakery there; I can still remember the smell of it! That day a couple of guys from the studio walked in, and one had just gotten fired. Well, my ears perked right up. *[Gestures with hands cupped behind ears.]* "Who are you? Where were you fired from, what department?"

By this time the doorman at the studio was a friend of mine. I would bring him my mother's homemade cookies; in other words, I was trying to get my foot in the door. If you were a smart punk from New York City you found ways to ingratiate yourself. I think I weighed maybe eighty-five pounds; I was a small punk.

My father found out about me hanging around there, and he socked me around a little bit. "Stay away from there." As far as he was concerned the movie studio was a bunch of bums, tramps, women with painted faces. That's how he understood it.

Anyway, I finally found out that this guy had been fired by his boss whose name was N. W. Palmer. He later became one of my closest friends, but at that time I didn't know who he was, what he did, and I couldn't have cared less. All I knew was that I had a name to go to. But the guy in his office wouldn't let me in.

One day Mr. Palmer walked by and I went up to him and hit him for a job. He said, "I don't know what you're talking about. You're just a kid. You're a child."

By now it was vacation time; I had ten weeks out of school. When Mr. Palmer came to work the next day there I was, sitting waiting for him. When he came back from lunch there I was. When he went home there I was. This went on for nine weeks. That ninth week I was getting nervous because I knew I had to go back to school. Finally he said, "Come on up with me." It was the first time I saw the inside of the studio except for the night I snuck in.

He told me he was head of the electrical department. What do I know about electricity? I said I know enough to stay away from it, not to stick my finger in the socket. So he said, "All right, I'll tell you what. I'll give you a clean-up job, for your persistence." So I got the job, at seven dollars a week. A lot of money. I didn't go back to school, and by the third week I was making twelve dollars a week, with overtime. It meant that every Saturday night I could go out, shoot a little craps. I was a typical New York kid.

When the studio shut down I got a job being a handyman and usher for Fox Theaters. When I got there they said, "We'll put you in a theater close to where you live." How nice. So they put me in the Audubon Theater on 168th Street and Broadway. There I got the same seven dollars a week.

It was a split-week house; in other words, they changed the movie twice a week, and they changed the vaudeville acts twice a week. My job, to start with, was to go downtown to the Fox exchange on 46th Street and pick up the film that was going to run on Thursday, Friday, Saturday, and Sunday. I'd pick it up Wednesday night. To bring it to the theater I had to go by bus. They wouldn't allow that kind of film on the subway in those days because it was flammable. Well, it took forever. But I was young, I was strong, and full of ambition.

After delivering the film Wednesday night I'd go home and have to be back at the theater at ten the next morning. Between ten o'clock and the time the theater opened I'd put posters up in the windows of the stores.

When it came time for the theater doors to open we would go and put our uniforms on. I'd stand in the back; I wasn't an usher but a bouncer. A light-weight bouncer.

Now I get myself promoted downtown, to a special messenger. A special messenger meant that if an outlying theater did not get its film in time they'd call the exchange. The exchange would get another print and send it out with the messenger—in this case, me. Those theaters had to have their films the day before.

Eventually, the studio reopened and I got my old job back. One night I was sitting cleaning the spotlights and I saw my father come in. Oh, I smell trouble. Wow! It seems that my mother was crying at home because I was killing myself with overwork. (I'd get home at three o'clock in the morning when I was working in the studio.) My father gestured for me to come down and said, "Come on home." It was about two in the morning.

I said, "No, Pop, I'm going to stay here." He hit me hard enough to knock me clear across the floor. It was practically the only time he ever hit me, but darn it, I was never so mortified in my life, in front of all those people.

He took me downtown and he taught me the embroidery business, what he had done all of his life. It took me about four days to learn it, and I made more money per week working with him. I was doing what they call piecework, machine work. In other words, the manufacturer would send just the collar of a dress over, we'd embroider it and send it back. All the time I was there, whenever I could, I went back to the studio and begged to be taken back. But the guy didn't want any part of me; he'd have such trouble with my parents, my God. But somehow I convinced him to give me back the job.

I said to Pop, "I'm sorry, you can hit me all you want, but I can't stand your business," not realizing I was breaking his heart. He would never be able to put "AND SON" on the door.

Once I got back in the studio, I decided I'd better figure out what job I wanted. I was tired of watching everybody. I'd learned that the director was the one who was doing everything; he was a *macher [big shot]*. But then I also realized that there was another guy who could change the director's mind, and he was the cameraman. So I concluded that the cameraman in those days was "it." Then I found out that you couldn't be a cameraman until you learned how to run a camera, and you had to own one. So, just for the hell of it, I priced a second-hand camera; it was $3,500. It might as well have been $3 million.

Well, I went to a place called the New York Institute of Photography, which I had seen advertised in the magazines. There I learned how to make still pictures, and I became what I still call a photo hack. I wasn't great, but I experimented and did some good things. And I learned a lot from my boss at the studio. So when it came time to study how to use the motion picture camera I thought, "What do I need the school for? I'm there every day. I'll learn there."

I did just that and got into a lot of trouble one time. I opened a camera and ruined a scene. I admitted it to my boss and not to anybody else because they would have killed me. So, by trial and error, I became an assistant cameraman. Now, I looked around and looked around, I tried here, I tried there. There were a lot of studios in New York, out in Long Island especially, about 1920. Famous Players was a big one, in Astoria. *[It is now Kaufman-Astoria Studios, home of the Museum of the Moving Image.]*

Finally I got a call one day to come over to Famous Players, and became third assistant cameraman on my first real feature picture, *Zaza,* with Gloria Swanson. It was the biggest movie that year. Three cameras on every scene. She would only do a scene once, so we had to get all the angles at the same time. It was directed by Allan Dwan, a mean bastard. In those days they were pretty arrogant guys. They were the bosses, the real bosses. The producers didn't know anything about picture-making. You know, they were glove salesmen; they only knew how to handle business and sell the stuff.

Anyway, on the third day of shooting *Zaza,* Swanson was doing a big scene. There were six of us around the camera: three cameramen and three assistants. In the middle of the take the guy playing music hit a sour note. In those days the director used to have a little megaphone wrapped around his wrist. When the guy hit the sour note, the director unwound the megaphone, threw it, and hit the musician right behind the ear. Well, little me, eighty-five pounds, I was going to kill the son-of-a-bitch.

I went right to the front office and told the guy that hired me, "I thank you for everything, but unless you can transfer me to another picture, consider this my resignation." I told him what had happened.

He said, "Good for you. You've got the guts to quit, huh?"

I said, "It doesn't take guts. It's breaking my heart. I can't afford to work with this guy because if he ever does that to me, I'll kill him and get a bad name in the business for being hot-tempered. So it's better that I just step out now."

So he transferred me to another picture called *Three Miles Out,* directed by Irvin Willat, another miserable bastard. It was a C-picture; the sets were on a boat; Madge Kennedy was the star. Willat had improvised what they called a sea-going tripod. They set the camera on the tripod and suspended it on a pipe. On the pipe they put an iron ball, like a bowling ball. On the bottom of the ball was a nail. We put a numeral *8* in chalk on the floor. Then, when the camera was going, it followed the nail in the shape of the *8.* You'd get the rise and fall and the pitch of the waves that way.

My job was to crank the camera. Nobody can understand what a thrill that was. But right in the middle of the first take the crank slipped out, and Willat took a swing at me, he got so mad. I ducked, then back to the office, "I'm quitting."

There are no other pictures there to put me on, so now I'm looking for a job and, sure enough, there was a small company that had just formed, called the Film Guild, and they were going to make a picture from a book called *The Scarecrow,* by Percy McKay, which was eventually released as *Puritan Passions.* Glen Hunter, a big star on Broadway in those days, was going to be the lead.

The company consisted of a bunch of guys who had gotten together at Yale. I didn't realize it then, but there were quite a few *fegeles [fairies]. [Waves arms to indicate flying, fairy-style.]* I didn't know it; I thought they were just a bunch of sissies. We never heard the word "homosexual" or "faggot."

We made this picture, called *Puritan Passions,* with a new girl as leading lady. She was a gorgeous sixteen-year-old named Lucille Langhanke. She became Mary Astor.

When the time came to make a second picture, they wanted to save some money, so they went over to a little studio over the 92nd Street ferry, the Pyramid Studios. Same star, but they were looking for some other girls, so I made some tests. One of the girls turned out to be Clara Bow. She had been in one picture. She got the part. She felt that I had a lot to do with it, because I was in love with her. I fell head over heels in love with her, but right now. But head over heels.

We finished the picture, and, naturally, I wooed her. She lived in a typical brownstone in Brooklyn, near Fulton Avenue, and I lived way up in the Bronx, in the classy part, as far as you could go before New Rochelle. We used to sit on the top step whenever we got back from where we ate, which was always a Chinese restaurant. We were in love; we were crazy in love. I was the only guy around that her father trusted a damn. She was a crazy dame, but she turned out to be one of the great actresses, at least until sound came in.

By this time I'd saved a little money, about $800. In the middle of the picture an agent had come on the set and offered Clara a contract. I think she offered her $100 a week. Well, Jesus Christ, that was a lot of money. But it meant she had to go to Hollywood. Apparently, the agent had seen her first picture where she played a hoyden; it was called *Down to the Sea in Ships.*

She said she'd go on the condition that her father could go with her. So she went to Hollywood and left me with my heart broken. I was so in love with her I couldn't see. I was nineteen or twenty at the time, and she was sixteen. This love lasted practically a lifetime.

The minute I finished the picture I was on, I took out my $800 and away I went, following her. I'll never forget it. I went by train, and it took five days and nights. My God, it went on and on and on. She knew I was coming, and she was living in a hotel with the lady agent who was assigned to her by the producer B. P. Schulberg. I went to see her, and then got me a room on

North Kingsley Drive and Hollywood Boulevard for five dollars a week. I took my camera with me because I knew I could always find some little company that could use it.

Clara did very well. They picked up her option and they gave her more money. She kept saying to me, "It's silly for you to live where you live." She had been up to see where I lived one day, and she practically hit me on the head. It was terrible, just a room.

By this time she and her father had gotten a bungalow in a typical Hollywood bungalow court on Sunset Boulevard. I moved in with them on one condition: that I pay the maid. She had to have a maid because she worked long, hard hours.

Well, the agent didn't like our arrangement one bit. She was a good friend and a very nice woman, but she didn't like it and tried to talk us out of it. She didn't get anywhere, so she cautioned, "At least keep it quiet. Don't tell anybody. For God's sake, don't let Schulberg find out about it." Well, he did find out, and he fired me. I was working for him and his production manager, Sam Jaffe (who was also his brother-in-law). Schulberg fired me personally. It was the first time I'd been asked to come into his office.

He asked, "You're the guy?"

I said, "I'm the guy. I'm not doing any harm."

He said, "You're not going to, either. You're taking an awful chance with a big investment of mine. Where do you work now?"

"Here," I said.

"Not any more, you don't."

Now I'm still looking for a job, and I'm an Easterner out West. I don't belong to the western affiliation of the union. Back East I was in the cameramen's union, but I can't get in the union out here. Anyway, I couldn't get a job until eventually one day a call went out from Famous Players. It wasn't Paramount yet. Anybody who had an Akeley camera could come and work at Famous Players for seventy-five dollars a day.

I knew where there was an Akeley camera, but I didn't know how to work it. It was one of those cameras that could do anything. It was invented by a man called Carl Akeley, who used it while hunting wild animals in Africa. Famous Players was making a picture called *Shadows of Paris.*

I got there and went to my friend Ray Lissner, the assistant director, and asked him, "Suppose I get the camera, can you help me?" He agreed, so when I was back in New York for a week I went to my friend Larry Kemball, who had the Akeley, and begged him to let me have it. He let me have it on the condition I take his cameraman with me. A lucky break since I didn't know how to work it.

So the cameraman came with me. We went to the studio and set the whole thing up. All I did was to roll it (anybody could do that), and I was getting $40 a day; the cameraman was getting $35 for running it. That was the going rate. We stretched the job out to five days, and when it was over with I went to the cashier and collected the money, paid the cameraman, thanked everybody, and left with my $200. That night I took all my friends to the Coconut Grove, woke up in the morning a big broke party-giver.

By that time, the heat of the love affair had cooled down some. We never broke it off; I never got jealous or anything. We had started to get married about four times, but we always got into a fight on the way. Anyway, she wanted to live her life. I still couldn't get a job, so I decided to go back to New York.

By now Clara is a big star. But big. She's the star of stars. About 1926, before sound came in. I was still in New York. The next part of the story is unbelievable; such a coincidence.

I had a cousin in the men's clothing business, the manager of a big store on 39th Street and Broadway. He was also a model, a good-looking guy. He called me one day and asked if I'd like to go to a dance up where he lived in Washington Heights. I told him I didn't like to dance, but that I'd go anyhow. At one point in the evening he came to me and said, "Boy, there's a dame here who found out that you're from Hollywood, and does she have the hots for you." I was used to hearing this.

So he introduced me to her, and while we were dancing she asked if I'd take her home. She was not too great—a little double *zaftig,* but, "What the hell," I thought, "what have I got to lose?" She was apparently from a rich family because she lived on Riverside Drive. Her name was Mildred Gershowitz, of the famous Gershowitz's deli at 96th and Broadway, and later that week she became Mrs. Sam Jaffe.

But that night over a cup of coffee on the way home she asked, "Do you know a man called Sam Jaffe?"

"God," I thought. "Think quick! What should I say? Should I tell the truth about him?" At that time, I hated him. But God was good; he tapped me on the shoulder and I said the most glowing things about Sam Jaffe that you could ever hear. She had only known him a short time when she went to California. He had wooed her over the telephone and with letters. He had gone to Texas on location and stopped in New York on her birthday and proposed to her. He had proposed to her before, and she couldn't make up her mind. All she knew was that he was a big shot from Hollywood, and he was Schulberg's brother-in-law. Schulberg at that time was very famous.

Anyway, that night Mildred said, "I want you to come to my birthday party. Sam's going to be there."

I told her, "Before I come to your birthday party tomorrow night you'd better tell Sam that you met me, and the circumstances. Be sure and tell him what I said about him." My little mind is going again. I wasn't working at the moment, and he was head of Paramount production. By this time I'd become an assistant director.

The next morning, Sunday, my phone rang. A man's voice asked, "Is this Artie Jacobson?"

I said, "Yes."

"You son-of-a-bitch. Can't you stay out of my life?"

"May I ask who this is?"

"This is Sam Jaffe."

I said, "Well, I agree with you on one thing. I am a son-of-a-bitch. But obviously, God doesn't want me to stay out of your life. Mildred asked me to come to her birthday party and I told her . . ."

To make a long story short, everyone got very drunk at the party, including me, and I hit Sam Jaffe for a job. He told me to come and see him in Hollywood. So back I go.

I gave myself a few days, and then went to his office. Well, he didn't see me that day. He wouldn't see me the next day, either; nor the next, nor the next, nor the next. I guess he had sobered up and realized what I had done to him. He finally saw me on Saturday night (I had been waiting since Monday). He had been going in and out of his office through a back door in order to avoid me. At one point I had said to Jean, his secretary, "I think I'll get a sack and put it over my head so you won't have to look at me." She had been looking at me for eight hours a day.

Apparently he didn't want to go through with giving me a job because he was scared to death to tell Schulberg. He wouldn't dare assign me to a picture with Clara, and he didn't want my name to be brought up in front of her. He didn't want her to know what was going on with me because she would raise such hell.

So now Jaffe hated me even more. He said, "I'll never forget this. You hit me for a job, didn't you?"

"Yup," I said.

"And I said I would give you one?"

"Yup."

"All right. I'm a man of my word," he said. "Come with me."

He took me to a guy named Charlie Sewell, who asked me what I had been doing. I told him I had been a first assistant director at $75 a week. Sam interrupted and said, "Are you kidding? You have to earn your buttons before you can become a first assistant at Paramount at $75 a week."

Charlie was head of the prop department, and I ended up getting a job there as a member of the swing gang. It was a job I never heard of. They swing the furniture from the bins onto the truck onto the set. The set dresser goes with you and tells you what to pick up. Then you take the truck over to the stage and unload it. All that for $27.50, on the time clock! I had never touched a time clock in my life. But that was nothing. I was not even allowed to go out the front gate, which was across the street from Oblat's Restaurant. (This was long before they had a commissary, so it was the closest place to eat.) I had to walk all the way to the back, which took ten minutes each way. With a half hour for lunch I ended up with ten minutes to eat.

This went on week after week until pretty soon I ran out of energy. I was making about forty dollars a week, but I was falling apart. They gave me the dirtiest, toughest jobs they had. They gave me a Ford truck to drive to the public dump where I was supposed to pick up and load all this crap—garbage, cans, trash— onto the truck, then take it out to the Paramount ranch and dump it in the back to eventually go on a set. I vomited three times. I knew what was going on, and I hated that man with a passion.

After about six months of this they called me in and made a prop man out of me. A promotion. A prop man's job is, before a scene starts, to brush dust off an actor's shoulder, or shine his shoes, or whatnot. Well, no matter what the reason, I will never brush off anybody's shoulders or shine his shoes.

Throughout this whole time I kept out of sight. There were a lot of people working in the studio who came from the East who would have recognized me, and I didn't want them to. I wanted to be known still as an assistant director. One day I had to take a great big empty crate from the prop room to the wardrobe department, which was near the front gate. I waited until seven o'clock at night so I wouldn't be seen. I was wrestling with this goddamn thing, trying to get it up the steps when a voice said, "Artie Jacobson."

I turned around, and it was a dear friend from New York, Bill Goetz. In those days he was just an assistant director, but of the Goetz family. He was an assistant director living in a bungalow at the Ambassador Hotel, so you can imagine. He had met Schulberg in a card game and had come to work for Paramount. He asked me, "What the hell are you doing?"

Next day, I'm sitting on a stool in the restaurant and a little guy sits down next to me. He tells me he's been watching me. He says, "Don't worry about the time. Go home and change your clothes and come see me on Stage 5. You're going to be a second assistant director." I could have kissed him.

I get to Stage 5, and who's standing there to welcome me but Bill Goetz, who is the first assistant director on the picture. He had seen Sam Jaffe that morning and he had laid him out. (Jaffe told me this in later years.) Jaffe had said to Goetz, "What am I going to do with Schulberg?"

Goetz told him, "Leave him to me. This guy is going to be more help to me . . ." and Sam gave him the go-ahead. So that's how I became a second assistant director again.

The first assistant director read the script, then broke it down, scene by scene. Then he took a great big board with a lot of strips, and on each strip he wrote the scene number, a description of the action, which actors played in it, how many extras were needed, whether it was day or night lighting, whether it was location or studio, until the whole board was laid out with the entire picture.

The first assistant ran the set; he was the boss, under the director. He carried out anything the director wanted done. He also directed the background and the extras. He was responsible for hiring the extras, although they came through the casting office. He saw to it that everything was right, and he kept the whole thing rolling.

The second assistant did everything he could to help the first assistant. The first assistant would allow him to do a lot of things, if he wanted to. But if he was a bastard, he kept his second under his thumb.

Well, I got to do the picture. It was with Loretta Young, and she was fourteen years old. When the picture was finished, they signed Bill to do another immediately, and I was assigned to it, too. Bill let me do everything. He gave me a lot of freedom.

Now we go on location. The director is a Frenchman, Harry D'Arrast. Bill and Harry do not get along. Harry was used to things a certain way, and so was Bill. One day, on the way back from location, Bill said, "You know what I'm going to do? I'm going to start another picture soon, so I'm going to lay back on this one. I already have my reputation, so I'm going to let you take over. I want you to do the first's work so that when we get back to the studio all the director can think about is you, about what a bastard I am and what a great guy you are for saving the day." So it happened. And sure enough, when the next picture rolled around and Bill wasn't available, I became a first under this director. For the second time I was a full-fledged first who had earned his buttons. It was 1927.

I got to be very good friends with most of the directors; some of them were such wonderful guys. Some of them were bastards. I had a fist fight with Henry Hathaway. The only reason we didn't kill each other that night was that the stuntmen pulled us apart. He was a bastard and so was I. We later became very good friends.

If the director could do me a lot of good, I'd kiss his ass a couple of times. Only if it was necessary, and never publicly.

In 1944 I was working on a musical called *Something for the Boys*. One day a man came on the set, walked up to me and asked if he could have lunch with me. I said, "Sure, if you pay for it. It's got to be awful fast today—we're only taking about forty minutes for lunch so we can finish the picture."

He said, "I'll pay for it. First, I want to tell you who I am. My name is George Seaton, and I'm going to direct a thing I've written called *Diamond Horseshoe* for Betty Grable. And I'm going to reproduce the nightclub on stage. I want you to be my assistant."

"Why do you ask me?" I said. "You don't know me."

He said, "My wife Phyllis knows you, and she told me, 'The first thing you have to do is get Artie Jacobson as your assistant. All you have to do is direct, he'll do the rest.'"

So I took a chance, since he was Phyllis's husband and she was a friend. The first thing I did was talk George into something. I said to him, "Don't let it come from me, for God's sake—it will be nothing but trouble—but ask for a week's rehearsal with the cast. But don't do it until the set is up." Nobody had ever heard of that before. "This marking places out with chalk and tape—that's a lot of crap. Get the people in and rehearse it. You can iron out the bubbles. You're the writer."

My job with George was to break him in. So when Friday night came, I told him, "George, I'm going to dismiss the whole company. I want you and I to sit down right here on the set. We're going to start shooting Monday morning. We've just finished five wonderful, quiet working days. Starting Monday morning at eight o'clock all hell is going to break loose. There will be at least 250 to 450 people on the set. And tumult. I'm used to it, but you're not, and everybody is going to look to George Seaton for guidance. The grips, but everybody, will be asking 'What do you want us to do?' Unless you tell them what you want, nobody can do anything. The first guy who's going to come to you is the cameraman. Don't worry about the extras or the music. I'll take care of all that. And don't you answer any questions, except from the cameraman or the actors. Send all the others to me. That's what I'm here for."

He said, "God bless you."

But I warned him, "Remember, now, it's going to be very different—not like this week."

He said, "I know, I've been on sets."

"But you haven't been on a set as a director. That's a whole different story. You come on, you get in your chair and sit there. Don't go running around. Let me do all that; that's my job."

When we were making the picture *Somebody Loves Me*, Betty Hutton was the queen of her company and acted accordingly. People would dismiss her behavior because she wasn't the brightest gal in the world and she was raucous. The second day she called me over and said, "I see you around the set all the time. Do you work here?" I explained to her that I was assistant director to Perlberg and Seaton. I was there in case I could help in any way. In this particular case, she and the director weren't getting along. I helped, eventually, by transferring messages between the two of them. I was right in the middle. My job was to keep the feathers from being ruffled. If they got ruffled, I had to go in there and smooth them out. She asked me what I did exactly, so I told her, "I'm an ass-kisser."

She looked me right in the eye without cracking a smile. "You're what?"

"I'm an ass-kisser. I kiss asses."

She said, "I don't believe it."

"It's very simple," I said. "Turn around. Bend over." I kissed her ass, and from there on we were friends.

=

Let me tell you about *Miracle on 34th Street.* George had written, with his friend Al Davies, a thing called *The Big Heart,* which he carried in his pocket for years. Zanuck couldn't imagine it. He couldn't see Santa Claus in a court of law in New York City. So nothing was coming of it.

Came the time when, for some reason, there was no assignment for George, and he's sitting around on his *tuchis* doing nothing for $3,500 a week. So one day, over lunch, I said, "George, what about *The Big Heart?*" It was still in his pocket, but in the meantime he had taken it upon himself to go to New York and talk to Jack Strauss, who was Mr. Macy. He talked to Bernard Gimbel of Gimbel's. He had it all okayed, but still nothing from Zanuck. Finally, about a month before Thanksgiving and the Macy's parade, George went to Zanuck and he gave in.

Well, as soon as he got the green light, we had to get everything ready, get the whole company to New York and be prepared to shoot the parade. We needed nine cameras for all the angles. The parade only went for two and a half hours, from 77th Street and Central Park West to 34th Street and Broadway, and there were no retakes, no going back and doing it again.

The cast was wonderful: Ed Gwenn, Maureen O'Hara, John Payne. Mr. Gwenn fell apart after he read the script and couldn't call George fast enough. "When do we start?" He was absolutely insane about it. He was a wonderful man, and we got to be great friends, he and George, my wife and I.

Before we went to New York there was one stumbling block. We couldn't find a child. She had to be a strange child, five or six years old, who didn't believe in Santa Claus. One night at four in the morning I sat straight up in bed. I had all these things going around in my head, and I said, "Jesus, God. Natasha!" I called George right then and there, before I forgot.

Natasha was a little four-year-old we had seen while we were making a picture up north. Well, she turned out to be Natasha

(Natalie) Wood. She was a child prodigy, an accomplished pianist who spoke English, Russian, and a smattering of two other languages.

The director was crazy about this child. He was so crazy about her that when he got back to Hollywood he asked the parents to bring her down. He had a little something that he would like her to do in the picture, one little scene that involved a scoop of ice cream melting on the sidewalk, having fallen off its cone. Naturally, the child cries at the empty cone in her hand. So they came down here and he put them under personal contract.

George was delighted with the idea. "Why the hell didn't you think about this sooner? We've been agonizing so, and she's perfect." So she became the little girl in *Miracle on 34th Street*.

Anyhow, now we start to make the picture. One of the things we had to figure out was how to accomodate Mr. Gwenn, who had a little problem. He never knew when he was going to urinate, and he refused to allow anybody else to play Santa Claus in the parade. He wanted to do the "Ho, Ho, Ho, Merry Christmas!" So we dressed him very, very warmly, and we rigged a funnel with a long pipe trailing out of the sleigh. How would they get wise? That's picture-making.

We had five windows where we put cameras to get our angles. George and I were on top of a station wagon so that we could shoot certain scenes and then we could beat the parade by twenty blocks and get some more angles before we wound up on 34th Street, where he climbed out and onto a marquee.

At one point they came to me and said, "We're in trouble. We're going to lose one of our key spots. That camera has to come out of that window." It seems that Papa didn't know that Mama had given permission to put a camera in the window (for which she was to be paid). Papa wouldn't be able to see the parade because our camera was in the way, and he wanted it the hell out of there. A couple of bucks did the job.

So now we're going to work in Macy's, the real Macy's. Jack Strauss would give us anything we wanted, anything at all. We had a scene on the mezzanine floor. They were to get out of the elevator, walk all the way down and around a corner, onto an escalator. They rode the escalator down to the main floor, where there must have been ten thousand people. We couldn't afford that many extras. When George showed us what he wanted to do, a Hollywood grip said he thought he could figure out a way to do it. He figured it would be just like landing an airplane. When a plane lands, it lands nosewheel first, and goes down gradually, on a slant. Sure enough, this worked on the escalator. When the step went down, the wheel under our dolly went down, too.

The next scenes we wanted to shoot were with the real people. Rigging that store with the lights and cables was really something. While we were getting ready, somebody came to me and said, "We've got *tsuris [trouble]*. Building Safety and Fire Department, right there."

I asked, "What's wrong?"

"Number one: There are people who are stepping onto those escalators, and POW! bright lights! They're going to be stumbling all over the place trying to figure out what's happening. It's too dangerous. Number two: the fire department says we can't have these cables on the floor."

Again our resourceful grip whispered in my ear. He suggested we string the cables up the back sides of the pilasters. We put every lamp on a rheostat which enabled us to bring them up slowly.

That's the kind of guys we have in this town. We have guys here who couldn't make it in a college of arts and sciences, but they sure as hell make it as a grip. They get good money for it, and the longer they work, the more experienced they get. They can do more goddamn things.

We had a problem with Bellevue Hospital, I remember. Gwenn was supposed to go by car from the front of Macy's right to the hospital. The unit manager supposedly made all the arrangements. He had in fact been unsuccessful, but had neglected to tell us. So we went out that morning to shoot these scenes, and it was cold. And we had old man Gwenn, who was not a well man by that time, sitting in a car all bundled up. The unit manager had somehow disappeared.

When we started to do the scene, the guards outside the hospital stopped us. George improvised immediately. He brought the car up as far as they would let it come, and the camera then panned and showed the building. It worked all right. We found out later the reason they wouldn't let us in was because they didn't like the way the hospital was portrayed in Billy Wilder's *The Lost Weekend,* which had been filmed a couple of years earlier, in 1945. Wilder had shown Bellevue as a terrible place, so the hospital people didn't trust anybody in the picture business.

The previews for *Miracle* were unbelievable. You should have heard the applause at the courtroom scene, where we proved beyond a question of a doubt in a court of law that he was really Santa Claus. In those days we used to give the audience cards so we could get their reactions. We put all the cards on Zanuck's desk, and he ordered another preview for the following night. Of course, it was the same reaction.

Working in pictures got me a paycheck every week, and it's allowed me to get a pension so I can live the way I do. I actually retired after working on *Camelot* in 1967. My hips were starting to bother me; I was looking for a place to lean, which is no good in my job.

September 1985
Culver City

ARTHUR JACOBSON

FILMOGRAPHY (partial)

(As Cameraman)

1923   *Zaza* (dir. Allan Dwan, Famous Players–Lasky)
         Puritan Passions (dir. Frank Tuttle, Film Guild)

1924   *Shadows of Paris* (dir. Herbert Brenon, Paramount)
         Three Miles Out (dir. Irvin Willat, D.W. Griffith)
         Grit (dir. Frank Tuttle, Film Guild)

(As Assistant Director)

1929   *The Wild Party* (dir. Dorothy Arzner, Paramount)
         Chinatown Nights (dir. William Wellman, Paramount)

1937   *I Met Him in Paris* (dir. Wesley Ruggles, Paramount)

1938   *Sing You Sinners* (dir. Wesley Ruggles, Paramount)

1944   *Something for the Boys* (dir. Lewis Seiler, Twentieth Century–Fox)

1945   *Billy Rose's Diamond Horseshoe* (dir. George Seaton, Twentieth Century–Fox)

1947   *Miracle on 34th Street* (dir. George Seaton, Twentieth Century–Fox)

1952   *Somebody Loves Me* (dir. Irving Brecher, Paramount)

1967   *Camelot* (dir. Joshua Logan, Warner Bros.)

≡

AL KELLER

**First Assistant
Camera Operator**

≡

*Al Keller was fascinated with cameras from the time he was a boy,
making home movies with his brother in the twenties. The years spent
under the legendary cinematographer Joe Walker at Columbia Studios were some of the most rewarding in a long and satisfying career
of filming some 160 features.*

*Keller is a tall, twinkly-eyed old shoe, who bears a slight resem-
blance to Telly Savalas. Well into his seventies, he is still possessed of
an enchanting enthusiasm for his profession and so devotes much of
his current time to the American Society of Cinematographers.*

My family and I moved out to California in 1920, and our house
in East Hollywood just happened to be two blocks from the old
Vitagraph Studios. My brother and I, who were already thrilled
with the movies, found a spot to crawl under the fence outside
the studio. We'd wander through the sets after everybody had
gone home.

I had a friend, Ed Harris, whose mother had bought him one
of those little 9.5mm movie cameras. We could buy fifty-foot rolls
of Will Rogers shorts and other comedies, and we'd show those
with Ed's projector. We also made some of our own films, though
I wasn't happy with the results. The pictures looked dim and blurry.

Cameraman Al Keller, shooting aerial background process shots as independent contractor to Columbia Studios, 1936.

My brother and I saved up to buy our own projector, and when a friend of ours bought a 16mm camera, we just borrowed it from him and began to improve our product. We started making our own short films. Our first effort was called *A Loose Nut,* and it starred my kid brother, Frank, as a lunatic who escaped from an asylum. The next one was about three boys who wanted to buy a car, and to get it they had to become prizefighters. That was called *Ford Preferred.*

Then my brother had an idea for a film that we called *The Golden Age.* It was dedicated to Clara Bow, whom my brother had a big crush on. It was about a high school boy who saves an actress from the attentions of a drunk.

In 1923, through a friend of mine whose father was a director, I got work as an extra. At last I was in a real movie studio. It was exciting, but what really fascinated me was what the cameraman was doing. I couldn't take my eyes off him.

I watched him crank that beautiful Bell & Howell 2709, cranking with his right hand, with his left hand on the pinion up there. I saw how he would change speed. If the action slowed down, he would slow down. He would compensate with the shutter for the exposure. He really had it down pat.

After the Crash, when my family was pretty much wiped out, I got a job as a messenger at Columbia Studios. I'll never forget the night I delivered a script to Jeannette MacDonald. She came to the door in a negligee, with a backlight.

Shortly after that I heard that Frank Capra was starting a picture called *Rain or Shine*. It was a circus movie, and I heard by the grapevine that they were going to shoot it out at the Jeffries Ranch. They were going to need four or five cameras, so I screwed up my courage and went over and applied for a job as a loader. That means you load the camera, but don't get the idea that it's a simple job. It's a big responsibility because you have to get the right film in there. It has to be done in the dark, and you can't make any mistakes. I'd go out with a black changing bag, put a black cloth over the bag and around me, too, to be sure that no light leaked in there.

Eventually I wangled a job as a night film-loader, which meant I could sleep in one of the three darkrooms they had that was never used. I cleaned it out and it became my apartment. I took showers in the new writers' building. I promoted some furniture pads, brought a pillow from home, and actually lived at Columbia Studios for almost two years. The price was right.

As a loader I didn't get a chance to really get to know Mr. Capra, but I used to listen very carefully and watch his directing technique. When he gave instructions to the cast he would always talk in the third person, even with extras and bit players, to sustain the mood. I never saw any other director do that.

By 1932 I was attaching myself as best I could to Joe Walker, a first-rate cinematographer. The best I could get with his crew was third assistant cameraman, but I really admired him and wanted to work with him. I worked myself up to first assistant, and I worked on *Miracle Woman, Lost Horizon, Theodora Goes Wild,* and many others. Those were some of the best years of my life.

September 1985
Hollywood
Pacific Palisades

Editors' Note: Al Keller died in 1990.

FILMOGRAPHY (partial)

(As Film Loader)

1930   *Rain or Shine* (dir. Frank Capra, Columbia)

(As Assistant Cameraman)

1931   *Dirigible* (dir. Frank Capra, Columbia)
          Platinum Blonde (dir. Frank Capra, Columbia)
1932   *The Miracle Woman* (dir. Frank Capra, Columbia)
          Forbidden (dir. Frank Capra, Columbia)
          American Madness (dir. Frank Capra, Columbia)
1933   *The Bitter Tea of General Yen* (dir. Frank Capra, Columbia)
          Lady for a Day (dir. Frank Capra, Columbia)

1934	*It Happened One Night* (dir. Frank Capra, Columbia)
	Broadway Bill (dir. Frank Capra, Columbia)
	One Night of Love (dir. Victor Schertzinger, Columbia)
1935	*Love Me Forever* (dir. Victor Schertzinger, Columbia)
	Let's Live Tonight (dir. Victor Schertzinger, Columbia)
1936	*Mr. Deeds Goes to Town* (dir. Frank Capra, Columbia)
	Theodora Goes Wild (dir. Richard Boleslawski, Columbia)
	The King Steps Out (dir. Josef von Sternberg, Columbia)
1937	*Lost Horizon* (dir. Frank Capra, Columbia)

≡ THE DEAL MAKERS ≡

Sam Jaffe, agent, in the 1930s.

SAM JAFFE

Agent

Sam Jaffe looks like an agent, like a man who has seen it all. Now eighty-four years old, he is balding and slim, sporting contemporary leisure clothes offset by the requisite California tan. Greeting us at the door of his modest apartment, he starts talking immediately, not waiting for any questions. He knows what he wants to talk about and is not particularly interested in what we want to hear. While not exactly bitter, he is certainly a disappointed man. There is no doubt he would have much to contribute if he were still involved in the business, but he is a dinosaur, a relic of the old Hollywood, and he knows it.

I started out in the distribution end of the business with B. P. Schulberg in New York, at a company he started called Preferred Pictures. Schulberg was my brother-in-law; he was married to my sister. I told him I wanted to come out to Hollywood, that I must see what was going on. So I came out here and got a job as a prop boy around 1921.

It was so easy to see what was going on because the whole studio was not much bigger than this flat. It was an open stage and there were three shops in the back: a carpentry shop, a plaster shop, and a prop shop. That was the whole studio. We worked in the sunlight, and if the wind was blowing on the tablecloth we'd put an ashtray on it.

Within three or four months of observing, I became the studio manager. But there wasn't anything to observe. The whole operation was right in front of me. I knew when the producer was not coming, if the star was coming late, that the production manager never came, that the art director was renting furniture for too much money. I was an eager little boy watching everything. It wasn't long before I realized, "This is all wrong. Schulberg should come out here and be the producer and let me take over the studio manager's job." And that's how my career in Hollywood began.

After Schulberg came out he asked me if I thought I could be a production manager of the studio, and I answered, "With this little finger." Schulberg and I became successful. We made a lot of pictures. We had Clara Bow, we had William Wellman.

Paramount was doing badly at the time, and they offered to buy our company if we would come in and run the studio. Paramount was then on Vine Street and Sunset Boulevard, and I got them to sell that property and made them a big profit. I bought the studio they have now; I bought that property. It was called the Robert Brunton Studio.

When Mayer and Schulberg broke up, Mayer wanted me to join him at Metro. His offer was very tempting because Irving Thalberg had just moved over from Universal, and he had Harry Rapf there, too. I was very flattered, but I felt an obligation to Schulberg. I remained with Schulberg because I was always very fond of him and he gave me my chance. I was very devoted to him.

The destruction of Schulberg is a whole story in itself. As I said, he was married to my sister, and I lived with them for a while when I first came out. When he was working well—that is, when he was normal and well—he would come home with his scripts, have dinner, and everything was great. But when he was broke I continuously lent him money—as Eddie Cantor and a few others did. Other people let him down.

I think Schulberg in those days made $6,500 a week, so you can imagine how that kind of money affected him. Ben couldn't take that kind of success. He went crazy. He gambled, he screwed, and he drank. He was screwing every girl that came along. He was handsome, he was intelligent, but the business was going down, and he was fired, finally. He ruined himself.

He was so dear to me. I loved this man. I had such great respect, and my heart was breaking for him. I said to Schulberg one day when he was down, "You know, Ben, I've learned a lot from you—what to do and what not to do—and seeing what happened to you frightens me. I know if I do what you did I'll be in the gutter."

He said, "Well, I don't think there's any chance of your doing it." He was so wonderful. That's when he was down, and writing letters to everyone to borrow money. Painful. I think it was 1949 when he put those ads in the trade papers pleading for jobs.

So I would say that he just couldn't handle all this money. It was the same thing with Zanuck. Here he was, the head of a studio, making a fortune, doing well, screwing every dame, running around, and then deciding to give it all up and go live in France. He made terrible pictures and lived with some prostitute. The story is so sad. When he was an old, sick man, he came back to his wife, Virginia, and she took him back until he died. It's a fascinating story, but not an uncommon one.

Darryl Zanuck needed Virginia. David Selznick needed Irene. When they gave up those partners, they gave up something that was very basic. Not only the relationships themselves, but the balance those women provided in their lives.

I was shocked when I was representing Jennifer Jones and the studio said to me, "We're going to put a clause in her contract that David can't call up and ask to read the scripts and see the rushes."

"Gee," I said. "You can't do that. That's such an insult."

They said, "Yeah, but he drives everybody crazy."

This was the mighty David Selznick they were talking about. I worked with him at Paramount. He was brilliant. He was knowledgeable. He was a producer who knew what stories were like. Look at the list of pictures he made. They weren't mistakes. He didn't promote them, he produced them. To see this man being shunted around was heartbreaking. But, in a way, he, too, brought it on himself.

I was more fortunate than many, in my background. My father was a very, very religious man, and as a young boy I was a rabbinical scholar. I think that helped me in my life here in Hollywood. I had ideals, I had basic principles, I had a family, relationships, and all that. I always remember something my father said to me years ago, when I was a poor little boy on the Lower East Side. He said, "You know, success is much harder to cope with than poverty." At the time I thought it was a nice thing for an old man to say, and I guessed it was from the Bible, but I didn't understand it. Later I realized what he meant. It did come from the Bible, not from my father's experience. He didn't know about success; he was a poor man. But he was right in his teachings.

There isn't any poverty of any kind like I had growing up. My mother never learned to speak English; she died speaking only Yiddish. My father worked as a glazier, and he spoke English and could also read and write in it. I slept in a bed, all my life until I left for Hollywood, with my father and two brothers. I never saw pyjamas in my life until I went on the road. We had no pyjamas. My father took his clothes off and got into bed in his underwear. We all got into bed that way. When I was a film salesman and went on the road, I saw these guys in their pyjamas. When I came back to the house I would hide my pyjamas. How could I put them on when my father had none?

I also worked with Selznick when he was at RKO, and when he left, I left. I was there about a year—eighteen months. When

Selznick formed his own studio I went to Columbia. Harry Cohn wanted me, but it was a mistake. I knew it was a mistake when I took the job, but he romanced me until I accepted. I was there for about a year and a half.

After Columbia I could have gone back to Metro, but I decided I'd go in to the agency business instead. I wasn't sure that I'd like it, but I felt it would give me some security. That's what was uppermost in my mind, being a poor boy. I felt that the agency could do it for me, and it did. It was my own agency, the Jaffe Agency. I had Humphrey Bogart, Lauren Bacall, Freddie March, David Niven, Joan Fontaine, Barbara Stanwyck, Mark Robson, Robert Wise, Lee J. Cobb, Zero Mostel, Mary Astor—I can't begin to think of all of them.

Back then the movie business was made up of creators. People like Selznick, Thalberg, Schulberg, Zanuck, Wallis—those were really great creators. They were brilliant. When I was at Paramount we made fifty-two pictures in a year, and Metro made fifty pictures, and Fox made fifty pictures, and they were all very important pictures. When I was at Paramount we had Lubitsch, we had Mamoulian, we had von Sternberg, and we had the Marx Brothers. Now Paramount makes maybe ten pictures a year. So every picture that is submitted to them means a lot. The costs are so outrageous.

Cameramen today are getting $10,000 a week. When I was making pictures they were getting $750. Cutters now get $4,000, $5,000. A director who has failed after three pictures is only getting a million dollars. *A million dollars.*

In my days studios used to put the brakes on and say, "Wait a minute. We're not going to pay that kind of money." And the studios would confer with one another and agree on limits to what they would pay a particular person. It was a business, with a system that developed people.

How many stars are being developed today? Very few, because if a producer has a package, he doesn't want to take a risk with an unknown girl. In the old days Paramount, Columbia, MGM all had rosters and they nursed their people along. Clark Gable wouldn't have happened but for the old studio system. They brought people along, gave them the right parts, publicized them. Sure, they were under contract (and they were slave-labor contracts) but it was a better business.

I made *Born Free* after I retired and was living in England. I had left Hollywood and went to live there. Lester Cole was living there then, too, and of course I knew him very well because I represented him. You see, I knew that *Born Free* was no great job to do because all you needed was pages. You couldn't change that basic story. I felt sorry for Lester so I thought, "What the hell? I don't need a great genius, I need a scriptwriter," so I called him to give him the job. It was *rach mones [compassion]*.

He got $10,000 for it, but they wouldn't put his name on it. Mike Frankovich said, "He's a commie. He'll drive me crazy." They were still frightened in those days, even in the early sixties. A lot of careers and lives were ruined in the McCarthy era. There were suicides, divorces, all that.

When I retired twenty-five years ago, I decided that I wanted another life. I'd been here for thirty-five years. I found it difficult staying here because I found that the same people were coming in and out of my life. I was still living in the same house. I felt I had to get out, so I went to England. While I was there I couldn't make up my mind, so I made three pictures: a small picture called *Damon and Pythias;* a picture with my son-in-law, starring Vincent Price; and then I did *Born Free*. When I left here I didn't think I wanted to come back. What do I come back to?

Well, now I am back, but, as they say in the fight game, I've hung up my gloves. Now I go to UCLA, where I read de Tocqueville and Kafka and Rousseau and Adam Smith, and I don't know about these stars anymore. They don't interest me. I go to the *[Motion Picture]* Academy, and some of the pictures I like are failures, and some of the pictures I don't like are successful. It's a different world to me.

My career in the movies was very exciting. My work was creative. It was also an education. Every picture was an event. There's no other business that's comparable. I had to read a lot, I had to study a lot, I had to understand a lot. I had to learn about sound and all the other technical things. I had to be involved in everything, and that meant I learned about people, too.

When I came here I knew everybody in the business, including the electricians and the doormen, so that when I walked down the street I was recognized. Now, I'm from Memory Lane. They say, "Oh, Sam Jaffe. I remember that name." I'm a historical figure. But that doesn't bother me. I accept life as it comes. I'm eighty-four and I don't want to work anymore. I don't want to make a picture. If I walk in with a script, gray-haired Sam Jaffe, eighty-four years old, they're going to help me sit down. I've done all that; I've had all those anxieties.

People say to me, "You want to make a picture?"

I say, "Make a picture? I'll die from aggravation."

March 1985
Beverly Hills

SAM JAFFE

CAREER HIGHLIGHTS

1920–1921   Studio Manager, Preferred Pictures, Mayer-Schulberg Studio

1922   Production Manager, Producer, B. P. Schulberg

1923–1929   Production Manager, Executive Manager, Paramount

1930–1932   Production Manager, Assistant to David O. Selznick, RKO

1933   Assistant to Sam Briskin, Columbia

1934   Partner, Schulberg, Feldman, Jaffe, talent agents

1935   President, Sam Jaffe Inc., Sam Jaffe Ltd. (later, the Jaffe Agency)

FILMOGRAPHY (partial)

(As Producer)

1944   *The Sullivans* (dir. Lloyd Bacon, Twentieth Century–Fox)

1961   *Damon and Pythias* (dir. Curtis Bernhardt, MGM)

1965   *Born Free* (dir. James Hill, Columbia/Open Road)

1973   *Theatre of Blood* (dir. Douglas Hickox, United Artists/Cineman)

JOSEPH J. COHN

Production Manager

≡

Joe Cohn's slim publicity file at the Academy of Motion Picture Arts and Sciences Library contains a faded, undated memorandum from MGM publicist Howard Strickling outlining Cohn's career. According to Strickling, Cohn was "the last word where production problems are concerned." In his decades of motion picture work, beginning on the East Coast at the Fox Film Company in 1915, Cohn emphasized that filmmaking should be closely integrated, cooperative work. Viewing his own contributions as purely behind the scenes, he preferred no screen credits.

Cohn worked in scenario and film editing before landing a job at the Samuel Goldwyn Company as a cashier and purchasing agent. In 1919, when Goldwyn acquired the Triangle Studio in Culver City, Cohn moved to California as business manager, becoming production chief in 1924, when the merger with Metro and Mayer occurred.

Today, nearly one hundred years old, Joe Cohn can still conduct an interview, keep two secretaries busy, escort ladies to dinner, and display a wicked sense of humor. He is neatly dressed in slacks and a bright orange sport shirt when we arrive early one morning at his Beverly Hills home.

Still supremely modest, he downplays the importance of his position at MGM. He seems genuinely unaware of his legendary status.

When we ask him to sign a release, he quips: "Does this mean I lose the house?"

Joseph J. Cohn, longtime production manager for MGM, in the 1940s.

My wife never understood what my job was. She would go up to friends at parties and ask, "Exactly what does Joe do?"

I used to say, "I pick up the garbage." I saw what went on.

I was the production manager of MGM, helping decide things like where we would make the picture and how we would make the picture. I was the production manager of the studio *[1924]*, and then I was made an executive *[1938]* in charge of a number of productions.

I would go to Mr. Thalberg and say, "How do we handle this picture—importantly or scrounging?" This was regarding the budget. I remember on *The Big House [1930]*, I went to him and asked him how we wanted to handle it, and he said, "I think we should handle it importantly."

Usually the management—the top management—decided how to do the picture. Everything was spelled out as carefully as we could. We had a marvelous organization. We had very good people and I had a very good staff. Cedric Gibbons was the head of the art department, and he had very good men working for him.

I got involved very early. I would approve the sets—where we built them, how we built them. I approved the plans, just like you would if you were building a house. We almost never went against the director, if he needed more, if he needed less. We weren't a penny ante outfit. If the assistant director or the director needed twenty people, we didn't say, "Can't you get along with eighteen?" The result was that there was a meeting of the minds.

A perfect example of this was the first *Mutiny on the Bounty* [1935]. The whole picture was made in California. We sent a cameraman and a second-unit director to get some shots of Tahiti, but outside of that the whole picture was made in California, on Catalina Island, and we helped lay it out. It didn't look too different at all. We didn't go on the basis of cheating on the picture; the picture was important.

Directors had a great deal to say, but they didn't have complete say, the way they do now. We utilized what tricks we had, what background we had. I had a hand in that.

MGM was a very loose organization. We had producers who were paid a great deal of respect. I'll give you a perfect example. We were going to make a Tarzan picture [*Tarzan the Ape Man, 1932*]. A man by the name of Bernie Hyman was the producer. The Tarzan pictures used to gross $500,000. Bernie Hyman wanted that swimmer—what's his name? Johnny Weissmuller. (I forget my mother's name sometimes.) He was then a model for B.V.D.s. Somehow or other, we finally got him. I went to Mr. Thalberg as to how we wanted to handle it, because we had a budget of about $600,000. He said, "Joe, the pictures haven't grossed that much. Do what you can to take it down."

So I went to Bernie Hyman and we eliminated little things. Finally, I went to Thalberg and said, "We can't eliminate certain things from this picture without harming it. What Bernie wants on the picture is going to cost money."

Mr. Thalberg said, "Joe, I've been talking to Hyman for three weeks. You talk to him now."

I came back a week later and said, "We can't take anything more out. We can take out maybe forty or fifty thousand dollars, from $600,000."

He said, "Well, do the best you can."

We didn't take an *atom* out of the film. And we made the picture for about $600,000 or $650,000. Needless to say, the film must have grossed about a million and a half. For that period, it was a lot of money. That was the first Tarzan movie that we made. Sol Lesser used to make them for $400,000, with Elmo Lincoln and those people.

The financial end was a rather loose arrangement. If we had a producer who wanted to do something extravagant or over budget and we couldn't convince him against it, we usually went to Mr. Thalberg, sometimes Mr. Mayer. Mr. Mayer rarely interfered, but he interfered a great deal at times. He liked the "Hardy" pictures.

We had a sort of stock company. We had the swimmer, Esther Williams. Jack Cummings, Mayer's nephew, didn't get the breaks. He wasn't treated any better than anyone else. He went up to San Francisco and saw the swimmer, and Mr. Mayer didn't know he brought her down. She made more money for the studio than anyone else. Finally, one day I said to Mr. Mayer, "Did you know about this?"

And he said, "No, I didn't know." He called Jack to his office. I'm trying to give you a picture of what it was like.

I was the executive in charge of the Andy Hardy pictures and the Dr. Kildare pictures. Mayer had a phobia about Mickey Rooney. He thought he was getting out of hand and overplaying the role. Mickey was a magnificent talent; he could do everything.

Anyway, there was an incident in a Hardy picture. Mayer came out of the theater, and he assailed me. Mickey was having dinner in the picture, and he pushed the plate away and he said, "I don't want it."

Mayer came out and said, "How can that boy insult his mother like that?" He was so offended that we cut it out of the picture. I'm trying to give you a picture of how it was.

Mayer used to take scripts up to Marie Dressler when she was living in Santa Barbara or someplace, when there was a thought that she would never work again. She was very ill, but very great, and the character she played in *Anna Christie* with Garbo, she was wonderful. Frances Marion pushed her a great deal. They were great friends. Dressler was kept on the payroll for a long time; that's how Mayer was.

Correspondingly, Lionel Barrymore was kept on the payroll for a long time, even though he couldn't get around. He had very bad arthritis. We wanted to use him in Kildare, and I said, "He can't walk." He thought he could.

Carey Wilson and I went up to see him, and we asked, "Lionel, can you walk?"

"Oh, yes," he says. He could walk three steps through sheer will power, but then he had to put his hand onto something. Well, we put him in a wheelchair and that's how he did the role.

Barrymore was able to keep working, and that way we were able to keep him on salary. Mayer was always good about that. Cedric Gibbons was kept on salary for quite a while. A lot of monetary things like this weren't even discussed; they were taken for granted. It was the way the studio was run.

When I was production manager, if I heard of a very good production unit manager, I would hire him. I would put him on the payroll and say, "Break the script down, efficiently. How can we shoot it so we don't have to keep an actor on salary for ten weeks for two days' work?" No one forced me to hire anyone; I did what I wanted, pretty much.

At times movies did run over budget. But we didn't think in those terms unless there was a major degree of insanity. We tried to keep it within bounds, and no one was on my back saying, "Well, we're running $12,000 over or $22,000 over." We knew it.

On the first *Mutiny on the Bounty,* we did a lot of stuff on backgrounds, and Frank Lloyd said we were doing more stuff outside. Well, we went out for a couple of days and then I took the company back in. No one said to me, "You shouldn't do it." And I didn't go to Thalberg about it. At times (and rather rarely) I did say, "Can we eliminate so-and-so?" I could *suggest.*

Also, if the unit manager came and said, "Joe, instead of moving this scene to the living room, why can't we continue it in the bedroom? We have a bedroom built; we can do some more work in there." I wouldn't dare make the decision.

I'd call up the very capable producer, in this case Hunt Stromberg, and say, "Hunt, Eddie Waller has a very good idea. I'm going to send him up and let him explain it to you." I would let *him* do it—and let *him* take the credit for the idea. That would elevate him a little more. That's the way the studio was run.

I would never change the design of the set. That was up to Cedric Gibbons. I could say, "We don't need an extra wall there," or "Why don't we move the desk out further?" but Gibbons had such good people working for him. There was a great viewpoint of economy, which no one really realized.

When we made *Ben Hur [1926],* the picture had been started under different management. I had made a previous trip to Europe to figure out whether or not we could make the picture cheaper—or less expensively. (I hated the word *cheaper.*) I came back and said the picture could never be made for $600,000. We had the whole Colosseum built in Rome. And then Thalberg insisted that the whole picture come back.

Cedric Gibbons designed the set, and it was built two or three miles outside the studio. The unfortunate thing was that where we built it, the fog came in every day. Finally, we get all the people there—an enormous number of people. Thalberg didn't think we had enough people, but I said we had enough. Fred Niblo laid out where he wanted the cameras.

We had shot one scene when the fog raised a little, and then we dismissed the company. We were waiting for the fog to lift, and then we had to send out for more extras—about three hundred. We got some extra police, and the police ate more sandwiches than they should have. They ate two sandwiches each, instead of one. It wasn't a problem with the budget. We ordered enough, but with the added people, we didn't have enough. So I turned to Charlie Stallings, the a.d. *[assistant director]*, and I said, "Have they come in with the extra food?"

He said, "No."

And when you wait, two minutes are like ten. Two minutes later I said, "Charlie, have the sandwiches come in?"

Niblo said, "Don't rush it."

I said, "If it isn't soon, the people will have a riot here. They need to be fed." I also said, "Charlie, get the horses out on the track." The director really should say that. We got the horses, and Niblo said, "We're going to have a riot if people don't have their food."

You see, authority is something that you take. When you have to.

I had an office in the main building, where Mr. Mayer was, but finally I moved my office to the studio itself so I could get to the set fast.

I didn't believe in writing notes to directors. If you could speak to them face-to-face, it was a great deal more effective. We never interfered with the director's shooting unless he was doing something really wrong. And the directors, if you showed them anything at all that made sense, they would go along with you or improve on it. It seemed to me that's how it was. We were very fortunate because we had such good directors, and also very good assistant directors and unit managers.

You see, a lot of directors had been there from the silent days, when some of them were actors. A lot of these directors knew a lot of the tricks. Some of them came from the silents and some from the theater. Thalberg brought George Cukor from New York. Woody *[W. S.]* Van Dyke was marvelous. He could do anything twice as fast as anyone else, and he could handle actors. Carey Wilson was afraid to go near Woody Van Dyke with any criticism.

Once we were using a girl who was a cello player, and we put her in an *Andy Hardy* picture, thinking we might develop something. I looked at the rushes and I thought maybe we could get by, but Carey Wilson thought they weren't any good, and I actually agreed with him. I said, "Go down and see Woody Van Dyke."

He said, "No, *you* go down and see him."

So I went and said, "Woody, the girl isn't too good."

He said, "Joe, she isn't too good at all."

I said, "Let's retake it."

He said, "No, I don't want to do it now. If I do it now, then it will kill her and give her a sense that she's not coming across. I'll do it at the end of the picture; it will be better then." And we listened to him.

After Mr. Mayer left, Eddie Mannix, Benny Thau, and I were put in charge of the studio. Later, Benny put Sol Siegel in charge, and that was its downfall. When I left MGM, it was because my contract was up. I had no desire to stay on. Studios were run in such a different manner than I had been accustomed to.

August 1993
Beverly Hills

JACK
CUMMINGS

Producer

≡

Jack Cummings came to Hollywood from his native Canada. A nephew of Louis B. Mayer, he began at MGM as an office boy and, not unexpectedly, worked his way up to producer.

When we arrive at his house, he greets us at the door, unshaven and still in his pyjamas and robe. He admits he has forgotten all about our appointment, but nevertheless graciously ushers us into the living room. It is filled with antiques and a grand piano, and on the walls are original works by Diego Rivera and Milton Avery. On a side table is a framed photo inscribed "Uncle Louis."

Once Cummings starts talking, there is no stopping him. We talk for several hours, well into the afternoon. And he has never gotten out of his robe. Fully dressed, he might have given us the entire history of MGM.

Once, Mr. Mayer was having problems with one of his daughters. He tried to reach me in New York, and in the process made a big man of me. I was just Mr. Cummings from Los Angeles until eight messages came in saying: LOUIS B. MAYER, URGENT, GET IN TOUCH IMMEDIATELY.

I got in so late I didn't want to call him. At eight o'clock my phone rang. "I left messages for you. Where the hell were you? Don't you ever get home at night? Get out of bed and come on over. I'll make you an omelette like your grandmother used to make for you."

"Where are you?" I asked. He gave me the name of his hotel. "You're in New York?"

"Yes, I couldn't wait for you to call."

"I'll be right there."

When I got to the hotel, he was in one of those funny, short-sleeved shirts he used to wear, and it was in shreds. I asked him if he was all right.

"I have to come to New York to see you, *macher.*" Big shot. He used to call me that.

He told me about the trouble he was having with his daughter that he blamed himself for. I tried to comfort him, but it was no use. He started to tear at himself. I said, "Whoa, where's your coat and hat?" I wanted to get him out of there, walking. We left and went into the park.

We talked and talked. Finally, after hours of walking he said, "You know, I think you're right. I'm glad I came to New York." The point is, the great Louis B. Mayer was human. He had a heart, and he could be hurt. I guess I was sort of like a son to Mr. Mayer, the son he never had.

In the case of my dear friend Lester Cole *[one of the "Hollywood Ten," a group of writers blacklisted during the McCarthy era]* Mr. Mayer showed real compassion. You must understand that there was real fear. The day the indictment came out from the government, Lester called me and I said, "Get your ass to the studio. You must come in. Don't give them a chance to break your contract because you didn't show. Come."

So he came. He was visibly shaken. Because from now on, they took off the boxing gloves, and this was bare-knuckle stuff. I told him to be prepared, because it was going to be very rough. He was very depressed and frightened. He had a family, a wife and two kids. Suddenly, the power of the United States government had shown itself, and it was no longer child's play. It got to be about 12:30, and I said, "How about some lunch?"

"Oh, I couldn't eat," he said.

I said, "I don't care whether you're hungry or not. I'm inviting you to lunch, and you're coming with me, and we're going into that commissary. You're going to show your mettle. Now come with me."

"What's it going to do to you?" he asked.

"You worry about yourself; don't worry about me." And we went down.

Everybody turned away. The moment we appeared in that place, where ordinarily you couldn't hear yourself think, you could cut the silence with a knife. The woman who normally seated us hung back, and I asked her, "Are you going to seat us or not?" Lester was trembling. So was I—trembling with anger. I mean, here was a guy being judged before he has a trial!

Mr. Mayer sent for me. He said, "You always talk so nicely about this fellow. The government's indicted him."

I said, "Yes, that's right. But I believe in the right of free speech." Now, Mr. Mayer was my uncle and he was very concerned.

"Is he a Communist?" he asked.

I replied, "I don't know. I never asked him what his politics were. I hired him as a writer."

Mr. Mayer asked what he could do. I asked if he wouldn't like to meet Lester. I told him I thought they would find much in common.

Lester didn't believe Mr. Mayer wanted to meet him, but I took him to the office and left the two of them alone.

Three hours later he came to my office, practically in tears. He had had to reevaluate his opinion of Mr. Mayer. He said he had found more humanity, more understanding . . . that L. B. had talked to him like a father.

We used to fight, though. One of our memorable fights was over a producer named Benny Ziedman. Benny was a wonderful little man. He had worked for Paramount and Warner Brothers as a producer, and suddenly came upon hard times. We all tried to get him a job. Finally, he got a job at Metro. He fished out an old script called *The Youngest Profession*. And the picture played, of all places, the Roxy in New York. No Metro picture had ever played the Roxy. Well, we all pounded him on the back and said, "You little bastard."

One evening I walked into Mr. Mayer's office and here was Harry Rapf, obviously denigrating him, saying, "Well, you see, L. B., it was somebody else's script that he took. He had nothing to do with it."

I said, "Excuse me, Mr. Mayer. Are you by any chance talking about Benny Ziedman?"

He said, "Yes."

I said, "You mean the man that made the picture that for the first time in Metro history played the Roxy?"

He said, "Yes."

I said, "Well, I hope before you make any decision you will think of the implications to the rest of us. Is the reward for making a picture that plays the Roxy being fired? Because that's how it looks to me. The same scripts were lying around for other people. I didn't find it; Benny Ziedman found it, and he turned it into a cinematic triumph."

Harry said, "Well, you don't understand . . ."

I said, "No, Harry. *You* don't understand."

Mr. Mayer said, "Harry, that's the end of it. Forget it." To me, he said, "That was very nice. What you spoke was the truth. Thank you for being here." He was grateful then, but not always, for my two cents' worth.

In the next few days they said they wanted a picture made in a hurry, because they were going to lose a release date. I said,

"Name it." So I got hold of an old picture, one that had been made many, many years ago, on which I had been the unit manager. I said, "My God, we can bring this up to date. Who's available?" Lana Turner was available; George Murphy was available.

I was told they were going to let go of Chodorov and Fields, the script team, in about a month. I said, "Don't let them go, give them to me. I'll have a script in two weeks. We've already got something to go on." So they came to my office and, by God, in two weeks we had the script for *Two Girls on Broadway*.

Merrill Pye was my art director, and I said to him, "Let's have dinner tonight, then we'll go over to the scene dock and we'll see what they've got there. We have a dance routine for George and Lana. She's no dancer, but she's a great mover. We'll put a dancing skirt on her and show off those great legs. He'll twirl her, and we've got something."

We saw some great columns. I said, "Hey, Merrill, this will be great. We'll paint those columns white, and we'll hang black velvet in between, and we'll put bars of light so they'll be coming through it. No steps, just a ramp to make it easy for Lana. We'll put some black stuff in the foreground, a shiny floor, and we can reflect it." The whole set cost fifteen hundred dollars and we did it in three hours.

Now, the point is, they had a system at Metro where a man named Bernie Hardin had to okay your script. So we sent it to him, and he called me in. He has problems with page four, page seven, page eight, page nine, page ten. I said, "Bernie, how long is this going to take? They want this picture right away."

"When it's ready," he said.

All right. Sylvan Simon was the director. I told him, "I know you're fast, but you've got to be plenty fast. I'm putting this picture in production right now."

"Without Bernie's okay?" he asked.

I answered, "Don't you open your mouth. I don't want to hear one word from you."

He did the picture in fourteen days. And each of those fourteen days I'm talking to Bernie, who is still on page four. Finally, I asked him, "Bernie, what are you doing tomorrow afternoon?"

"Why?"

I said, "I want you to see the picture."

Well, he just went white. Next thing, Mr. Mayer called and asked, "How could you? You know my system."

I said, "Why don't you examine your system? You wanted the picture, you got the picture. You made the release date. Now what the hell is wrong?"

"To do this to Bernie . . ." he said.

I said, "What difference does it make who I did it to? The problem is your system. Don't blame me. I did what I was asked to do."

So then we took the picture out to preview. Mr. Mayer went to it and afterwards he sent for me. Now he's going to fire Merrill Pye, my art director. Why? He says, "That little picture. To put that kind of a set on a little picture. That set must have cost seventy-five thousand dollars!"

"Which set?" I asked.

"The one with the great big columns, with that whole thing that stretched . . . it was enormous. I know about sets. I know what that must have cost."

I said, "No, you don't, Mr. Mayer. You really don't." And I told him how Merrill and I had done this, and what it really cost. They were upset because Eleanor Powell was having a romance with Merrill Pye. I said, "I wouldn't fire him, I'd give him a raise! He deserves credit." So in the end he didn't fire Merrill Pye.

Another time I go into his office and he is absolutely white with rage. I said, "My God, you're going to give yourself a heart attack. What the hell's the matter?" I learn this is about Cedric Gibbons, the head of the art department. More Oscars than anyone in the business. "What's the trouble with Gibbie?" I asked.

"Goddamn it to hell. Arthur Freed has picked up all these great guys from New York, and he won't hire them."

I said, "Mr. Mayer, don't blame him for that. He's merely carrying out the terms of an agreement between the Art Directors Guild and the Producers Guild. You're a signatory to that pact. They can't work unless they're here for six months. Conversely, guys from out here can't work on the New York stage unless they serve a six-month apprenticeship. It's all equal. What the hell has Cedric Gibbons done? If he did anything else you would be sued. This is the greatest art director that the business has ever had, bar nobody. And he's been a wonderful and loyal employee. Why don't you hear his side of the story? Let him tell it to you. Then maybe you won't want to fire him."

"You," he said. "You little son-of-a-bitch, you wouldn't let me fire Benny Ziedman. You wouldn't let me fire Merrill Pye. Now you won't let me fire Gibbons. But there is one son-of-a-bitch I *can* fire."

I said, "Not me, not me. I quit!"

September 1985
Beverly Hills

Editors' Note: Jack Cummings died in April 1989.

FILMOGRAPHY (partial)

(As Co-Producer)

| 1935 | *The Winning Ticket* (dir. Charles Riesner, MGM) |
| 1964 | *Viva Las Vegas* (dir. George Sidney, MGM) |

(As Producer)

1936	*Born to Dance* (dir. Roy del Ruth, MGM)
1937	*Broadway Melody of 1938* (dir. Roy del Ruth, MGM)
	Yellow Jack (dir. George B. Seitz, MGM)
1938	*Listen Darling* (dir. Edwin L. Marin, MGM)
1939	*Broadway Melody of 1940* (dir. Norman Taurog, MGM)
1940	*Go West* (dir. Edward Buzzell, MGM)
	Two Girls on Broadway (dir. S. Sylvan Simon, MGM)
1942	*Ship Ahoy* (dir. Edward Buzzell, MGM)
1943	*I Dood It* (dir. Vincente Minelli, MGM)
	Broadway Rhythm (dir. Roy del Ruth, MGM)
1944	*Bathing Beauty* (dir. George Sidney, MGM)
1946	*Easy to Wed* (dir. Edward Buzzell, MGM)
1947	*Fiesta* (dir. Richard Thorpe, MGM)
	The Romance of Rosy Ridge (dir. Roy Rowland, MGM)
	It Happened in Brooklyn (dir. Richard Whorf, MGM)
1949	*Neptune's Daughter* (dir. Edward Buzzell, MGM)
	The Stratton Story (dir. Sam Wood, MGM)
1950	*Three Little Words* (dir. Richard Thorpe, MGM)
	Two Weeks with Love (dir. Roy Rowland, MGM)

1951	*Sombrero* (dir. Norman Foster, MGM)
	Kiss Me Kate (dir. George Sidney, MGM)
	Give a Girl a Break (dir. Stanley Donen, MGM)
	Excuse My Dust (dir. Roy Rowland, MGM)
	Texas Carnival (dir. Charles Walters, MGM)
1952	*Lovely to Look At* (dir. Mervyn Le Roy, MGM)
1954	*Seven Brides for Seven Brothers* (dir. Stanley Donen, MGM)
	The Last Time I Saw Paris (dir. Richard Brooks, MGM)
1955	*Interrupted Melody* (dir. Curtis Bernhardt, MGM)
	Many Rivers to Cross (dir. Roy Rowland, MGM)
1956	*The Teahouse of the August Moon* (dir. Daniel Mann, MGM)
1959	*The Blue Angel* (dir. Edward Dymtryk, Twentieth Century–Fox)
1960	*Can Can* (dir. Walter Lang, Twentieth Century–Fox)
1961	*The Second Time Around* (dir. Vincent Sherman, Twentieth Century–Fox)
1962	*Bachelor Flat* (dir. Frank Tashlin, Twentieth Century–Fox)

Producer Frank McCarthy (left) on location of *Sailor of the King* (Twentieth Century–Fox, 1951).

≡

FRANK
McCARTHY

Producer

≡

Frank McCarthy is the epitome of a southern gentleman schooled at the Virginia Military Institute—gracious and welcoming, yet shy and careful. He is practically standing at attention when we arrive at the door to his modern house high in the hills above Los Angeles. He apologizes for not having shaved, saying he likes to rest when he has no formal social obligations. His living room displays an impressive art collection, and his study is filled with photographs and mementos from friends in government and film.

McCarthy, who was born in Richmond, Virginia, in 1912, pursued several distinguished careers. A brigadier general, he served under General Marshall in World War II and was an assistant secretary of state. He was also a teacher, reporter, and theatrical press agent before finally settling in Hollywood. His first movie job was as a technical adviser to Brother Rat *in 1938. He won an Academy Award for best picture for* Patton *in 1970.*

Ideally, the producer is responsible for absolutely everything. The producer should be the one to shape the whole budget and to make sure the picture stays on budget, which is harder. There are all kinds of circumstances that can cause a movie to run over. It can be difficult stars, it can be bad weather, it can be all sorts of unexpected emergencies. It's up to the producer—all subject to approval, step by step, by the studio head—to choose and supervise the writers, read every word they write, call for alterations, fire them if necessary, see the script through.

Choosing the right writers is tremendously crucial because the single most important element in a film is the story, every time. If the material isn't good, there's no way all the other elements can make it a good film.

The most important quality a producer should have is the ability to look at the overall picture and to analyze it, to visualize all its various aspects and fit them together. I would say it takes creative coordination. People don't usually think of the producer as being creative, but I think he has to be—because if he's not there's no way he can supervise creative people like writers, directors, and actors. He must understand the creative process to be effective and successful.

I loved working in the old studio system. Here's how it worked. Darryl Zanuck kept a great chart in his office, under his desk blotter, which showed all the stars, directors, art directors, and others he had under contract. You could sit in his office and cast an entire picture. You would try to select people that were already under contract, because you got a better deal than you did going out and hiring somebody on the outside. Besides, the contract people were wonderful, talented people. There was never a better art director than Lyle Wheeler; there was never a better musical director than Alfred Newman. If you didn't get Wheeler or Newman himself you got a member of his staff, for whom he was responsible. It was absolutely marvelous to have your own stock company, so to speak. Zanuck always knew who was available and, more important, what people were being paid. That way it was relatively easy to make up a budget.

Actors were at first cast in small parts, and they were brought along. If an actress did well in a small part Darryl would say, "Let's try her in something bigger next time." There was real team work, combined with a healthy amount of competition and some envy among directors and producers; but it wasn't bad, because everybody was pacified in terms of that weekly paycheck.

Zanuck had a big input into every movie that was made in that studio, and he was a wonderful supervisor. He looked at the rushes every single night. If you worked for Darryl you worked five nights a week and sometimes Saturday, too. That first year, he had me come to the dailies every single night with him. I could watch what he did. He would say, "That scene is terrible. Shoot it over again." The director, the producer, the art director would all be there, and anybody else who was concerned.

When the movie was completed the producer and the director would put together the rough cut. As a matter of fact, by contract the director had the right to submit his own first rough cut, and even the producer couldn't touch it. But most directors, with some exceptions, would collaborate with the producer on the rough cut, so that by the time it got to Zanuck it had already been through a certain period of refinement. Still, Darryl was so canny. He would often make a slight change that would bring the whole picture together. He just had the surest eye in the world.

September 1985
Beverly Hills

Editors' Note: Frank McCarthy died in December 1986.

CAREER HIGHLIGHTS

1935–1936 Press agent for theatrical producer George Abbott

1946–1949 European Representative, Motion Picture Association
of America

1949–1962 Producer, executive, Twentieth Century–Fox

1963–1965 Producer, Universal

1965–1972 Producer, Twentieth Century–Fox

1972–1977 Producer, Universal

FILMOGRAPHY (partial)

1938 *Brother Rat* (technical adviser, dir. William Keighley,
Warner Bros.)

1951 *Decision Before Dawn* (co-producer, dir. Anatole
Litvak, Twentieth Century–Fox)

1962 *The Longest Day* (military adviser, dir. Andrew
Marton, Twentieth Century–Fox)

(As Producer)

1951 *Sailor of the King* (dir. Roy Boulting, Twentieth
Century–Fox)

1967 *A Guide for the Married Man* (dir. Gene Kelly,
Twentieth Century–Fox)

1970 *Patton* (dir. Franklin Shaffner, Twentieth Century–
Fox)

1977 *MacArthur* (dir. Joseph Sargent, Twentieth Century–
Fox)

≡ STORY

BY ≡

Eleanor Wolquitt, reader (third from left), in Calcutta, 1950, attending the wedding of two crew members during the filming of Jean Renoir's *The River* (United Artists, 1951).

ELEANOR
WOLQUITT

Reader

Eleanor Wolquitt returned from serving as a Wave (Women Accepted for Volunteer Emergency Service) officer (the youngest ever) in World War II and decided to try pictures as a way of escaping the teaching career everyone expected for her. After a short time in Hollywood, she came to New York and became an outside reader for Twentieth Century–Fox, and later a story editor for Robert Rossen and Kirk Douglas.

Some years ago she quit her job in order to become a screenwriter, a lifelong dream. Her limited success has not destroyed her optimism. She is a small, startlingly pretty woman in her early sixties, whose bright blue eyes are still filled with stars.

My first movie job was with Sol Lesser, who, along with Sam Goldwyn, was one of the most successful independent producers in Hollywood. Where Goldwyn was noted for quality, Sol Lesser's success was based largely on the Tarzan films: he had the rights to the Edgar Rice Burroughs books. But he always aspired to quality, so he hired very good writers, paid them well, and then imposed his will on them.

Later I worked with a very august German writer, Curt Siodmak, who'd been a top writer before Hitler. *[In those days he spelled his name Kurt.]* He was the brother of Robert Siodmak, the director. Curt's big book, which is still a classic, was *Donovan's Brain.* Well, Lesser hired him, and together they hired me to help him with the English idiom in the dialogue for the film *Tarzan and the Fountain of Youth.* When you consider that it was "Me Tarzan, you Jane" type of talk, it's kind of wild, but that's what we did. We went to Palm Springs to work on the dialogue so that it would be smooth: "Me Tarzan, you Jane," I suppose, instead of "Icht Tarzan, du Jane." Actually, Curt was very good with the English language, but I guess the producer wanted me as a kind of insurance.

Eventually I decided I'd like to see if I could become a reader, so I began by reading a novel and making my own synopsis and comment. It was *East Side, West Side* by Marcia Davenport. When I took it over to MGM all my writer friends laughed and thought I was crazy because it was a classic catch-22 situation: you could not become a reader unless you were a member of the Story Analysts Guild on the West Coast, and you could not become a member of the guild unless you had a job. But I went ahead and submitted my synopsis anyway, and went home to wait by the phone. One day it rang, and Metro asked me to come down to the story department to talk about the book. They said they had in fact already bought the novel, but they liked my recommended changes and comments. And, while they could not put me on staff because of the studio rules, they asked me if I would consider substituting in the summer while their people were on vacation. And so I did, and it was good experience.

Then one day Al Bleich called to tell me there was a possibility of a three-week job with Jean Renoir. I got the job. I was hired to help Rumer Godden, whose most famous novel, *The River,* was being brought to the screen. I was to assist with the American idiom in the dialogue, and then it was decided that I would go to India with Renoir. Three weeks turned into a year, and it was probably the best professional experience of my whole life, and a pretty damn good personal experience, too. I learned so much.

Returning from India, I decided to stay on the East Coast. In New York I again submitted my own unsolicited synopsis of a book, this time to Twentieth Century–Fox, and they called to say they liked it. They gave me one or two more books to synopsize, and then offered me what they called a "permanent outside reader" job. New York readers were never allowed to form a guild or union. They had been successfully fought on that. There was a staff of four or five in-house readers, at fifty dollars a week. But one could do what was outlawed in Hollywood, and that was called "outside reading," which was really piecework. You were paid by the book instead of a weekly salary, and there were no fringe benefits. You couldn't even keep the books you read for synopsis.

When Fox asked me if I would consider becoming a permanent outside reader I assumed it meant they would guarantee me enough material to pay the rent. I agreed because their New York story department was always known as the best in the business. In the middle forties the studios would take from their reading ranks their most promising people and promote them to what they called "junior writers." And from junior writer you could graduate to senior, or regular, writer.

Under the old studio system the story departments were important. Reading and story editing were two separate jobs then. I think the ambition of most readers was to become writers rather than story editors, but some were very satisfied when they became story editors. The pay was good and there was plenty of prestige.

The reader system worked this way: I would usually get galleys from publishers before the book was published. They were mainly of average length, 300 to 500 pages, and they were mostly novels. The top page of the reader's report would say what the material was—novel or nonfiction, whether it was a manuscript, galleys, or finished book, and how many pages it had. On the other side of the page was the name of the reader and the date. Also on that side, who had submitted it: an agent or a publisher. Right away you knew all about the material and who read it.

After reading it, I would write a three-page, single-spaced synopsis, and a one-page comment. For that I was paid $8, e-i-g-h-t dollars. If I did a French book (I was the only one there who could read French), which meant first mentally translating the book and then doing the three-page synopsis and one-page comment, I was paid twelve dollars. If you did a longer synopsis, which you did when you recommended a book, you were paid twenty dollars.

I once recommended a Françoise Sagan novel. I'd read it in a rush, overnight, in French, and had written a three-page, single-spaced synopsis, a one-page comment and a thirty-page, double-spaced synopsis because I had recommended it. Fox bought it for a huge sum of money, and I remember *Variety* at the time saying it was one of the highest prices ever paid for a book. That was done on the basis of my synopsis, because none of the executives could read French. My reward was twenty dollars.

After the reader turned in a manuscript or galleys with the synopsis and comment, an initial decision would be made. Then the synopsis would go on to the West Coast for Darryl Zanuck's consideration.

Needing that eight dollars would create its own time pressure. If you worked on salary there, you might possibly work on one thing all week and you'd still get fifty dollars. They called us—the outside readers—the "galley slaves."

My assignments came from a man who was sort of the bridge between the editors and the readers. Material arrived from agents, publishers, and, in our case, from a British woman named Peggy

Purdell, whose job it was to wine and dine anybody that might give us an early, early look at galleys.

As readers we always came across things; but it was not customary for us to submit them for consideration, though I tried a few times. I had once seen a story in the *Herald-Tribune* about a man named Mickey Marcus, who was an American war hero and who had died in Israel. It was a fantastic story, so I took it into Fox and, though they agreed with me, they said they couldn't use it. Nor could they even do a story based on the man's life because the British market in those days was so resistant to anything having to do with Israel. Many years later another studio bought it and made it into a film called *Cast a Giant Shadow,* starring Kirk Douglas.

In the days when there was still no divorcement and the studios still owned their own theaters, they had contract players; so part of the reader's job was to look for material that might be suitable for a Gene Tierney or a Betty Grable or any of the Fox stars. We also looked for parts for character actors like Clifton Webb, who'd made a very big splash in *Sitting Pretty.* If you read a book or galleys in which a subsidiary character might provide a good role for Webb or whomever, you could mention that in your comments.

Readers had to be really objective. There was stuff I didn't like, but which I recognized could be a good movie. A good reader could not recommend just what he or she liked. The question was: Will it make a good movie? Not: Do *I* like that kind of film?

A reader could not really sell material to a studio; but if the reader said no, that was usually the end of it—because no one would then bother to read the full material. But a yes would usually start it up the ladder.

We were told that Darryl Zanuck did not want baseball stories, whimsical themes, ballets, or musicals. I once got a set of galleys of a book that was called *The Year the Yankees Lost the Pennant* by Douglass Wallop. I absolutely flipped for it, went in, and suggested that they make a preproduction deal immediately, that ideally it should be a musical done in the legitimate theater, and then a movie. I was told, "Eleanor, it's the three things: baseball, fantasy, and a musical." So they passed on it. Of course it became *Damn Yankees* on Broadway and the movie was made at Warner's.

These things went in cycles. Somebody would say, "Westerns are out." So they would be out, and then along would come *Shane,* and westerns would be in again. Then it would start all over again.

Like the reader who passed on *Gone with the Wind,* I have my own little cross to bear. Mine was a first novel I was told was going to be a best-seller. I read it and found it utterly appalling. I still have my comment, in which I said the book was cheap pornography, a poor man's *King's Row.* I turned it down flat. The editor called me in and said, "Eleanor, you're right, but Jerry Wald said it was going onto the best-seller list and would stay there."

I said, "Well, if you're going to change my comment you have to take my name off it." And I must say, they were very good about it. They sent my synopsis and comment with a covering note saying, "We agree with Eleanor, but if Jerry Wald likes it, we recommend you buy it." That book was *Peyton Place,* which kept Fox going for a long time. Believe it or not, I would still write the same comment today.

I was reading on subways, I was reading at the beach, I was reading seven days a week. It was a sort of slavery, but of course nobody forced me to do it. I was barely able to pay my rent. Sometimes I would try to pick up a little extra money by reading a French manuscript for somebody like Helen Strauss, an agent at the William Morris Agency. But there wasn't much money in that either. I also did a little play reading for Leah Salisbury, who was a very fine theatrical agent. That paid four dollars a manuscript.

All along I thought that being a reader would help me in my career as a screenwriter, and it did, at least to an extent. Along with galleys of novels, I got to read original screenplays that were submitted, and I became familiar with the form.

I thought working in the movies would be the "dream factory" myth come true. But in fact I was very healthy about it. Maybe it was the war, but I could always see through the tinsel, and I learned to be amused and not impressed by it. Reading made me happy or I certainly wouldn't have stayed on ten years at eight dollars a book. I never decried Hollywood for what it was, nor did I ever try to make of it something it wasn't.

January 1985
New York

Postscript: Eleanor Wolquitt died suddenly in 1990, at the age of sixty-eight. We had been friends for nearly forty years.

When she was brought into the emergency room at Roosevelt Hospital, unconscious from a stroke, the attending physician asked what her profession was. Vivian Bell, who had worked at the William Morris Agency most of her life, answered firmly: "Screenwriter. And she was working on a definite project."

Although Eleanor appears in this book as a Reader, or Lowly Reader, as she always put it, she had written many screenplays, none of them ever produced. Her luck seemed to change in the year before her death, however. Arthur Williams, a television producer, asked her to write a treatment for a mini-series based on the life of Gertrude Stein, adapted from the biography The Charmed Circle.

At Eleanor's memorial service, I read a part of it to her friends. It was so moving that when I looked up for a moment (after choking up myself), I saw that Jessica Tandy and Hume Cronyn were both crying.

This project was very important to her. She once told my husband that she didn't want to die without a credit. But the final script was never written. This interview, then, will have to serve as her credit.

Sylvia Shorris
August 1993
San Francisco

JOHN BRIGHT

Screenwriter

═

Despite his many years in Hollywood and Mexico, John Bright still looks like a Chicagoan, born and bred. The years have not been kind to him, but his aura is still rough and tough, much like the persona he created in the gangster films he wrote for Jimmy Cagney during the thirties and forties.

He lives in a small apartment in Los Angeles, definitely on the wrong side of town and is looked after by a companion whose tongue is as sharp as his. He has recently suffered a stroke and his breathing is labored, but he still manages to sound cocky. When he gets warmed up, one can almost forget that there is a sign on his screen door that reads DAY SLEEPER.

I had no intention of going to work for the movies at all. It was sort of an accident. I was never really a movie fan. I went to California because I was chasing a girl. I started out as a newspaper man in Chicago, where I wrote a muckraking biography of the then mayor, Bill Thompson. With the advance Cape & Smith gave me for *Hizzoner Big Bill Thompson* I went to California with Kubec Glasmon, who had subsidized my book, and by then we were a team.

The way I got hooked up with Glasmon was that I was a soda jerk in his drugstore. Then Glasmon had a "Jewish bankruptcy fire" and collected the insurance for his store; the proceeds helped

Screenwriter John Bright (far right) with director Lucky Humberstone and George Raft, for Paramount's *If I Had a Million*, 1932 (Paramount photo).

get us set up in California. It was about 1930, and we decided to become partners.

⁀The first thing we wrote was a novel called *Beer and Blood,* later known as *The Public Enemy* when it was bought for the pictures. At Warners we were assigned to an old hand who told us the difference between technical terms like *lap dissolve* and *fade out,* but otherwise he contributed nothing. The two of us found that writing together was a hit-or-miss kind of thing. We shared the construction and the dialogue, everything. I guess screenwriting is so often a collaboration because it's the only way it's bearable.

After that first success, Glasmon and I became a well-known team, as well known as Hecht and MacArthur. Our next assignment was another Cagney movie, *Smart Money*, and we went on to write Cagney's next three pictures. They were mostly gangster movies and they made Cagney a star. The films were written specifically for him. He had an astonishing personality, so we sought to tailor *The Public Enemy* script to fit it. He was not originally scheduled for the lead, but for a much smaller role. But when I met him I decided for the first time to play Hollywood politics, and talked William Wellman, the director, into giving him the lead. He, in turn, sold Zanuck on our idea, saying it was his. That was my first introduction to the Hollywood double cross.

Zanuck called us in and announced, "I've got an idea to build up Cagney's part," and that's how Jimmy was made a star. Zanuck had risen to head of Warner Brothers by dint of many double crosses. He was a tin-pot Mussolini, but a very capable man, and because of him Warner Brothers had very high morale. In my naïveté I thought all studios were like that, and didn't find out until much later how isolated we were.

Zanuck ran his studio really well. Most of the directors I worked with—in addition to Wellman, Al Green, Mervyn LeRoy, Howard Hawks, Roy del Ruth, to name a few—left my scripts alone. The writers were respected. (Treated like shit, but respected.) These were Zanuck productions, his personal productions, and he insisted that they shoot the scripts as written. *The Public Enemy* endured very few changes at the hands of Wellman. The same was true of *Smart Money,* mainly because it was directed by Al Green, a literal-minded hack who didn't have the imagination to usurp my work.

I was friendly with Zanuck in those days. He wanted to make an actor out of me. He proposed it at a wild stag party—a surprise party that had been thrown for him—that involved everything, including a lesbian show by two prostitutes. I remember commenting to myself that here were the leading creators of the nation's entertainment, including children's pictures, and they were behaving so obscenely. Speculating whether the girls were on the level or not, were they having orgasms or not, while these wretched little creatures were involved in angleworm antics. I was so shocked and revolted at the absurdity of it that I decided to lock the whores in. And I did, but the guys broke the door down trying to get at them.

Anyway, at this party I told Zanuck, "I'm flattered at the invitation to act, but I'm afraid it would boomerang. As an actor, if I became a star then I would demand to control the product. That would result in absolute bankruptcy for the studio, and it would have to revert to orange groves. So, thank you, no thank you." I had no interest in being an actor, though in those days I was handsome. I never regretted turning it down.

All this time I had been under contract to Warners and had gone on strike by myself in 1932, about the time of my fourth picture. I had written several hits that were making the studio a lot of money, and they were still only paying me $250 a week. Glasmon double-crossed me, so I went out alone.

His refusal to go on strike with me caused a fight, but we had gotten back together again. He was exactly ten years older than me, and I had always looked up to him as a more sophisticated man, beginning when I worked in his drugstore in Chicago. But as I became more sophisticated myself I no longer felt the need to take any crap from him. And so we began to move apart. Eventually, we also moved apart politically; I went left and he went right, like the opportunist he was.

The next year, ten of us (the original ten, not the Hollywood Ten) got together and decided we needed a union. It was a random group of writers who all met at the Knickerbocker Hotel.

Present besides me were Lester Cole, Glasmon, Courtenay Ter-
rett, John Howard Lawson, Samson Raphaelson, Edwin Justus
Mayer, Louis Weitzenkorn, Brian Marlowe, and Bertram Bloch.
We had three meetings to debate tactics, and out of those meetings the Screen Writers Guild was born. Jack Lawson was our first
president.

The craft unions had already been established, the IATSE
[*International Alliance of Theatrical Stage Employees*], but there
was still no Screen Actors or Screen Directors Guild. They
followed later.

It wasn't director interference that led me to involvement with
the formation of the Screen Writers Guild; it was money. Simple
as that. Zanuck was actually inclined to favor the formation of
the union.

In 1939 I was almost rich. Berg and Allenberg, then my agents,
were crazy about a story I wrote called *The Tin Goose,* which was
for Cagney. It dealt with Bert Acosta, the last of the pre-instrument-
directed pilots, and a very colorful guy. I had heard his story and
was intrigued with it and wrote it as an original screenplay. My
agents, who were characteristically greedy, asked $150,000 for it,
which was an enormous amount of money in those days. When
three studios showed serious interest in it, they boosted the price
to $200,000. The deal hung fire over a weekend, I remember—the
weekend Hitler invaded Poland. After that, every studio dropped
The Tin Goose because from then on nothing but military aviation
was relevant. I never sold it.

I became fully aware of the blacklist only after the Hollywood
Ten were already in prison. A mass blacklist was not yet in effect,
but it was promised. I found out while I was doing a picture at
Paramount for a producer and professional charmer by the name
of Bob Fellows. I was doing very well with the script of a
melodrama called *Dynamite.* It was going so well, in fact, that

Fellows asked me if I would consider leaving Paramount with him and joining his new tie-up.

I said, "Of course, Bob. Who's your partner?"

Here I must interject a background piece. Fellows had told me that he'd been an informer for the FBI, tracking down Nazis. They used to meet every Wednesday evening to compare notes. One particularly pregnant evening, the great man himself, J. Edgar Hoover, was present. He came to talk to the Los Angeles contingent. It was right after Stalingrad when he told the group, "Forget about Nazis; they're defeated. The Russians defeated them for us. Our enemy is Russia. Therefore, concentrate on exposing Communists."

I asked Fellows why he was telling me all this and he said, "Well, it has to do with my offer. You see, my new partner is John Wayne. Of course, he has to be pleased. He likes your work but he hates your politics."

He asked if I'd be interested in telling my story, the story of my political background. At that time I was a member of the Communist Party. Smelling a rat, I played dumb and asked him what might follow, and he said, "You won't be mentioned. All you have to do is give us the names. That would be satisfactory to Wayne."

I told him I'd have to think about it. I knew then that the storm was about to break, so I went to Mexico. I wouldn't be an informer, so I had no alternative. I had some very good prospects down there; I was confident that there would be work for me. Among the people I knew in Mexico was the actor Pedro Armendariz, who was a very close friend and a great help to me. My wife set up a decorating business of her own and was fairly successful at it. We were both happy to be living in Mexico.

The union allowed me to write pictures in double versions (in English and Spanish). Since I couldn't take the job of a Mexican, I wrote the screenplays and a Mexican wrote the translations. The first double-version picture I wrote was *Rebellion of the Hanged,* based on one of B. Traven's books. *Mexican Trio* came next, based on another Traven novel.

Double versions worked this way: I would write the script in English, but because I was blacklisted the translator would get full screen credit. These films weren't released in the United States because they were felt to be too left-wing, but they were big hits in Mexico and in Europe.

I stayed on in Mexico until I was deported in 1959. The events surrounding my deportation remain a mystery. At that time there was a lot of political heat on Mexico, focused particularly on expatriate Americans. I was in the midst of writing a novel, and my wife, Mura, was planning a visit to Cuernavaca. Before she left she made me promise that I wouldn't go to a big fiesta at Albert Maltz's house. She thought it would be a wonderful opportunity for a mass arrest of all the writers. I reluctantly promised, but it turned out she needn't have worried. I got arrested in my own house.

It wasn't technically an arrest; it was billed as a routine check on my papers. I wasn't concerned, having just recently attained the status of *inmigrado* (an immigrant who is allowed to work) and was in the second stage of becoming a citizen, so I knew my papers were kosher. But instead of driving me to *Gobernación* (the Mexican state department) they hauled me off to the detention jail. I was able to get in touch with Mura to tell her to contact Bill O'Dwyer, the American ambassador at the time. He was in the process of arranging a habeas for me, which would have saved my ass in Mexico. That was apparently the reason for the haste of the people who were trying to get me out. They knew all about it.

I was in jail for about ten days. They wouldn't allow my wife to come and see me, but they did allow a friend of hers whom I said was my mistress. (They allowed a mistress but not your wife—typical Mexico.) She smuggled in food and money and took several notes out to O'Dwyer.

I adjusted to the time spent in jail very well. I learned early on how to get toilet paper and cigarettes, and I learned that there were some five thousand people in that can, mostly Cubans, awaiting deportation to Batista, which would be a death sentence. But Papa Cardenas (former president of Mexico) was the road-block to their deportation, and so as a result the Cubans were just languishing in jail. Unlike the rest of us, they had privileges, very special privileges, including the right to go out and play handball. By cleverly using their handball signals they could warn us that the gestapo was coming. If we saw *cuidado* (be careful) on the handball court, that tipped us off and we got back into our cells.

We had immunity from the guards because of the illegality of our arrest. My own guard was a wetback who had been deported from the United States, so he was very sympathetic. When I learned that O'Dwyer was about to materialize with my habeas, I tried to stall for a day but couldn't. They handcuffed me and drove me to the airport. The pilot asked why I was handcuffed, and removed them. At least I was free. On the plane I confronted my next immediate problems: I was still in my bedroom slippers (because of the handcuffs I hadn't been able to put on my shoes) and, of course, I had no papers and no money. Several of my fellow passengers belonged to an orchestra that was en route to a command performance for Eisenhower in Washington. They were mostly refugees and were very sympathetic to my situation. They even took up a collection for me, so I had about $20 when we landed.

I expected to be arrested by the FBI once I arrived in the United States, of course. I couldn't figure out any other explanation. I figured that the FBI wanted to get their hands on me and that the Mexican government had complied. That's what I thought I was walking into when we landed in Brownsville.

I still was not through the gates. I was a suspicious deportee in bedroom slippers. There were three lines of people coming into the country, and I looked the immigration officials over to size up the little petty bureaucrats. I decided on a big red-haired Texan, a good-natured guy, and I got on his line. As I got further up I noticed a thin-lipped woman working with him. She was a bad one, and I knew it. When it was my turn she said to him, "If he has no papers, call the FBI." By then, it was four o'clock in the morning, and he told her he didn't want to wake up the boys at that hour.

So he turned to me and said, "Well, no papers. How can you prove you're a citizen?"

I said, "Well, I was in World War II, in Intelligence, and one of the ways we caught POWs who were trying to pass as American citizens was to test their knowledge of the comic strips. All of them spoke good English, in fact some of the Germans were even born in the United States, and yet we caught them by the dozen on the basis of comic strip characters. With their fancy intellect they hadn't bothered to acquaint themselves with something that every American knows. I'd like you to question me about the comic strips. Who is Olive Oyl? Who is Popeye? I know the answers to those types of questions."

That satisfied him and he passed me. I told him that I had been scooped up in Mexico by *Gobernación* on a technicality (which could have happened), so I didn't have too much explaining to do.

After that I had no more trouble with the authorities. I went ahead and tried to pick up my career, but television had arrived in my absence. I learned that, despite the revolution in Hollywood and the enormous changes that have been made, one rule is constant: you're as good as your last picture. My last kosher picture had been ten years earlier, so I was a has-been. I think that aspect of the blacklist has been overlooked. The fact that I hadn't worked in Hollywood was actually held against me. Dalton

Trumbo picked up his writing career, but only after a long wait. This man, who had been earning $150,000 a picture, was now working for $2,500 a shooting script.

September 1985

Los Angeles

Editors' Note: John Bright died in August 1987.

FILMOGRAPHY (partial)

1931   *The Public Enemy* (with Kubec Glasmon, dir. William Wellman, Warner Bros.)

Blonde Crazy (with Kubec Glasmon, dir. Roy del Ruth, Warner Bros.)

Smart Money (with Kubec Glasmon, dir. Alfred E. Green, Warner Bros.)

1932   *The Crowd Roars* (with Kubec Glasmon, dir. Howard Hawks, Warner Bros.)

Taxi! (with Kubec Glasmon, dir. Roy del Ruth, Warner Bros.)

If I Had a Million (co-story, co-dirs. Ernst Lubitsch, Norman Tavrog, Stephen Roberts, Norman McLeod, James Cruze, William A. Seiter, H. Bruce Humberstone, Paramount)

Three on a Match (co-story, dir. Mervyn Le Roy, Warner Bros.)

1933   *She Done Him Wrong* (with Mae West and Harry Thew, dir. Lowell Sherman, Paramount)

1936   *Girl of the Ozarks* (co-story, dir. William Shea, Paramount)

1937	*The Accusing Finger* (dir. James Hogan, Paramount)
	John Meade's Woman (co-story, dir. Richard Wallace, Paramount)
	San Quentin (co-story, dir. Lloyd Bacon, Warner Bros.)
1939	*Back Door to Heaven* (dir. William Howard, Paramount)
1940	*Glamour for Sale* (dir. D. Ross Lederman, Columbia)
1942	*Broadway* (with Felix Jackson, dir. William Seiter, Universal)
	Sherlock Holmes and the Voice of Terror (dir. John Rawlins, Universal)
1945	*We Accuse* (documentary, prod. Irvin Shapiro)
1948	*Close-up* (dir. Jack Donohue, Eagle Lion)
	I Walk Alone (co-adaptor, dir. Byron Haskin, Paramount)
1949	*The Kid from Cleveland* (dir. Herbert Kline, Republic)
1951	*The Brave Bulls* (dir. Robert Rossen, Columbia)
1954	*The Rebellion of the Hanged* (in Spanish, co-dirs. Emilio Fernandez, Alfredo Crevenna, Mexico)

Lester Cole, screenwriter, with family and supporters, 1948.

LESTER COLE
Screenwriter

═══

Lester Cole was born in 1904 in New York City. He first went to Los Angeles in 1927 as a stage manager for Max Reinhardt's production of The Miracle. *In the thirties Cole worked as a reader (making thirty-five dollars a week) for film studios in New York and wrote plays, eventually landing an offer from Paramount.*

A tall, robust-looking man, Cole now lives on San Francisco's Potrero Hill, in a modest apartment where he makes lunch for us. Despite a life marked by bad luck, missed opportunities, and hounding by the federal government, he shows no trace of self-pity or bitterness. He is still passionately involved in various political and social causes, and he continues to write and teach.

When I got my first writing assignment, I went to L.A. by train. I was one of only three passengers. It was the Depression, remember. Well, the treatment I got. I had a room to myself, and when I'd go to the dining car they'd be bowing and scraping all over the place.

It was like I had a private railroad car. After a while the engineer heard that I was going to Hollywood, that I was a big star. He asked if I would like to come up front and see California as the train came in.

One of my first screenwriting assignments was called *If I Had a Million,* starring Lionel Barrymore. There were ten separate episodes, and I wrote one of them. There were also ten different directors, all of whom got credit. You never saw such a list of credits in your life.

Soon I moved to Fox, where I made $300 to $350 a week, and had the wonderful experience of working with S. J. Perelman. Sid, of course, was a well-known musical comedy and comedy writer by then. We were put on a musical comedy that Winfield Sheehan, the head of the studio, had bought on a trip to London.

We finished the first draft of our screenplay, and Buddy De Silva liked it very much. But Sheehan apparently didn't. In fact, he hated it. "How the hell did these guys so alter the story I bought? This is the worst insult I've ever seen," he said.

The story editor had an office above ours, and we could hear through the pipes when he was talking. He had a big voice. We heard him say, "Cole and Perelman? Let them go? Okay, Mr. De Silva."

Well, we preempted him by going straight to De Silva, saying, "Listen, we don't like this. We're quitting." He just sat there and stared at us.

Years later De Silva told us what had really happened that day. It turned out Sheehan was drunk when he bought the play, and he'd gotten hold of the wrong script.

After Fox I went to a little place called Republic Studios. It was one of the independents and they made mostly cheap westerns— $60,000- to $100,000-pictures. They had one guy there who did pretty good work, and I did two or three pictures for him.

Then, in 1936 along came *The President's Mystery*. President Roosevelt was a great mystery fan. It had originally been written as a magazine promotion. The magazine had advertised for ten top mystery writers to contribute an episode each. They were in such a hurry to get it out that one writer didn't know what the hell the next was writing. There was a general outline, but nobody knew where one episode ended and another began. The promoters had hoped to sell it for a million dollars but, in desperation, finally settled on $2,500 to Republic.

At that point, having done a couple of pictures there, I brought out my friend Nathanael West to work on it with me. Together, we wrote a story following this basic outline: A U.S. attorney in Washington, bored and tired of it all, leaves to go fishing up in New England, some state where there are fruit growers—Vermont or New Hampshire—and after he leaves, his wife is murdered. The lawyer is accused because they didn't know where he was. Meanwhile, he's gotten involved with a beautiful young woman who is part of the farm workers' group. They form a cooperative, have a mini-revolution, get the canning factory, and that was the picture.

Burt Kelly, the guy who made it, loved it. The head of the studio, Nat Levine, loved it too. But the owner, Herbert Yates, was outraged. He yelled, "You idiot, this is a picture that will promote Roosevelt."

"Well, what's wrong with that?" I asked.

He asked Levine, "How much did this picture cost to make?"

Levine said, "I think between $95,000 and $100,000."

Yates exploded. "You goddamn fool, I've got $250,000 on Governor Landon. Keep this picture until after the election."

Well, Roosevelt didn't need our picture to be reelected, and Yates eventually relented. When it was released, the *New York Times* ranked it one of the ten best films of the year, and it was also a big success at the box office. Yates made his money back, and then some.

For the main part my screenwriting assignments were collaborations, and that was for two reasons. The studio felt that if they had two people on a script they could get it written faster, and then it would be cheaper. The other reason was learning experience. When I started, to give me experience, I was put with experienced writers. As I became more adept they would bring young writers to work with me, to learn from me.

I wrote a picture called *Hostages* at Paramount in the early forties. It was a picture they knew I was particularly suited for, because it was about the resistance in Czechoslovakia.

The way that script went through the studio shows how things worked and what led me to help found the Screen Writers Guild. When the script was finished, Buddy De Silva (who had recently come aboard as a producer) read it and said, "Oh, it's great, Lester. We're going to start shooting; we've got the cast all lined up. There's just one little thing in here . . . it won't take you five days to fix this. You know, you've got a scene in there where the Nazis come to visit this woman's father, and she is so outraged that he's working with these Fascists that she runs out and joins the underground. Then she meets the leading man, they fall in love, and they work against the Fascists. Look, just make one switch here. You know, you're making this gorgeous woman into a political person."

We were already in the war, mind you, and for anybody to get any sympathy she had to be against the Nazis. De Silva continued, "Look, just one scene has to be changed. She's there, she knows from nothing, a beautiful dame. In comes this handsome guy; he's one of them, one of the pro-Nazi Czechs. He comes in, looks at her, she looks at him and that night they're in bed together. From then on, Lester, she goes wherever he goes. Politics, no politics, she's got what she wants."

I was absolutely shocked. I said to him, "We can't do that. Hey, there's a war on, don't you get it?"

"Yeah," he says, "but this is a movie, for Christ's sake. It's a movie and we've gotta have some sex in there, something real." I refused. After a lot of arguing, he says, "Listen, Lester, think it over, and I'll do the same. Twenty-four hours. I'll give you a call tomorrow, and you can tell me what you think then."

Of course my feelings didn't change, and I told him so, told him I was sorry, but that I was leaving. "No you're not," he said, "because I've changed my mind. We're going to do it your way." I couldn't believe my ears. It was the first time in all my years that I actually retained control of the script to that degree. So I thanked him very much and went ahead and made the other necessary changes—smoothing it out, fixing the dialogue. In two weeks I was finished, and we shook hands as I left.

The good feelings completely dissolved at the preview, when I realized De Silva had gotten another contract writer, Frank Butler, to write it his way after all. He had just switched the whole thing around, and no one had breathed a word of it to me.

That's the way Hollywood was. Directors and producers routinely usurped a writer's work. That was one of the reasons we formed the guild. With the coming of talkies, playwrights were brought out from New York. In 1927 they had formed a union or guild in New York, and they had called a strike and won. There, also, it was a question of control of material. It was the same issue, aside from royalties and other things that were involved. When these writers came out to Hollywood and found out what was going on there, they were understandably furious. I was one of the younger ones then, but there were some Pulitzer Prize–winners among them.

So things began to brew among the writers, and one day they went from a simmer to a boil. It was 1933. At Paramount, Brian Marlowe, a playwright from New York, and I were called in and told, "Look, fellows, it's up to you as patriots to save this industry. These goddamn trade unions are ruining us. When they've got contracts there's nothing we can do. We're going to ask you, as patriots, to take a 50 percent cut in salary."

We later learned that this announcement was being made simultaneously in every studio in Hollywood. So, as Marlowe and I were walking out we said to each other, "Hey, did you hear what he said about the unions? They've got contracts, they can't do anything to them. What are we waiting for?"

That same day we sat down and wrote out a statement of purpose, called in ten or twelve fellow writers, organized a lunch meeting at the Hollywood Knickerbocker Hotel, and that was the beginning of the Screen Writers Guild.

From then on, when one of my pictures appeared in the *Hollywood Reporter,* my name was blacklisted from the credits. My collaborators' names were always there, but mine was always blacked out. That was just the beginning.

By that time I had written six or seven films, and because of my participation in organizing the guild I was blacklisted at MGM. Irving Thalberg had said, "That son-of-a-bitch will never work here unless he gives that whole thing up. I don't want that kind of troublemaker here." They weren't calling us Commies yet, but we were troublemakers. Later on we were known as Commie troublemakers who were trying to take over the industry. The attitude lived on at MGM even after Thalberg died. The top writers there were part of a right-wing coalition called the Screen Playwrights. They tried to beat us, but we won in the election and knocked them out. But they wouldn't recognize us until we threatened to strike, and then we went into negotiations. Our bargaining committee met with the producers in 1941.

I think we helped writers a great deal with that guild. The fact that it is still operating today, although much changed, says a lot. I served on the board in various capacities for many years, and was vice-president during the House Un-American Activities investigation.

I missed out on getting residuals from television for every one of the blacklisted films I wrote under assumed names. Under the influence of the anti-Communist hysteria, the guild passed a bylaw of the new constitution which fit right in with the producers' stand on the blacklist. So they wouldn't recognize me as a writer in the guild at that time.

In 1945, after writing *Blood on the Sun* for Jimmy Cagney, I came to MGM. Jack Cummings wanted me for a picture. When my agent told me that I was wanted at Metro, where I thought my name couldn't even be mentioned, I couldn't believe it. They wanted me to do the script for *The Romance of Rosy Ridge* by McKinlay Kantor—the story of a young man returning from the Civil War, set in the mountains of Missouri. When I went to see Cummings it was the first time in my life I had crossed the threshold of the MGM studios.

We shook hands and he said, "Look, it's only an eighty-page novella. Sit right here and read it, and tell me whether you like it and really want to do it. I think you're the guy for it."

It was a fascinating story, beautifully written, but as I read I realized the guts of it weren't there. Sitting there I couldn't come up with the missing part, so I told Cummings, "Look, I've been waiting since I first came to Hollywood to work at MGM." (My salary was going to be a thousand dollars a week, more money than I had ever gotten.) "I can't take a chance. Are you willing to gamble on this with me? Let me go home and see if I can find what's missing."

Cummings asked, "What do you think it is?"

"The *why. Why* did this man come to this place and stay on?" He looked at me in some surprise when I said, "I can't afford to come here after all these years, spend three or four weeks, try to do a treatment for you, fail, and then get fired. I have too many enemies here who would gloat over it."

He agreed, and so I took it home, found what I wanted, and brought it back. Cummings then saw what had been missing, and he liked my ideas. I wrote the script and did three more for MGM.

In between *The President's Mystery* and *The Romance of Rosy Ridge* I wrote another of my favorite screenplays, and that was an adaptation of Nathaniel Hawthorne's novel *The House of the Seven Gables*. Burt Kelly was the producer at Universal. They were initially frightened of this film because I introduced something that was not in the book. I decided that because the book took place in the 1850s, I would make the character truly radical by getting him involved in the abolitionist movement. Well, it really brought some sensational things into the script, and generally it was very well received. Universal was afraid it wouldn't sell in the South, but it ended up selling.

Out of some forty films I wrote in my lifetime, these three were about the only ones on which I worked in collaboration with the producer. It helped me enormously in being able to express myself freely, and I felt, as a result, that these were the best pictures I ever wrote. The producers defended what I wrote; they fought for it. Sure, we would argue about things, we would agree or disagree, but I was never arbitrarily edited or censored in any way.

During the time I was blacklisted I wrote eight or ten films, the last being *Born Free,* in London in 1965. There I also wrote a couple of plays. I put my real name on my plays, but on screenplays I called myself Gerald L. C. Copley, and I used that name on *Born Free.* For writing that classic I got the glorious sum of ten thousand dollars, and it was considered generous.

I was always very conscious of the fact that you could make trash or you could make something worthwhile; that you had to fight to make something worthwhile, and this is what I always tried to do. That's why the organization of the Screen Writers Guild and control of material became some of the big concerns of my life. I think helping to form the guild was my biggest accomplishment. I still feel loyal to the things I believed in then. I'm still fighting, to the degree that I still can.

February 1985

San Francisco

Editors' Note: Lester Cole died of a heart attack in August 1985.

FILMOGRAPHY (partial)

1932   *If I Had a Million* (co-story, co-dirs. Ernst Lubitsch, Norman Taurog, Stephen Roberts, Norman McLeod, James Cruze, William A. Seiter, H. Bruce Humberstone, Paramount)

1933   *Charlie Chan's Greatest Case* (co-adaptor, dir. Hamilton MacFadden, Fox Film Corp.)

1934   *Pursued* (co-story, dir. Raoul Walsh, Warner Bros.)

Sleepers East (dir. Kenneth MacKenna, Fox Film Corp.)

Wild Gold (co-adaptor, dir. George Marshall, Fox Film Corp.)

1935   *Hitch Hike Lady* (dir. Aubrey Scotto, Republic)

Too Tough to Kill (co-adaptor, dir. D. Ross Lederman, Columbia)

Under Pressure (dir. Raoul Walsh, Twentieth Century–Fox)

1936   *Follow Your Heart* (dir. Aubrey Scotto, Republic)

The President's Mystery (dir. Phil Rosen, Republic)

1937   *The Affairs of Cappy Ricks* (dir. Ralph Staub, Republic)

The Man in Blue (dir. Milton Carruth, Universal)

Some Blondes Are Dangerous (dir. Milton Carruth, Universal)

1938   *The Crime of Dr. Hallet* (dir. S. Sylvan Simon, Universal)

The Jury's Secret (dir. Ted Sloman, Universal)

Midnight Intruder (dir. Arthur Lubin, Universal)

Secrets of a Nurse (dir. Arthur Lubin, Universal)

Sinners in Paradise (dir. James Whale, Universal)

1939   *Winter Carnival* (with Budd Schulberg, dir. Charles Riesner, United Artists)

I Stole a Million (story only, dir. Frank Tuttle, Universal)

1940   *The Big Guy* (dir. Arthur Lubin, Universal)

The House of Seven Gables (dir. Joe May, Universal)

The Invisible Man Returns (with Curt Siodmak and Cedric Belfrage, dir. Joe May, Universal)

1941   *Among the Living* (with Garrett Fort, dir. Stuart Heisler, Paramount)

Footsteps in the Dark (with John Wexley, dir. Lloyd Bacon, Warner Bros.)

1942   *Pacific Blackout* (with W. P. Lipscomb, dir. Ralph Murphy, Paramount)

1943   *Hostages* (with Frank Butler, dir. Frank Tuttle, Paramount)

Night Plane from Chungking (with Earl Felton and Theodore Reeves, dir. Ralph Murphy, Paramount)

1944   *None Shall Escape* (dir. André de Toth, Columbia)

1945   *Blood on the Sun* (dir. Frank Lloyd, United Artists)

Objective Burma (with Ronald MacDougall and Alvah Bessie, dir. Raoul Walsh, Warner Bros.)

Men in Her Diary (adaptor, dir. Charles Barton, Universal)

1947   *Fiesta* (dir. Richard Thorpe, MGM)

High Wall (with Sidney Boehm, dir. Curtis Bernhardt, MGM)

The Romance of Rosy Ridge (dir. Roy Rowland, MGM)

1950   *Chain Lightning* (under pseudonym, story only, dir. Stuart Heisler, Warner Bros.)

1965   *Born Free* (under pseudonym Gerald L. C. Copley, dir. James Hill, Columbia/Open Road)

NANCY GREEN

Studio Representative

===

Nancy Green grew up in Baltimore, where she was an avid theater-goer. During World War II she ran USO camp shows, and from there found a job as a producer in New York. In 1946 the theatrical agent Kay Brown recommended her to David Selznick.

She is now in her late sixties, as lively and enthusiastic as she was in the frenetic days of working for Selznick. She is married to Jules Green.

I always wanted to be a stage actress, starting when I was just a little girl right up until my early twenties. I realized I was finally a movie fan when I found myself hanging around stage doors, waiting to see people like William Haines after their personal appearances. I even cut my hair in bangs after seeing Louise Brooks and Claudette Colbert.

The Selznick job came to me through a theatrical agent. I had worked my way up in the legit theater business in New York and had produced two plays. It just so happened that the agent for those plays was a gal named Kay Brown. Kay had worked for Sam Goldwyn and for David. She had sort of mothered Ingrid Bergman and was in charge of a lot of David's study-options contracts.

It turned out she had been watching me produce, and one day she called and announced, "You're going to work for David Selznick as his eastern representative."

Nancy Green, East Coast studio representative for David Selznick, in the late 1940s.

Naturally, I was flattered, but I reminded her, "Kay, I don't know the first thing about movies. I'm a theater person."

"That's why you'd be good. I told David you don't know your ass from your elbow about the movies, but that you'd be damn good at it."

I went to the interview because the job intrigued me. In fact, I loved the idea because, basically, the job was seeing all the Broadway shows. I was supposed to go to every show, looking for talent and stories.

I became the talent scout and story editor in 1946. I also ran the whole so-called creative part of the New York office. Besides me, there was always somebody legal there, and always somebody in charge of foreign distribution. It was Betty Goldsmith then, and Selznick sold a lot of his stuff then to foreign countries. It was one of the ways he stayed solvent.

Elsa Neuberger trained me as a story editor. She was almost retired—she was not a kid. I learned so much from her. I'd been used to reading and producing plays, but reading a manuscript was completely different because it was a narrative. I also found, much to my delight, that I was a fast reader without having to be trained.

Among the many things Elsa taught me was you didn't go by your own taste. You went by your belly reaction: would this work as a film? It didn't mean you liked it. That's terribly important. Obviously, you had to like it on a certain level—you had to have some feel for it—but nobody knew for sure what was going to work.

Elsa knew that I could deal with people, and she introduced me to all kinds of people I didn't know. I didn't know as many publishers as I did writers; I didn't know as many literary agents as I did talent agents. And I had to learn the routine of finding stuff before anybody else.

Elsa Neuberger also taught me how to "read." First, you'd get the advance *Kirkus Report* and then read all the stuff in the *New York Times*. You'd see what was coming out way ahead of time. You also had to keep up with the gossip columns, and you had to know writers.

When she knew she was leaving, Elsa spent about six months making me read stuff after she had, to help me get a feel for what could possibly make a movie. And that's about as far as anybody could go.

There was no such thing as a typical day. It depended. If we weren't in production I'd come in and go through the memos from David, read the mail and dictate any correspondence, and then go over my book. This was yet another thing Elsa taught me. My book had every literary agent, every manager, every publisher, every writer I was interested in. It was probably my most valuable possession.

With one of my assistants, I'd go down the list of materials we were expecting to see. Someone would say to call back in a week or two weeks, or two months, and I'd mark the date in my book. So each day I had a list of who to call to see whether that manuscript was ready.

Then the phone calls to people I'd just heard about. I was constantly getting mail from David with a tear sheet from *Vogue* or *Harper's* enclosed and I'd have to make appointments to see those models. After Lauren Bacall was discovered in *Vogue* by Slim Hawks, the producers all went the same pattern. Sometimes it was frustrating, as when I had a very eager Julie Harris I wanted David to see, and he didn't think she was attractive enough. The fashion model who got to see him would say, "Oh, I never thought of acting. That might be fun." I frequently had to swallow my hostility over things like that.

Part of my job was reading all the magazines and getting to know people, which was helped by taking someone out to lunch every day. There were really only two places: "21" and the old Ritz. Chances were, in either place, you'd run into some writer and could make a date with him. It was important to be seen.

The Ritz was like a small club. There was a little bar there and everybody knew the bartender. The clientele were almost all eastern story editors and talent people, so the bartender knew all of us. You'd leave word with your secretary that you could be reached at the Ritz bar, and it was like a second office. A lot of people never went back after lunch—they just conducted their business out of the bar.

Most of my friends were creative people. I met Wolcott Gibbs on Fire Island one summer, and through him I met all the *New Yorker* people. I think I met Irwin Shaw through Charlie Addams and his wife. We all shared a house together one year. I got to know Tennessee Williams during the period that Audrey Woods had him. To a great extent the business was social. We were all part of the same crowd, and we were all developing at the same time.

Literary agents like Harold Ober were very important—much more important than talent agents then. You had lunch with them just as much as you did publishers and editors and writers. I met most of the writers I knew through their publishers, like Harold Guinzberg at Viking, Bennett Cerf at Random House, Cass Canfield at Harper's, and Roger Straus at Farrar, Straus. They'd give me names of writers they thought were hot, and I was sometimes invited to parties in their homes.

My agenda always depended on whether or not David was in town. When he was there, I'd arrange interviews for all the people I'd seen in plays or who'd been brought in by agents, or for any of those models he'd been interested in. If he thought someone was interesting, he'd offer a study-option contract. It might be a seven-year contract, which meant the person was exclusively at David's disposal for the duration of the contract. There was no way of getting out of it. And this is where David and others like him made some of their money.

Under the terms of those contracts, actors got increases of maybe $50 or $100 over that whole seven-year period. If a producer had a Doe Avedon and he wasn't using her, he'd lend her out to another studio. This happened even to the big stars. An actress who was hired at something like $700 a week would be loaned out at $1,400 or $1,500.

Pretty soon, though, actors wouldn't sign at all, deciding instead to take their chances going picture by picture. The agents got smarter about it, too, and that was really the beginning of the end of the old system.

Whenever David was in town, it was frantic—mostly because he was always late, always trying to do too much. He was ceaseless. His energy knew no bounds. He smoked a lot and ate well, but wasn't fat. Just a big bear of a man.

After everybody had been seen for the day and he'd told his secretary to go out for dinner, he would ask me to stay and have dinner with him. We'd order room service at the St. Regis, and that's when he'd tell me these marvelous stories about his father, about casting Vivien Leigh and other stars, and about how tired he was now, and how hard it was to be a big gambler without any money. They were not apocryphal, but they were fascinating. I can remember him and Alexander Korda yelling and screaming at each other, threatening to sue one another over *Odd Man Out*—over who did what in the film, who'd given the most to it—and then the three of us going out to a very civilized dinner. David could be utterly charming.

Talent was found in so many ways, but David and I had an interesting little system. On Wednesday and Saturday matinee days we'd see six shows. We'd stay for fifteen minutes at one, ten minutes at another, and we'd be running all over New York looking at people. Sometimes you noticed that special something, and sometimes you didn't. I found Maureen Stapleton and Julie Harris when I was working in the theater.

When David was out of town I searched for talent on my own. The scouting end was just as intense and competitive as the story end of the business. I had to see every Broadway play, and when I heard somebody was hot in a show in Boston or New Haven I'd have to go up to check it out. I remember being sent immediately to see *No Time for Segeants* because word had suddenly gotten around that Andy Griffith, somebody nobody had heard of, was very good. I was to try to get in there and get an edge, find out what he expected.

I sometimes saw plays five nights a week. I quickly learned to take a dim view of any critic being able to like anything after awhile. When you see that much you can't handle it—you lose your ability to judge.

If you really wanted to be good at your job, the thing you had to do was recognize a Marlon Brando when he was the son in *I Remember Mama* instead of waiting until *A Streetcar Named Desire*. David sent me to sign Marlon after *Streetcar*. But Marlon Brando would not see anybody from Hollywood. He wasn't even remotely interested in a movie career.

To help me, I turned to my friend Jessie Tandy, and she arranged a meeting. I've never been so scared in my life. He had a reputation for doing things to embarrass people, like walking out stark naked with an erection.

Jessie pushed me in the door and said to Marlon, "This is my friend Nancy," and was gone.

Marlon looked at me and said, "You look scared."

"I'm terrified," I said.

"Why?"

"Because I've heard all these terrible things about you," I said.

He laughed, and then we became friends. I still remember him sort of purposefully flipping this buffalo nickel when, finally, he asked, "Is that a male or a female buffalo?" I bent to examine it more closely and he squirted water into my eye. I loved that trick, and so he took me around the corner so I could get one for my son Tony. Despite our getting along so well Marlon was never going to sign for a film with David Selznick.

After I saw or read a play that interested me I'd either write a synopsis or I'd call David and tell him about it. A lot of people didn't have any guts about buying things; in fact, most of the plays weren't bought before they were shown. It was different from books that you'd get in manuscript. With plays you pretty much had to wait for a Broadway opening, unless it got brilliant reviews out of town.

Another way we found people was through their agents. They were always calling and asking to bring their clients around. Walter Matthau came to me through his agent, Jane Brody. I can't tell you the number of times I took him up to see David. I thought—I knew—he had talent. Unfortunately, though, for the most part it was still the day of the beautiful people—the Marlon Brando, Charlton Heston types—and Walter wasn't one of them. David just couldn't be convinced.

Knowing writers socially was essential, and if they liked you enough they might give you a break. Irwin Shaw actually gave me pages of *The Young Lions* right out of his typewriter. Everybody was after that book, and when I asked him about it he just said, "Come on up and I'll give you the pages." It was a coup for me to get the first crack at it, even though David decided not to buy it.

If you saw someone you thought had real potential you'd set up a screen test at one of the studios up around 125th Street. You'd either provide a scene or let the person choose his own. Or, if you were looking for a specific part in a specific picture, you'd use a scene from the actual picture.

The test would last about five minutes, sometimes a little longer because of the set-ups. Somebody, usually the director, had to read the lines, like a cue. They'd do a close-up, a three-quarter, both sides, a full-length, and content. That was it, very short.

David had a shrewd sense of talent and beauty. I've always remembered what he said about Gene Tierney: "Do you know why she made it at all? Because her mother apparently either didn't have the money, or had the good sense not to have her teeth fixed." He named two or three girls who were beautiful but perfect, and said, "They're a dime a dozen."

David was congenitally, notoriously late. And by late I mean a good two hours. His waiting room at the St. Regis suite was always full of the most amazing people, and part of my job was to keep them entertained while they were waiting. I'd sit there and talk to Graham Greene or Truman Capote or Robert Penn Warren, and David would burst out every fifteen minutes or so, saying, "I'll be right with you . . . I feel so terrible." This happened all the time, but they'd just sit and wait. It was marvelous fun for me.

But there was one time when David really got me into a tight spot. He'd called and asked me to go over to a hotel and meet a man named Vittorio De Sica. I was to befriend him and see if he needed anything. Well, the name meant nothing to me, this being the late forties. I knew he had something to do with the Italian film industry, but who was he?

I looked forward to the conversation. But David had forgotten to tell me that De Sica didn't speak a word of English. And I didn't speak a word of Italian. So there we sat, not knowing quite what to do. Finally, David arrived and rescued me. He, of course, wasn't bothered in the least by the language barrier. His idea of speaking Italian was to put an *o* on the end of everything, as in, "I'll phon-o you tomorrow."

The amount of research David demanded for his pictures was unbelievable! Everything was researched a hundred times. He was a perfectionist who would rather make a fool of himself than have anything go wrong, no matter what it was. No one could ever say that he hadn't researched every possible part, or selected exactly the right person for it.

His memos were endless. They were mental masturbation. He would go on and on in tremendous detail about something that didn't warrant that much explanation. Or they were outrageous, like, "Please get in touch with Albert Einstein and see if he would like to play the old man in . . ." If he thought he could get Einstein, he'd try. And he'd say, "Don't go to his aide, go right to him." Or, "Please go past his agent." These dictated memos were almost daily occurrences so we called him the Great Dictator. I think they were his form of analysis and catharsis.

My favorite memo came from Rome, where he was casting *A Farewell to Arms.* He asked me to start looking immediately for Italian actors in New York because he couldn't find anyone there. It really said: "Please start looking for Italian actors. Can find no one over here."

David was way ahead of his time about building up people to become stars. He decided in the late forties that personal appearances should come back again. He sent me Louis Jourdan, Rhonda Fleming, Rory Calhoun, Shirley Temple, John Agar, and Bert Shevelove. Bert had been the biggest guy at Yale, and later became a big director. He and I put together a little show using old material, where Louis and Rhonda could sing, with clips of their pictures. We went to places like Rochester and Buffalo, wherever the pictures were showing.

David was, of course, with Jennifer Jones by the time I came to work for him. And, as everybody knows, he was obsessed with her, which is kind of funny because he didn't get around to seeing her screen test until a year and a half after Kay Brown had gotten it. Meanwhile, Jennifer had done *Hello Out There,* the Saroyan play, and she'd even tried to see him in his office. He was always too busy. But once he finally saw her screen test he fell completely in love with her. And then he went all out promoting her.

David was really kind of treading water then. I think he was just exhausted, and he loved Jennifer, so she became his focal point. Once big budgets went out, he thought he was through. He told me, "I'm not capable of being in the business anymore because nobody can afford me. I know I take too much time, but I can't work any other way."

By the time I arrived on the scene, David was beginning to decline. Nobody knew it unless he worked there. People were still sending him marvelous material, and everybody wanted to work for him. But I knew; he told me. Still, David always had people who believed in him, even when the chips were down. He had loyal friends. Danny O'Shea was one. A brilliant lawyer who started with him here and stayed a very long time. And Mac, his PR man, used to say, "You'd sit with David and you'd listen, and while you were with him, you were absolutely sure he was going to do everything he dreamt of because he always had before." When David died, things hadn't been going well for some time. He couldn't quite make the transition, couldn't make his style conform to the times.

Dealing with people was my forte, I guess, and David recognized it right away. He said something to me early on that stands out as a pretty sexist remark today. He said, "One thing you must never forget if you want to stay in this business and have a career in it: Keep wearing your Arpège. Keep looking the way you do. Keep remembering you're a woman. Because you're attractive, and that's your advantage. You get the scripts, you get the person by being charming. We'll get somebody else to do the 'hondling' of the contracts."

That was David Selznick.

January 1984
New York

Editors' Note: Nancy Green died in December 1989.

William Fadiman, story editor and producer, in 1954 at Columbia (Photo by Cronenweth).

≡

WILLIAM
FADIMAN
Story Editor

≡

William Fadiman began his literary education at the University of Wisconsin and the Sorbonne. During his active career of more than forty years as a story editor for several major Hollywood studios, he also worked as a journalist and critic.

Fadiman is an attractive, fastidiously groomed man who gives a somewhat daunting first impression. He is supremely urbane and self-confident, yet is also a chain smoker, a cougher, and a pacer— clues to his shyness. He lives in a well-kept house near the Bel Air Hotel. Our interview takes place in his upstairs study, which is lined with books and memorabilia from his years in what he calls "the word business."

(Before the interview begins, Fadiman gestures toward a long, thin horizontal frame containing seventeen business cards documenting his positions at various studios.)

See those seventeen pictures up on the wall? That's a career in the musical chairs industry called motion pictures. Now look behind the shutter there. *[Next to the window is a single framed card bearing a large question mark.]*

My first job was in New York City when I left college, and I was an agent for an organization called George T. Bye. The thrill of that job, which paid $25 a week, was that I represented people like Heywood Broun, Eleanor Roosevelt's column, Westbrook Pegler, and people of that ilk . . . high-class journalism. That was very thrilling for me. I was a young boy at that time.

After that job, I went to what was then called RKO Radio Pictures, in about 1934 or 1935. There I became what was called an assistant story editor. The job of a story editor, or an assistant story editor, in New York then and now, is to contact publishers, writers, agents in an endeavor to ascertain the value of written materials, long before they reach the stage or print. Each person, therefore, competes valiantly and dishonestly with every other story editor, in an effort to ascertain that which is valuable to him or her and to the studio.

Leland Hayward was, at that time, the person who figured out that what were known as corollary or subsidiary rights in a contract for books could be immensely and intensely valuable. In a sense he invented what are now called motion picture rights. He specialized in selling that which was in small print and of no consequence to publishers whatsoever. That was the beginning of an enormous agency called the Myron Selznick Agency. Leland Hayward became the East Coast partner of Myron Selznick, and I was in charge of what was called the literary department, which consisted then of precisely the same thing I was doing before, except backwards. I would endeavor to find out ahead of time what was around, in order to get it for my clients.

When I left Leland Hayward, it was because I was offered a job by a man called Samuel Goldwyn, to head his story department. I went up to Leland Hayward's rather ornate office, in a penthouse of a building on Madison Avenue, and said, "Leland, I've gotten a very nice offer from Samuel Goldwyn, and I'm sorry, I'll have to leave." The following dialogue ensued:

He said, "What's he paying you?" I told him the figure (which I've forgotten) and he said, "Not enough." So he got on the phone and got me a better deal at Samuel Goldwyn! His agent's mentality couldn't stand it, even though the loss of an employee was important. He couldn't stand a bad deal, so he automatically became my agent for that particular job. He never took any commission, but he made his point.

At Samuel Goldwyn, I was New York story editor for about two years. During that entire period, Mr. Goldwyn, who never quite got my name straight, referred to me for some reason as Mr. Rosenthal. He was an interesting, curious, intelligent, and highly sensitized man about the world he knew best, which was motion pictures.

A lot of his malapropisms were invented by a man named Lin Farnol, who was his press agent. He invented some of them, if not all. Actually, Goldwyn was guilty of a great number of them. He was not a cultivated man; I believe he was a public school graduate, if that; I'm not quite sure. But he had enormous antennae for the public, and he had something that very few of the other executives of that period had, which was an innate and inexplicable taste for that which had quality. He produced many pictures of considerable distinction. He didn't know who the authors were (he had never heard of Charlotte Bronte), but it didn't matter. He had a feeling that something by this particular author was valuable.

He hired the finest *literary* writers he could find. That is, men and women of distinction in the world of print who had nothing to do with motion pictures, in the hope that he could transfer their genius and talent to the screen. Quite an odd, unusual, distinctive, and remarkable man.

I was also a story editor at Columbia. That job involved the use of what were ingloriously then called readers, who did synopses. One of the ways I had of augmenting my income was to write synopses to myself, under other names, which I then paid myself for. I figured that they got pretty good synopses out of me since I was the boss.

During my RKO period the studio was bought by a gentleman named Howard Hughes. I became an executive assistant to him. It's quite true that (a) he never actually saw the studio; and (b) he did say "Take it," when he saw it from an airplane in the sky. He never used the RKO studio for his own pictures. He hired space at the Samuel Goldwyn studios to work. Why, I can't tell you. His meetings were held, quite truthfully, at three, four, five o'clock in the morning. You went to a meeting via, usually, two or three different cars, on the theory that you would not know quite where he was when you got there. It was absurd because you could ascertain it, of course. But you went to car #1, then were picked up by car #2, and car #3, and so on, and eventually you got to his office.

Howard Hughes was an extraordinary man. One of the first things that happened when I got there was to be called to one of these three-o'clock-in-the-morning meetings. He said, "Your name is Fadiman?"

I said, "Yes."

He said, "I'm Howard."

I said, "Hello, Mr. Hughes."

He said, "I'm Howard."

I said, "Hello, Howard."

He said, "You're Bill."

I said, "Yes."

He said, "How many writers do you have under contract?" At that time, I had maybe thirty or forty. He continued, "I want the payroll cut by 25 percent by next Thursday." (This was Monday.)

I said to him, "Howard . . ."

He said, "Just a moment. You're going to tell me that you know that one of the writers has cancer, that one is about to get married, another is having a baby, and a fourth just broke his leg. You're going to tell me that you'd like to wait a little while on some of these. If you tell me these things, I will tell you not to fire those writers. If I tell you not to fire those writers, I will not get my 25 percent. I don't want to hear these stories. I want 25 percent of the writers' payroll cut by Thursday. Thank you, Bill."

Interesting man, very interesting. Corporate mentality, you see. But he was also a man of extraordinary personal generosity. He gave millions of dollars anonymously to ill people. I could tell you things about other people he kept under contract for twenty years, which was seventeen years after he left.

But this was a curious man. He had always a brown paper bag in front of him, which was his lunch, at three or four in the morning. It was always difficult to not want to ask for a bite, because you felt odd. But he never offered it to you.

Several years later I was in his office for a meeting with a rather distinguished agent, a man named Bert Allenberg. As one always does when you sit in an office, we started moving our chairs very slightly, to be more comfortable or to face him better. Our chairs were nailed to the floor. Very odd. We discovered why, later. He was getting deaf at that time. His electronic experts had explained to him that if the chairs were exactly at a certain position he could hear superbly. If the person moved three inches, it would be no good. So he simply nailed all the chairs down.

He had a passion for the film industry. It wasn't money; he had so much money that it didn't interest him. He also had some interest in an actress called Jane Russell, the one with the very large mammary glands. He in fact invented a special brassiere for her. He engineered it himself. She was under contract for twenty years, long after his leaving RKO. She was paid personally by Mr. Hughes. Quite an odd duck.

I soon moved to Metro, where I spent a good many years. In New York I was what is called the New York editor, and then I became the head of what was called the scenario department, located on the West Coast.

I had certain value for them. In the first place, I could write letters very well, and I did a lot of that. Second, I spoke a few languages. This was an area of cultivation in that era which was both welcomed and resented, simultaneously. That is, they resented their inability to function in certain areas, so they hired people like me, and many others who were equally intelligent.

Metro-Goldwyn-Mayer had offices all over the world then, and we used to get "material," which was the generic phrase, in literary form, in synopsis form, or sometimes in galley proofs. I would say we covered about twenty-five thousand pieces of material a year to buy enough for the hundred-odd pictures that we used to make a year.

Mayer's theory about big stars such as Gable or Garbo was: Do not let them appear in too many pictures. Make the people wait for the next Garbo or the next Gable film. And he did that by keeping them under seven-year contracts and paying them, in those days, enormous sums of money for doing nothing, and by loaning them out only if the figure was fantastic and the picture was one which would do the studio no harm.

Gable brings to mind my *Gone with the Wind* story. Part of my job at Metro was to go back and forth between here and New York to look at material. The head of the editorial department in New York was a man named Harold Latham, and we went through the routine of looking at the publishers' catalogs. I said, "Do you have anything very special that no one knows much about?"

He said, "Come on," and took me to a back room where there was a very large packing case.

I said, "What the hell is that?"

He said, "That's a novel." He picked up the cover and there were two and a half million words of manuscript.

I said, "What's the name of this?"

He said, "*Gone with the Wind.*"

I said, "What the hell kind of title is that?"

He said, "I don't know, but that's it." I asked who wrote it, and he said it was somebody named Margaret Mitchell. "We think it's a knockout," he added.

I said, "Two and a half million words?"

He said, "It's got to be cut and edited. If you like, you can read it." He was kidding me.

I said, "What do you mean, I can read it? What do you expect me to do with this box?"

He said, "Look, you're young. If you really want to read it, I'll give you two days to do it in, because we need it. If you can get it in a taxi, good luck."

I, being young and foolish, said, "Fine." So I got it into a taxi. I read, and I read, and I read. I had no time to give it to a reader to synopsize, so I had to do it myself. I wrote about fifty pages, quite a long synopsis. I sent it along to a man in the West Coast office. I usually didn't hear anything back, but this time I got a wire because I had praised it so highly. The wire said: SUGGEST YOU DISCUSS "GONE WITH THE WIND" WITH MR. NICHOLAS SCHENCK. He was the head of the studio, and he lived on Long Island. I had never seen him in my life. This was still when I was very young. So I called Mr. Schenck's secretary and, sure enough, I got an appointment in five minutes, and off I went on the Long Island Railroad.

At the station, there's a car and chauffeur to meet me and I'm driven for about two miles, and then I'm driven up a driveway which seems about another two miles. I get to Mr. Schenck's baronial castle and a butler meets me. I'm pretty nervous and pretty tense. I knock on his door. He said, "Come in," and I went in to Mr. Schenck's bedroom.

He was at that time ill with a very severe cold. He was sneezing and wheezing and coughing. I knew I was going to have a hell of a time up there. In a corner, unobtrusively, was his wife, who bore the name of Pansy. She kept bringing him orange juice. Nobody asked me to sit down, so I stood there.

He said, "You're Mr. Fadiman?"

I said, "Yes."

He said, "You got a story to tell me?"

I said, "Yes."

He said, "Louis told you?"

I said, "Yes."

He said, "Tell."

I'm standing there, nervous and tense, and I have to tell him the story of *Gone with the Wind*. Now, I'm interrupted every four or five seconds, or minutes, by the sneezing and the coughing, and the orange juice that Pansy keeps bringing. I'm really doing the best I can. I left out, I'm sure, at least two-thirds of it, but I did what I could, and I'm standing all the time. Finally, I finish.

I wait. He sneezes and he coughs, and he sneezes and he drinks orange juice and, finally, he asks, "Do you like this story?"

I say, "Yes, I do, Mr. Schenck, I do."

"It's going to be a big best-seller?"

"I think so, Mr. Schenck. The publishers are very high on it, and they're a pretty good organization."

"People are going to buy lots of copies?"

I said, "Yes, I think so, Mr. Schenck."

"It's going to make a good movie?"

I said, "Yes, I wouldn't be here if I didn't think so."

"Young man, *Gone with the Wind* is a title? *Gone with the Wind*? What does this mean?" I knew I was dead. "It's about what . . . a war? Who needs war?" I had nothing to say to that. Then, "Everybody dies?"

I offered, "Well, some do."

He repeated, "Everybody dies. It's sad. You tell Louis, 'No.'"

Well, back I go. I leave him sneezing and wheezing. I wire Mr. Mayer my most tactful wire, something like this: AM UNDER THE IMPRESSION THAT MR SCHENCK DID NOT LIKE "GONE WITH THE WIND."

Ultimately, as you know, it was bought by David Selznick, some years later. It was bought, by the way, for $52,000. That was the price at that time for *Gone with the Wind.* Metro ultimately bought the entire finished film from David Selznick, for I think $4 million. We bought the finished film, and we also loaned Clark Gable to Selznick.

Every company, including Metro, had many properties that they had bought many years before which had either not been lickable, or time had passed them by so they were no longer of any value. I, in my first year on the West Coast, compiled a careful list of these properties to explain to someone who'd listen that they could sell them to other studios and pick up some money. I went with this idea to someone and he said, "Nice idea. Do we need money?"

I said, "No, but the corporation has these things which are dead. You could pick up $50,000 here, $100,000 there. It wouldn't hurt."

He said, "Suppose another studio made a good picture out of one of those?" And I left the room. He had a point.

One of my more memorable encounters from that period involved Thomas Mann. We had a Tuesday morning meeting which was called, among us, the "overhead meeting" because all the expensive executives were present. The day before that particular Tuesday's meeting, Mr. Mayer had phoned me. I had an enormous office telephone, like a piano console with buttons connected to every nerve in the studio. The buzzer would not only ring, but flash red. So I was forever bouncing up in terror.

Mr. Mayer called me on the phone and said, "Do you know a man named Mann, a writer named Thomas Mann?" (He pronounced it *man.*)

I said, "Yes, I do, Mr. Mayer."

He said, "What's he doing?"

I said, "I don't know quite what he's doing. He's probably writing. He lives in Santa Monica currently."

Then he named an "original" (the word for an unpublished piece of material, in motion pictures, in narrative form). It was something that we bought some years ago, of some middle-European origin. It had turned out to be unlickable, and therefore pointless. We'd written it off from a tax point of view and forgotten all about it. He remembered it for some reason.

I said, "Yes, I do know it."

Mr. Mayer said, "Do you think he'd like it?" I said I had no idea. He said, "Well, you're sure he's good?"

I said, "Yes, he definitely is, he's a remarkably good writer."

He said, "What does he get?"

I said, "I don't know what he gets, Mr. Mayer."

He said, "If he's that good, whatever he wants, give it to him."

I said, "All right."

He said, "Can he come to our next story meeting?"

And here I must explain what a story meeting was at Metro. The executives, either because of occupational euphoria or ignorance, almost never read what we bought, and yet they had to make the decisions. So, of course, we evolved early on the synopsis system. But that wasn't satisfactory enough for me, because I felt they might not even read the synopses. So I evolved what became rather well known at the time: the Scheherazade system. I hired a lecturer and ex-actress, Harriet Frank, to go over with me the piece of material that was about to be presented. We would translate it into a play, almost in three acts. We would be ruthless in excising what we thought was not valuable for films, we occasionally would invent things that weren't even there, to make it better. Eventually, after a week or so, we would get together a recital. On the given Tuesday morning, Harriet Frank would come up to the executive meeting room, the "overhead room," and she would literally recite and dramatize a novel, a play, a short story, an original, taking twenty or thirty minutes, up to an hour. This was like going to the movies for these men; they adored it.

So I had Thomas Mann come this time, and Harriet told the story, this middle-European original story, doing the very best she could with it, and it was still trash. Everybody listened intently. Dr. Mann was sitting next to me. When she finished, there was that awesome silence that only took place when Mr. Mayer was in the room. You didn't dare utter your own opinion until you knew what he was going to say. He said nothing.

A silence that seemed to me to last about five years took place . . . It was probably three or four minutes. Finally, I nudged Dr. Mann and said, "Dr. Mann, I have a feeling that Mr. Mayer and the other executives would like to have your reaction to this piece of material, which is why we asked you to listen to it. Naturally, you can read it, but I thought you might be entertained by this system."

He said, "Very amusing." Then he got up, and he looked at me and clicked his heels. He said, "Mr. Fadiman."

I said, "Dr. Mann."

He walked the length of the room to where Mr. Mayer sat. He said, "Mr. Mayer. Gentlemen, there have been two mistakes made today. One, that you asked me. Two, that I came. Good day." He walked out, and everybody was a little flabbergasted.

Mayer turned to me as if it was all my fault, of course, and said, "What the hell does that mean?"

I said, "I guess that means he doesn't like the story, Mr. Mayer."

He said, "What did you tell him?"

I said, "I didn't tell him anything. I just invited him to come and listen."

He asked, "What did you offer him?"

I said, "I didn't offer him anything."

He said, "I'll be goddamned."

There were lots of odd stories of that nature, including this one about the well-known playwright Norman Krasna. He refused to write his material; he wanted to tell it to the powers that be. He had just married Al Jolson's widow, which involved with it a considerable fortune. I think it was four or five million dollars.

Anyway, we said to him, "Fine, if you insist on it," and he came and told his story. We didn't like it, and we turned it down right in front of him. He said, "You know, I'm so lucky, gentlemen. I have fuck-you money. Fuck you!"

Metro was the largest company, the most powerful, and the one with the most potency in name value throughout the world. We had "more stars than there are in the heavens." Mr. Mayer changed his birthday to July 4th so that we could celebrate two things on that day. There's a funny story connected with that. I didn't know about his new birthday, and there was a July 4th executive dinner conference, and we all came, and Mr. Mayer raised his glass and said, "To the president . . ." I immediately thought he meant the president of the United States. But he finished, ". . . Nicholas Schenck." It was an odd world.

The "Prince Story" is worth recalling. There was a fellow named the Prince of Wales, who was also briefly the king of England until he abdicated. We came in one morning and the *Hollywood Reporter* had the headline, and again Mayer turned to me as if I was responsible for everything, and asked, "What's he doing?"

I said, "I don't know what he's doing. He was just king of England."

"What do you think he gets?"

I said, "I don't know, but he's a very rich man, Mr. Mayer. I don't think it's a question of getting him."

He said, "Cable him."

I said, "Cable him what?"

He said, "Well, I'll tell you what I want. He was king of England, wasn't he?"

I said, "Yes."

"I want him to be the head of our European offices. I don't want him to do a goddamn thing. I just want him to be the head of the offices. How does that strike you?"

We all said, "That's marvelous, Mr. Mayer," but afterwards we decided it would not be marvelous, and we talked him out of it. But that's the kind of interesting man Mayer was. Without question, he was the czar of Hollywood, if there was such a term. He was the most important person. I think his salary was half a million a year, which was very high; I think it was the highest in America at that time. He once explained to us that he didn't care about the half a million because he paid taxes on it. But he wanted it to be the highest in America, period.

My being fired is another story. We were having a meeting to cut everyone's salary, including the writers', and reduce the payroll. We had a lot of them under contract, so we paid them half their money. I thought I did an honorable job for them; I really tried very hard to. When I got all finished I reported to Sam Katz, one of our vice-presidents. I said, "I think I've done the job, Sam. I've pruned the writers' list. I've cut down a lot of people, I've halved their salaries, I've settled their contracts."

"You've done a fine job. You really learned how to do it. Now let's talk about getting rid of you."

The work was so intense. I had so much reading and analyses to do that I didn't have much time for anything else. They also paid me, for those days, quite well. And the job carried with it a kind of glory. A personal story about the glory involved the famous restaurateur Mike Romanoff. His name was really Harry Ferguson and he was from Brooklyn, but we liked to believe that he was one of *the* Romanoffs—and by then he believed it himself.

He was a charming, charming fellow. Once or maybe twice a week I would lunch at Mike Romanoff's, as did most of Hollywood in those days.

As I passed by the long bar on the way to my table, I would be greeted by maybe twenty people: "Hi, Bill." "How are ya, baby?" "What's new?" "Nice to see you." Then I'd reach my table and have my lunch, and Mike would sit down. He was a very cynical man.

Once, he sat at my table and asked, "You want to make a hundred bucks?"

I said, "How do I make a hundred bucks?"

He said, "It will take me about five minutes, in this dining room, to spread the rumor that you've just been fired and can't buy $5 million worth of anything anymore. Then I want you to go back to that same bar you came through and tell me how many people say hello."

I looked at Mike and said, "I won't do it." Power was very consequential.

It was an era in which creativity could be bought by the carload because our figures, our money, Hollywood money, was fantastically superior to that which any writer in any part of the world could get, beyond the international best-seller.

For about two or three years we put on a trick, which was my idea, where we had prizes (I think they were very large sums like $100,000) for the best first novel, which we would then buy for films. The idea behind that was that the publishers would give us first look at everything in order to get the $100,000. It was a pretty clever device because we bought many more than the first novels; we'd pick up five or six more.

We would also make a best-seller for our own purposes. We would decide to buy a book, knowing that the star we wanted was either illiterate or unwilling to read it. But we also knew he'd know about it if it was a best-seller. We had regional offices in those days throughout the United States, so we would wire the heads of the regional offices to buy 100, 200, 400 copies of this book, all over the United States. They would buy roughly 30,000 copies, which cost us something like $75,000. We'd throw the books out the window, but the title would appear on the *New York Times* best-seller list for about two weeks or so. Then the individual star would say, "My God, I'm buying a best-seller."

This is why it was important for these seven men, who ruled Hollywood, who were very rich in their day, to have their industries and their business. Harry Cohn, the head of Columbia Pictures, once had an offer of a large sum of money for the studio. I had dinner with him one night and the subject came up. I said, "Harry, why don't you accept it? It's an awful lot of money." He'd worked a lot of years, and by then he had to be over sixty.

He said, "You know why not? I'd be rich, wouldn't I?"

I said, "Yes, you'd have a lot more money than you have now."

He said, "But who would invite me to dinner?"

That was what they lived for—the power. In those days, they owned their companies. They were the bosses. There was public stock, but they held most of it. And they owned movie theaters before divorcement came in. In this tiny world of about thirty thousand people, which is what Hollywood had in those days, they truly were kings, czars, emperors. And that mattered. To preserve their power those men were cruel, they were vicious, they were ruthless.

But they loved the power that stems from movies, and consequently they loved movies. They believed in movies. They had no interest in the fact that movies could be used for propaganda; they really didn't. That's why the whole McCarthy thing was genuine idiocy. They had no idea about putting anything into a film to sell ideology. The word ideology was a very large number of syllables. They wanted to make a buck, or many bucks, which is really only one syllable, and they wanted to please as many people as they could to get as many dollars as they could.

I know so many things which are unpleasant and ugly, but I see no particular point in discussing them. I could tell you a lot of stories of such treachery, and such dishonesty, such inhumanity to man by these men. But you have to understand what they were. They were pioneers. They hadn't any technology to work with; they just had their instincts. And their instincts were magnificent in terms of audience understanding.

Metro's pictures were known, not by Mr. Mayer, but through-out the industry, as "being shot through gauze." Everything was gentle and lovely. They figured out that people loved that, and they were quite right. It was never the point to educate people; we never tried.

September 1985
Bel Air

CAREER HIGHLIGHTS

1934–1942	Assistant Story Editor, RKO-Pathé, New York
	Eastern Story Editor, Columbia, New York
	General Manager, Leland Hayward, Inc., New York
	Eastern Story Editor, MGM, New York
1942–1947	Scenario and Story Editor, MGM, Hollywood
1947–1952	Executive Assistant to Dore Schary, RKO
	Executive Assistant to Howard Hughes, RKO
	Producer/Editorial Consultant, Columbia
1952–1961	Executive Story Editor/Producer, Columbia
1961–1967	Vice-President, Literary Operations, Script Development, Seven Arts
1967	Executive Literary Adviser/Script Analyst, Seven Arts/Warner Brothers

≡ DIRECTED

BY ≡

Script girl Florence Mack with Charles Bickford and Mady Christians on the set of *A Wicked Woman* (MGM, 1934).

FLORENCE MACK

Script Girl

Serving as a right hand to directors Clarence Brown, Richard Boleslawski, Charles Brabin, and W. S. Van Dyke, among others, Florence Mack worked behind the scenes for fifty years, doing detail work both on and off the set.

Now eighty-five, she lives at the Motion Picture and Television Fund retirement home, where we meet for lunch.

The first place I worked was in the casting office of the old Thomas Ince Studio in Culver City. It was 1919. When I went for the interview, I made up my mind that I would tell them, no matter what they asked me to do, that I was able to do it. A woman asked, "Have you had any experience in casting?"

I said, "Yes." Then I thought, "My goodness. I suppose it has something to do with fishing." So help me.

She sent me to the casting office, to a man named Horace Williams. The job was to answer the phone, and he soon learned that I didn't know one actor from another, or whether they were eighteen and trim, or sixty and fat. So he sent me back to the personnel office. The same woman asked me, "Well, have you ever worked on sets?"

I lied again and said, "Oh, yes." So they sent me to the Douglas MacLean Company. He and a young lady named Doris May were making domestic comedies. Douglas had been on the New York stage, and he would call the cast together about ten days or two weeks before shooting and everybody would tell him their ideas for improving the script. Putting in gags and so forth. My duty was to make notes. Every once in a while I would make a suggestion, and Douglas would say to put it in.

When they started to shoot I went along as a script girl. One of my duties was to give the cameraman the number of the scene. I found out that you watched the clothes, the props, and the dialogue to see that they all matched up. They were liable to use the wrong name or something. If you were shooting outside you had to be sure that the backgrounds were the same as they were when you started. You had to check everything for consistency.

Some directors liked to use their script girls as whipping boys. I worked for one director who was like that, but I used to protect myself by writing everything down, very carefully. I remember one who asked me one morning, "How are those clouds going?" And I said quickly, "From left to right." I had written that down the day before. He said, "You know, some of your answers are so appallingly stupid I wonder if you're in your right mind." I turned around and left the set, I was so mad.

March 1986
Woodland Hills

Editors' Note: Florence Mack died in June 1992.

FRANCISCO (CHICO) DAY

Assistant Director

≡

Chico Day was born Francisco Alonso, the third son of a Mexican bullfighter and the brother of the film star Gilbert Roland. We meet him at the offices of the Directors Guild of America. He has dressed for the occasion, looking very dapper in a blue blazer and charcoal gray trousers. Under his arm he carries a two-volume book entitled Chico Day's Snaps and Scraps. *He is justifiably proud of the many accolades he has received from directors, actors, and producers with whom he has worked.*

He has been described as having the patience of a saint and the sense of humor of Cantinflas (Mexico's legendary comedian). He also has an almost childlike innocence, firm in his belief that all people are basically good. After so many years spent on the front lines of the Hollywood wars, this good soldier has emerged unscarred.

I was born in Mexico, on the border, in Juárez. The way I got to work in the movies was that my brother, Gilbert Roland, was one of the Golden Era's most good-looking macho actors that ever lived. So I started out as an extra, the way Gilbert had. Soon, however, I became disappointed with the acting business. I was promised a part in *Ramona,* with Loretta Young at Twentieth Century–Fox, but it didn't happen. I was so disappointed that I said adios to the business of acting.

Chico Day, assistant director (far left), and his beloved boss, Cecil B. deMille (center), on the set of *The Ten Commandments* (Paramount, 1956).

I went over to Paramount and applied for a job on the production side. They said they wouldn't use anybody from the outside and that I had to start in the lowest possible position. So I started in the mail room, but from then on I progressed. I worked for the first time as an assistant director on a picture that Gilbert was in, *The Last Train from Madrid.* This was around 1936, and for twenty-five years I never stopped because everyone I worked with wanted me again. I did some of the biggest pictures at Paramount.

I have nothing but praise to offer about the wonderful old man *[Cecil B. deMille].* (We called him "the old man.") But I call him the old man affectionately because he had a heart this big. There was nothing small about this man.

My office for *The Ten Commandments* was right off the street from the garage where Mr. deMille parked his car. After he parked he would walk across the street and enter by the deMille gate. Consequently, mine would be the first office he would pass. One day an extra stopped Mr. deMille and asked him when he thought we were going to get started. Mr. deMille said, "Well, in about thirty days. We have to do all the interiors first." The man said nothing, but Mr. deMille said to him, "I can see by your eyes and by your expression that you need money." And he pulled out a $100 bill. In those days that was a fortune. He gave it to this man and said to him, "You can pay me back when you start working." That was the man that everybody called such an s.o.b. I knew him very differently.

Another time, his first assistant director on *The Ten Commandments* went to Egypt on location. (I was the second assistant on the picture.) Mr. deMille called me into his office and said, "Eddie, my assistant, is ill. I want you to take care of all the bills—medicines, doctors, hotels, automobiles, clothes, whatever." Now that is the s.o.b. as I knew him.

I also worked with George Seaton, who was really a gentleman. I did *Country Girl* and *Teacher's Pet* with him. George was once lecturing at UCLA, and he asked me to write out the duties and responsibilities of an assistant director. I wrote it all out and gave it to him, and he read it while I was there in the office. After he read it he asked me, "What does the *director* do?"

The assistant director is the first person on the set, every day, to check to see if there are any problems or faults with all the things he has talked over with the director the night before. He really prepares everything for the director. He sees that the cast is in make-up at the proper time, he sees that the wardrobe is lined up, he sees that the dressing rooms are comfortable. He is the one in charge of everything in front and in back of the camera at all times. He's the one who tells the director that everything is ready.

(And everything *better* be ready.) He keeps track of expenses so that they don't go over budget on extras or on overtime or meal penalties. If twelve hours have elapsed, there is an extra day's check coming to the actor. Of course there are exceptions to that rule, such as when you're on location. So the assistant director has to know all these rules and laws. We don't actually do the budget; the production manager does that. But the assistant does the breakdown of the script, the boards, and the schedules. Though the production manager has also already done that, the assistant director has to acquaint himself with the whole setup. There usually are both a production manager and an assistant director, though not always. But you really need both most of the time. And in big pictures you need more. When I was the production manager on *Patton,* for instance, I had seven production managers in Spain! I had one in England, one in France, one in Crete, and one in Morocco!

As for assistant directors, it depended on how many people we were working with. Usually, on call we had four. Then we augmented that to as many as ten. You know, that was a big production, with complex war scenes, so we needed a lot of assistant directors, and in some scenes they were dressed like soldiers.

The assistant director sees that the cameras are set up properly, according to the director's wishes. He is the one who knows where each camera should be, if they're ready, and so forth. He is also in charge of the crew. Now, the cameraman has charge of his own crew, the grips and the gaffer, but any time something happens within the crew, the assistant director is the one to solve the problem.

The assistant director sometimes directs a second unit. It's not done so much now, but it was done frequently then. I directed many, many second units, especially in westerns. I was out there on the range.

The production manager is the one who starts first when a film is getting started, because he's hired to break down the script, make up the schedule, and make the estimate. It becomes an estimate; it is never a budget. If the stars have special clauses in their contracts, the production manager handles them.

And he is the one that takes charge, more or less, of the budget. He controls it. Whenever something is going over budget, he makes it known to everyone concerned. The production manager should be very, very close to the director because many times the director and the producer are not really well balanced. And he is the one that takes care of that imbalance. He has to bring certain things to the attention of the director.

The second assistant director is more or less the runner for the first assistant. In fact, I once belonged to the screening committee for people that wanted to come in to the Directors Guild at that time. In my group I had four assistant directors. One of them, when screening a prospective member, would ask, "Have you got good legs?" The second assistant director is a very important person. He has to keep himself just as well versed in rules and laws and changes as anyone. He is the one that takes care of the production report, he is the one that takes care of the call sheets, he is the one that takes care of any infringement on the laws of any of the unions. If something happens, accidents or whatever, he has to put it on the production report. Plus the fact that he helps the first assistant in staging background action.

Let me tell you one thing about directors. DeMille was one and George Stevens was another that I worked with who never told an actor how to do it. If they were displeased with a scene they would just say, "We'll do it over again." I never heard either deMille or Stevens tell an actor how to do it. If they had anything to say to the actor they would go over to him and whisper; they would never embarrass him.

The most responsibility I got from a director was from Cecil B. deMille, on *The Ten Commandments*. I'm telling you this with all humility, but I knew more about the Bible than anyone on the set. I knew the spiritual interpretation of the Bible, which is the most important thing, not the words, but the interpretation. Mr. deMille had heard me giving instructions to the extras. In every scene I would take five minutes and tell the actors what the scene was and what it meant, both in the Bible and to the picture. The girl who was playing Miriam went to the associate producer, Henry Wilcoxon, and told him she would like to talk to Mr. deMille about a certain scene because she wanted to know what her feelings should be. Mr. Wilcoxon went to Mr. deMille, who said to him, "You tell the young lady to go and listen to Chico explain it to the extras."

This was immediately after the closing of the Red Sea scene, when we had 350 extras. In the scene of the original exodus we had 15,000 animals and 10,000 people. The assistant director directs the extras, but it has to be with the consent of the director. You know, if an extra says even one word he gets paid for a bit part. (By the way, Mr. deMille never called an extra an extra. He would always call them actors. He would say, "You are actors. You're nothing else to me but actors. That's why I'm paying you.")

Mr. Seaton also gave me a lot of responsibility. We had sixty-seven newspaper reporters in *Teacher's Pet*. George called them over before we started, when we were rehearsing, and told them that I was in charge of them. He said, "Whatever he tells you to do, you do, because he knows cameras, he knows angles, he knows everything."

So they all used to come to me and I would say, "You just do what a newspaper person would do. The only thing I can tell you is if I want you to cross over here or make some other move." And it was beautiful. It was like a symphony because everything was done the way they would really do it. These were *real* newspaper-men. We got a lot of free publicity on that picture.

There are several qualities you have to have to make a good assistant director. First of all, you have to have intelligence. You have to have personality. You have to be clean (you know, you're so close to the artists and everybody else). You have to have love for the job you're doing, and you have to have love for the person you are there to help, the director. Even if it doesn't get shown, there must be a mental love for the director so that he can call you anything he wants and you still love him.

In fact, I told several directors who I knew were temperamental, "If you want to say anything out of your heart or your soul, you say it to me. You can do that, and I'll never take it personally." I don't remember, ever, anyone really turning on me.

You have to have a lot of physical strength, too. I never sat down when I was working, because if I sat down I would feel tired. I never had a chair following me, like Mr. deMille did.

Maybe my style was different because of how I was brought up, how I was taught to respect other people and other people's property. We never left the house without kissing our mother and father. I made a family out of the people I worked with.

February 1985
Hollywood

FILMOGRAPHY (partial)

1929   *Bulldog Drummond* (dir. F. Richard Jones, Samuel Goldwyn Productions)

1932   *The Kid from Spain* (dir. Leo McCarey, Samuel Goldwyn Productions)

1937   *The Big Broadcast of 1938* (dir. Mitchell Leisen, Paramount)

        The Last Train from Madrid (dir. James Hogan, Paramount)

1938   *The Buccaneer* (dir. Cecil B. deMille, Paramount)

1939   *Midnight* (dir. Mitchell Leisen, Paramount)

1940   *Arise My Love* (dir. Mitchell Leisen, Paramount)

1941   *Hold Back the Dawn* (dir. Mitchell Leisen, Paramount)

1942   *Reap the Wild Wind* (dir. Cecil B. deMille, Paramount)

        Take a Letter, Darling (dir. Mitchell Leisen, Paramount)

1943   *No Time for Love* (dir. Mitchell Leisen, Paramount)

1944   *Lady in the Dark* (dir. Mitchell Leisen, Paramount)

1946   *The Perfect Marriage* (dir. Lewis Allen, Paramount)

1947   *Saigon* (dir. Leslie Fenton, Paramount)

1948   *Isn't It Romantic* (dir. Norman McLeod, Paramount)

        Whispering Smith (dir. Leslie Fenton, Paramount)

        The Sainted Sisters (dir. William D. Russell, Paramount)

1949   *Samson and Delilah* (dir. Cecil B. deMille, Paramount)

        Streets of Laredo (dir. Leslie Fenton, Paramount)

        The File on Thelma Jordan (dir. Robert Siodmak, Paramount)

1950   *The Furies* (dir. Anthony Mann, Paramount)

1952	*Anything Can Happen* (dir. George Seaton, Paramount)
1953	*Shane* (dir. George Stevens, Paramount)
	Little Boy Lost (dir. George Seaton, Paramount)
	Pony Express (dir. Jerry Hopper, Paramount)
1954	*Knock on Wood* (dir. Norman Panama, Paramount)
	The Bridges at Toko-Ri (dir. Mark Robson, Paramount)
	Elephant Walk (dir. William Dieterle, Paramount)
	The Country Girl (dir. George Seaton, Paramount)
1956	*The Ten Commandments* (dir. Cecil B. deMille, Paramount)
	Omar Khayyam (dir. William Dieterle, Paramount)
1957	*The Buster Keaton Story* (dir. Sidney Sheldon, Paramount)
	Teacher's Pet (dir. George Seaton, Paramount)
1958	*Spanish Affair* (dir. Don Siegel, Paramount)
1960	*The Magnificent Seven* (dir. John Sturges, United Artists)
1961	*The Last Time I Saw Archie* (dir. Jack Webb, United Artists)
	One-Eyed Jacks (dir. Marlon Brando, Paramount)
	Escape from Zahrain (dir. Ronald Neame, Paramount)
1965	*The Sandpiper* (dir. Vincente Minelli, MGM)
	Major Dundee (dir. Sam Peckinpah, Columbia)
	The Greatest Story Ever Told (dir. George Stevens, United Artists)
1966	*Seconds* (dir. John Frankenheimer, Paramount)
	Last of the Secret Agents (dir. Norman Abbott, Paramount)
	Nevada Smith (dir. Henry Hathaway, Paramount)

1967   *Valley of the Dolls* (dir. Mark Robson, Twentieth Century–Fox)

Caprice (dir. Frank Tashlin, Twentieth Century–Fox)

Planet of the Apes (dir. Franklin Schaffner, Twentieth Century–Fox)

1969   *Patton* (dir. Franklin Schaffner, Twentieth Century–Fox)

Hello, Dolly! (dir. Gene Kelly, Twentieth Century–Fox)

1971   *Vanishing Point* (dir. Richard Sarafin, Twentieth Century–Fox)

1972   *Rage* (dir. George C. Scott, Warner Bros.)

1976   *Islands in the Stream* (dir. Franklin Schaffner, Paramount)

1978   *Matilda* (dir. Daniel Mann, American International)

ANDRE DE TOTH

Director

André de Toth was born in Hungary and came to Hollywood in the early forties. For eight years he was married to the actress Veronica Lake, and directed her in several of his signature films noir.

We meet at a restaurant de Toth has chosen, where he is a regular, judging by the nameplate at our table. He is a robust, athletic-looking man, who appears a good deal younger than his nearly eighty years. His self-confident demeanor and rakish eye patch combine to make him look both striking and intimidating.

Though he never became a director of the first rank, he is proud of his body of work and speaks convincingly, with the authority of one who is used to having his orders carried out on the double.

Everybody wants to go to Hollywood. Being in the picture business in Europe, of course I, too, wanted to come; it was only natural. But there was no red carpet rolled out for me here. I knew how to drive a race car, how to fly a plane, how to ride a polo pony. But nobody gave me a car to drive, a plane to fly, or a horse to ride. So I ended up driving orange-drink trucks, until I got enough money to come back to Hollywood.

I started working on scripts. When the Kordas arrived, they knew me, of course (one Hungarian meets another), and I started working for them as a second-unit director. I had done second-unit work on *The Thief of Baghdad* in England, so I did it again on *Jungle Book*. I worked on *Lady Hamilton*, doing a little of

Directors George Sidney (left) and André de Toth (right).

everything, solving a little problem here, a little problem there. Actually, I was Korda's associate; I kind of represented him, so to speak.

As a full-time director, I was first hired by Columbia. On my first picture, of course, they assigned me a crew. But from then on, as a director, you usually had the right to pick your key people. That is only smart. Nobody, nobody in the motion picture business who was in his right mind would force a director to work with someone he doesn't like to work with. You see, some of the members of the crew know your faults so they can help you, because everybody needs a lot of help. Anybody who tells you he makes the picture alone is an idiot.

A director is really a writer. He writes with the camera, that's his pen, that's his chisel, that's his easel, that's his canvas. A director, I think, should have an overall knowledge. Not that you have to be better than your cameraman, or better than your special technicians, but you have to understand at least their problems. That's the only way you can appreciate what they do, and then you can ask them the limit.

The director has to make changes as he goes along, on the spur of the moment. If directing meant adhering exactly verbatim to everything, then a pharmacist would be the best director because he just follows directions.

The director is an artist. But you also have to have the cameraman because you can ruin a scene with the wrong lighting, the wrong photography. The director does not have to know exactly how to do it, but he must know exactly what he wants and ask for it. A good cinematographer, of course, adds to the picture by feeling the mood of the director. He adds additional shading or form.

There are two kinds of people you call directors. One I call selectors, and the other directors. There are magnificent selectors: William Wyler, David Lean, George Stevens, to name just a few. They shoot millions of feet of film, and then they sit in the cutting room and pick out the best of them. Then there are directors like John Ford or myself. I see the whole film before I get on the set. I see every single move. I see the light and the shade and the color. So I can shoot faster because I know exactly what I want.

People kind of tagged me as a certain kind of director, but I must say I am unaware of any specific style I have. It's me, and I'm doing it this way, period. Of course, my style is described as film noir or reality. I try to create reality. It's as I see it. I know right away where I want to put the emphasis, where I put the camera, what lens I use.

On my films, the director of photography doesn't exist. It has to be part of me. It's one. The cinematographer does what the story requires, and I have to translate it for him, make him understand, direct him like I direct an actor. I *contaminate* him. The same goes for the art director. He can create a set which is fantastic, and then comes a collision between the director's ideas and the visual requirements. Sometimes it just doesn't work.

In working with an actor, if you have a good one, then you almost don't have to talk to him because before you come on the set you have discussed the character he portrays. Once he understands the character it can be only one way. It's very simple. I discuss each character with each actor. It's very important that they should understand what makes these people tick, how they would react to certain things and why.

Actually, psychoanalysis is the best step to direction. Understanding of human beings is the key for a director's success—understanding motivations, understanding reactions, understanding that different people react differently to certain things.

If the actor gets out of the rhythm of the character, I intervene. As far as rehearsing goes, again, some actors need a lot of rehearsal, some lose it if you rehearse too much. The director has to feel it. What's so beautiful about directing is that there is no rubber stamp. I cannot tell you to rehearse it eight times and you have a good scene. Or not to rehearse it and you have a good scene. There are no such guarantees. The director has to be sensitive to the moment, to recognize what is required at that particular second. And that may change from day to day even with the same people, because an actor might have had a bad night with his wife, or he has a hangover, or he lost on the horses.

Now comes the difficult part: to balance it. Because it's an ensemble, right? One actor would like to do it now, another would like two hours of rehearsal; so how to get the common denominator, where you don't go along with one and destroy the other.

A second-unit director is the most useful, and usually the most hated, man. The job is kind of in between the devil and the deep blue sea. Usually, the second-unit director does scenes which are complicated to set up and would waste a lot of time, and which the director does not want to do. Or somebody's contract expires, the deal is about over, and so they have another unit shooting simultaneously. The good directors know their limits, and they delegate certain jobs to second units, who are experts in certain things.

You can do second unit right in the studio; it doesn't have to be on location. I did second unit for Selznick right here. Sometimes they send them to a far-off location, and because the whole unit cannot travel they send a smaller unit.

Sometimes a second unit is larger than the first unit. The second-unit director directs actors as well. It's a very difficult job, really, because it has to match the style of the director. A good second-unit director is unknown, so to speak, because you should never be able to tell where the director left off and the second-unit director picked up. Whenever I do second unit, I don't even take credit on it. I'm not directing as myself; I'm fitting into the director's style and work.

A director needs to be aware. He needs awareness of life, awareness of human possibilities, frailties, assets. He also has to be completely knowledgeable about the forces at his disposal. He has to know what a cameraman can and cannot do, so that he won't ask a cameraman to do something impossible. He has to know what an editor does, and he has to respect him. Acting is also good training for a director because, again, you're aware of the trials and pain of an actor.

The old producers loved the business, they loved to make movies. I had great respect for Harry Cohn. He was a picture-maker, a shrewd operator, and instinctively knew stories. We fought like dogs and cats, and he took me to court. It's in the law books: *Columbia v. de Toth*. I paid him $156,000 cash in 1946 or 1947. I had been wrong on contract technicalities. But while we were still in court he rehired me on my own terms. You had to stand up to Harry Cohn—you had to not just stand up to him but to argue—and once he discovered that you had integrity and a real point of view, he was a pussycat to work with. You could almost do anything you wanted.

The studio system never hampered me; it worked extremely well. There are people who work well under any system, and there are people who cannot work well under any system, no matter what. There are complainers and there are doers. I'm a doer, even if I make nothing but mistakes. When we were assigned to a picture under the studio system, if I didn't want to do it, I would say, "No, thank you very much." That's it. Sometimes they would suspend me for it, sometimes they wouldn't. They suspended me so often that they finally respected me. That's why I have never been on a long-term contract. I just wanted to do one picture at a time, pictures I was interested in. The studio system was hard, but straight. It worked. Look at all the talent. Look at the credits, look at the pictures of Michael Curtiz, from a western to a psychological murder mystery to *Yankee Doodle Dandy* to *Casablanca*. He could do anything. Why? He understood his metier. He understood the craft, and he understood human beings. He didn't speak Hungarian, he couldn't speak English; he couldn't speak. But somehow he communicated. That's more than language.

February 1986
Burbank

FILMOGRAPHY (partial)

(As Second-Unit Director)

1940   *The Thief of Baghdad* (co-dirs. Michael Powell, Ludwig Berger, Tim Whelan, United Artists)

1941   *Rudyard Kipling's Jungle Book* (dir. Zoltan Korda, UK)

1942   *Lady Hamilton* (dir. Alexander Korda, United Artists)

(As Director)

1943   *Passport to Suez* (Columbia)

1944   *None Shall Escape* (Columbia)

          Dark Waters (United Artists)

1947   *Ramrod* (United Artists)

          The Other Love (United Artists)

1948   *Pitfall* (United Artists)

1949   *Slattery's Hurricane* (Twentieth Century–Fox)

1951   *Man in the Saddle* (Columbia)

1952   *Carson City* (Warner Bros.)

          Springfield Rifle (Warner Bros.)

          Last of the Comanches (Columbia)

1953   *House of Wax* (Warner Bros.)

          The Stranger Wore a Gun (Columbia)

          Thunder Over the Plains (Warner Bros.)

1954   *Riding Shotgun* (Warner Bros.)

          Tanganyika (Universal)

          The Bounty Hunter (Warner Bros.)

          Crime Wave (Warner Bros.)

1955   *The Indian Fighter* (United Artists)

1957   *Monkey on My Back* (United Artists)

           Hidden Fear (also co-screenwriter, United Artists)

1958   *The Two-Headed Spy* (Columbia)

           The Day of the Outlaw (United Artists)

1960   *Man on a String* (Columbia)

1961   *Morgan the Pirate* (MGM)

1962   *The Mongols* (with Riccardo Freda, Italy)

1964   *Gold for the Caesars* (with Riccardo Freda, Italy)

1969   *Play Dirty* (United Artists)

≡ CAMERAS
ROLLING ≡

JIM NOBLITT

Grip

Jim Noblitt came to California in 1928 and began work as a grip at Paramount for seventy-five cents an hour. At eighty-three, Noblitt still looks like he could haul around lights and cameras as well as a man forty years his junior. He is plain-spoken, but answers our questions carefully and thoughtfully. He lives in a room in the Motion Picture and Television Fund retirement home.

A grip's main purpose in a studio is to handle the equipment for the cameraman, and to handle all the stage walls that are shifted during production to make way for trains, cameras, and other equipment, and to hang all the scaffolding that holds the lights. We report directly to the key grip; he's the head grip on the stage.

The number of grips on a set would depend on the size of the production. If you were on a large production like *My Fair Lady* you would have seven grips: a key grip, a best boy, and five grips. The best boy checks in the men in the morning and checks them out at night. If there are any absences, he gets competent replacements. He assigns grips to work on the scaffold and set the scrims and the flags on the lamps, as advised by the cameraman, who is on the floor lighting the set. Sometimes there are as many as two or three men on the scaffold. Those two extra men come back on the deck again to help with the parallels or dolly track, if the dolly has to be laid. They have to put the camera on the dolly to wheel it down the stage to pick up the actors or whatever they're photographing. I worked with quite a few cinematographers— Harry Stradling quite a bit, Bun Haskins, Phil Krasna, Les Shorr, Joe Byrock, Ted McCord.

On location you're up earlier, and you go to bed much earlier because you're so tired. In those days you worked in the sand and the dirt. The equipment was heavy, and you didn't have near the help on location that you had at the studio. When you were at the studio you had wheels. You could load your equipment on wheels and push. Out on location you carried it all. It was very tiresome.

We had a call steward at the union. It was customary when you were out of work to call the local and put your name in the book. The union tried to establish this as a rule, but they were never too successful. A lot of us would just call the department heads at the various studios. They'd put you on the gang, or in a room someplace, building equipment until they found a show for you, or a spot where you could work for a while. We were kept busy all the time. I worked for Paramount, Warner Brothers, and Fox. I got raises along the way, and there was always night penalty. Ten percent of your wages for night penalty.

I'll tell you one of the smart things, I think, for technicians to do on pictures when they're in production, is to keep themselves clean. The men who kept themselves clean every day and wore the nicest, cleanest clothes were on productions all the time. Those that didn't take care of themselves were seldom asked to go to a stage and work on a production. The grip boss was always dressed nicely, and he always picked out nice-looking people to work for him. Even if they were in overalls, if they were clean that was okay.

To be a good grip you have to have physical strength, and you have to listen and pay attention. You have to be quick to learn, and you have to obey the rules. I don't think anyone ever learns from anyone else; you just pick it up.

You can get so involved in a picture. I remember something that happened on one of George Cukor's sets. We were doing a scene in *My Fair Lady* on Stage 2. We had the dolly and all. We had the camera on the doorway, and Rex Harrison came through the door and walked toward the camera. The music started playing "I've Grown Accustomed to Her Face." I'm by the dolly watching him, the key grip's in the back, and the tears are running down my face. I was so intent on this scene. Mr. Cukor turned around to look at Rex, but he saw me and said, "For Christ's sake, Jim, what the hell is wrong with you? Do you mean to tell me that you're living this picture? And you're crying already, when we don't even have it on the screen yet?" He says, "Go have a beer, go have something. Go on, get out of here."

September 1985
Woodland Hills

Editors' Note: Jim Noblitt died in January 1991.

ED RIKE

Gaffer

Ed Rike went to work at a young age, lighting sets for movies at Warner Brothers. He was a loyal member of many crews, and he enjoyed his work until a back injury forced him to retire. He lives in a room at the Motion Picture and Television Fund retirement home.

We came out here to California in 1908, from Illinois. When my dad died I was a sophomore in high school, and I quit school and went to work. There was no use fooling around. I knew what I was going to be, and I had my mother to take care of.

I started out on the silents. We didn't have talking pictures till *The Jazz Singer [Warner Brothers, 1927]* with Al Jolson. I did the lighting on it. I actually worked with the cameraman. I set up all the lights. The cameraman would make suggestions and I made suggestions. We worked together. I worked with George Barnes for years. This was all at Warner Brothers.

I went out with different cameramen for different pictures. We worked in the electrical department. We were the riffraff, the grips and us, and we never had contracts. Only the cameramen had contracts.

If I was free I would be assigned to a cameraman. I was never off; I was always working. I was always on the "preference list" as they called it. We already had our union, 728; it's Local 80 now. They were part of IATSE *[International Alliance of Theatrical Stage Employees]*. But we had nothing like a forty-hour week. We worked as long as was necessary in the very early days. Later on, after you worked eight hours you got time and a half. Saturdays were also time-and-a-half days.

The crew ran from seven to ten or twelve people. It all depended on the picture. If you had a big hotel set, for example, you needed a lot of arc lights, and you'd need more electricians. I would say Warners had more help than any other studio, and that made working there easier. There were always plenty of men on the crews.

The cameraman wasn't really my boss, but he would tell me what he wanted, and we cooperated. The grips would move the cameras back and forth for the cameramen. It used to take four men to carry an arc light. It was heavy stuff.

I worked on all the big movies at Warner Brothers, on a lot of the Jimmy Cagney movies, including *The Public Enemy.* I also worked on all the Busby Berkeley musicals. I was the lighting man for him for years. I used to sit and watch them rehearse first. There were lots of pretty girls, but I was never on the make for any of them. I knew them all and they were all nice girls.

When I retired, all I got was my Social Security. We never got pensions. I went out on disability; I just couldn't walk no more. My spine went out.

February 1986
Woodland Hills

Editors' Note: Ed Rike died in July 1993.

George Folsey, cameraman, with Joan Crawford on the set of *The Gorgeous Hussy* (MGM, 1936).

GEORGE FOLSEY

Director of

Cinematography

As we arrive for our first interview with George Folsey, we find him chipping golf balls on the lawn in front of his gracious Spanish-style house. He is quick to inform us that the house once belonged to Greta Garbo. A slender, white-haired man who appears quite frail, he nevertheless speaks with vigor and passion about his work and his life.

The second time we ask to talk with him (several months later) he has to get permission from his nurse, as he has been seriously ill and is not allowed to exert himself. He agrees to a short interview but, as we begin talking, he forgets about the time—and so do we. Ironically, the man who brought the softness of muted light to black-and-white cinematography sits in the unforgiving harshness of a sunlit California day.

Throughout both our conversations, this legendary cinematographer, nominated twelve times for Academy Awards, refers to himself simply as a cameraman.

I started out as Adolph Zukor's office boy, at the Famous Players film company. When a job agency sent me there I had no idea what it was. I sat in an office that whole first day, and not a soul came in or went out. I sat there with a telephone operator named

Lily Mitchell. At six o'clock she said I could go home, and to be there at eight the next morning.

Well, the next morning the office which had been so empty was suddenly packed with people. In came Mary Pickford, Carlisle Blackwell, Harold Lockwood, Marguerite Clark, Hazel Dawn, Pauline Frederick, Paul McAllister—people that I had seen on the screen, that I was enchanted with.

I was told to take their names to a man named Bill Scully, so I did that. To find him I went down a long hall and entered a big double door. When I got inside, it was a big motion picture studio, with sets here and sets there. There was a costume ball going on. Over here was an Indian, there a northwest mounted policeman, and a fire, a piece of meat, and a guy on a ladder dripping blood.

From that day on I was hooked. I got to learn how to run the switchboard, I got to learn how to run the elevator, I played parts in pictures with Mary Pickford and Jack Barrymore. They'd just say, "Come here," they'd put make-up on you and stick you in the scene. The assistant director would tell you what to do.

It was exciting and fascinating, and I knew this was the business for me. I even got $6 a week. One of my duties was to get everybody's lunch. I used to get Zukor's sardine sandwich at a little Jewish delicatessen below the studio. I used to get Ed Porter's lunch from a Chinese restaurant, and two Pittsburgh stogies. Then they would send me to get Jack Barrymore's lunch. I used to go to a nearby hotel or restaurant, and I would be standing in the kitchen waiting where the food checker stood. She would give me pieces of sourdough bread and sweet butter, and then I wouldn't have to buy myself any lunch. That way I could save fifteen cents, and with Jack Barrymore's half-dollar tip, I was loaded. I was on my way. Great feeling.

Nobody had any assistants in those days. The cameraman didn't have any; there was a director, an assistant director, the actors, and the property men. The property men did everything. But that was the crew. There were no grips then. Now, Porter was both a cameraman and part owner of the company with Zukor, and he was terribly, terribly important technically. He was probably the only one who really knew what happened when a piece of film was developed. He supervised the developing, printing, and cutting of the film; he did everything. He was so busy that he didn't have time to load the magazines, unload them, can them and put them away. So he got his secretary to get him an assistant. One of the office boys, Joe Goodrich, became Porter's assistant and right away I thought, "There's a job I could do."

Pretty soon they sent me out to help a cameraman named Martinelli. I didn't know what I was doing, but I knew how to follow instructions. He told me just what to do. Then Emmett Williams asked me to be his assistant, and I was ready to go, but they transferred him to California, so I was dead. Then Lyman Buning asked me, and I became his assistant. We did *Snow White and the Seven Dwarfs*. We did that long before Disney did; we did it as a straight motion picture. I learned to do double exposures in the camera on that picture.

We did *Uncle Tom's Cabin,* which was a great film. Of course, we worked ungodly hours. By that time I was getting $8 a week. I worked with Lyman for about three and a half years, then went with a fellow named Larry Williams, Emmett Williams's brother. It was a good move for me because, nice as he was, Lyman wouldn't let me get ahead. Whereas the first picture that I'm on with Larry, I'm shooting second camera. It was a picture with George M. Cohan called *Broadway Jones.*

We were down in Florida, and I'm up on a platform shooting a second camera, and my foot is hanging over the side, shaking because I'm so nervous. I've shot the damn camera four thousand times, but now I'm shooting it in a real scene in a big picture, and it's the second camera.

I got to make a picture with a guy named Kenneth Webb, and then worked with a mournful French cameraman named Jacques Monterand. This is how I got to be a cameraman.

It was so early in the business that nobody knew what was going on except that a picture was being made. We made so many mistakes you can't believe it. We used to go on location, and the only person who knew where we were going was the director. We'd all get into cars and follow the director's car, not having the remotest idea of where we were going. We once took off from the 56th Street studio and ended up in Mohegan Lakes, outside of Peekskill, New York. We all stopped for lunch, ate, piled back in the cars, and off we went. Nobody asked questions. This time the director had found a farmhouse, in the middle of a teeming rainstorm at about three or four in the afternoon, and he announced, "This is where we're going to do it."

Everyone stayed till the end except me. I was sent back to New York to get crepe hair, make-up, costumes, film, black paper, tape, everything we needed. I packed the gear that we needed, got in an open seven-passenger automobile with seven people, a dog, a bird, and a pig. The pig was eating everything that was on the floor. He'd chew on shoes, so I sat with my feet up all the way to Peekskill. By the time we got there the pig had eaten the entire upholstery in the bottom of the car.

By this time I'm about eighteen or nineteen, and now I'm a pretty good assistant. I can do all kinds of things. About that time they decided that instead of making one negative and all the prints here and shipping them to Europe, they'd have some good sense and make *two* negatives and let the Europeans do their own printing. So to do that they have to have two cameras.

Under Monterand, I started on a picture with Jimmy Crane and Alice Brady. She was a big star for years. In the movie she played two parts: herself and her sister. They had split screens.

(They had split screens from the beginning—they did trick camera work in the 1890s in France and elsewhere in Europe.)

Anyway, I don't know whether Monterand was worried about the double exposures or whether he was genuinely homesick and uncomfortable in New York, but one night about ten days after the picture started he said, "I quit. I go back to France and I raise violets."

The director, Kenneth Webb, asked me, "Can you shoot the picture?" Well, by this time I'm nineteen years old, and I feel I can move the studio if you want me to. I'd never shot a picture in my life, but I'd been around with good cameramen, and I was always watching. I understood about lights and all that, so I said sure, and he made me cameraman.

Alice immediately said, "Gee, Kenneth, he's awfully young."

Webb said, "Don't worry. If he's not all right we'll change him." I didn't know this, of course. Alice was in love with Jimmy Crane. How are you going to make a woman in love look bad? So it went great, and on about the third day she offered me a personal contract (which I didn't take, but I was glad to have that reassurance).

It worked out fine and I became a cameraman. I had been getting $22.50 as a second cameraman. Cameramen's salaries were $75 to $100 a week; there was no logical relationship between the two salary levels. But I felt I could live on anything if I was a cameraman— that's all I wanted. It never even entered my mind to worry about the salary; I could do that some other time.

After the picture was finished a man named Scott saw it. He was working in and out of the Famous Players company, and he had another outfit he was going to be connected with. He offered me a job with them, at $175 a week! I think I was pretty bright for my age and for the amount of experience that I had, but I thought to myself, "The picture will finish, and I'll be through, and I won't know anybody else in the business. All the people here like me. The money is not as important as the job." And I turned it down.

But I did go to the management, and when I came in they said, "George, from now on we're going to give you $50 a week."

I said to J. N. Naulty, the studio manager, "That's awfully nice of you, and I appreciate it very much, but I've been offered another job."

A guy named Smith was also there, and asked, "Would you sign a contract with us for six months for $100 a week?"

I said, "Yes, sir." Boom, just like that. So I went from $40 a week to $100, at nineteen years old. Now, most kids would have gone out and bought a fancy car or something, but I got it all out of my system for about $36. I had never bought anything for myself—ever—but this day I went to John David's haberdashery store and bought about six pairs of cloisonné cufflinks for $6 apiece.

I went to night school to study photography. They taught us how to make the emulsion. A cameraman needs to know how to make the emulsion like a baker needs to know how they grow wheat to make flour. The class was a disappointment, so I found myself a book called *The Art of Composition and the Critical Judgment of Pictures,* which I studied very carefully.

I gradually learned about composition and about light, which is so important. When you light a scene, you try to assume that there is a kind of source light that shines on you. We try to avoid that because women in particular don't always look well lit from behind. You put what you call a key light (which is a spot light with a Fresnel lens on it and a place to put diffusion). It's a series of circles—bigger and bigger and bigger—of ground glass. The circles are ground in the glass so they can make it a kind of soft, diffused light that will light up a distance shot. If you put just a plain piece of glass there, the light would be very harsh. This is softer. Then you diffuse it further by either putting what they call a plain gel, or an oiled gel, or a plain gel with oil in the center. It depends on what you want. If the light is still too strong you can put nets on it. It's a little net that can be single or double.

So after that was done we'd read the light; we'd read it with a light meter. There was a time, of course, when we had no light meters. The cameramen had to judge by eye. All of the pictures I shot as a young man were without light meters until I came to Metro and worked with Karl Freund. He didn't invent, but he developed the light meter, and did a good job of promoting it in the business. They were very helpful because they enabled the cameraman to have the printing density always in the right place.

About printing density. Let's say you take a picture of someone, and it is developed and there isn't a sufficient amount of light on it. There are two ways of developing the negative. It can be developed by time and temperature, or it can be developed by sight, by looking at it with a green light. With time and temperature you put the film in at a certain temperature for a certain time. If it isn't developed sufficiently then it never will be.

Originally, film was developed exclusively by sight. They put the film in and then developed it in green light in most cases, sometimes in red. That was the beginning of orthochromatic film, film that is sensitive only to blue. For instance, the sky in all those early Hal Roach comedies was always blue.

Then they invented panchromatic photography for the furniture business, so they could copy grains of wood, with yellows and so on. That eventually gravitated to the picture business, and we began to use panchromatic film with filters. Now we could put a filter on the sky and that would pull the white cloud out because it would darken the sky. Before that, the cloud and the sky were white, so you couldn't see them. Panchromatic is sensitive to all colors. It was a tremendous improvement, and we used it for a long time.

Then came Technicolor. Technicolor is a black-and-white film. With Technicolor you have three negatives: blue, green, and yellow. If there was a quality in the blue, you'd get the blue quality in black and white. After they got all this done and developed, they would bleach that negative. All three negatives would be bleached. They would take that film and print it like they do a funny sheet: they print a yellow, a blue, a green, a red, whatever that combination is, one upon another. There's perfect registration, so they'll print a blue and run blue dye over it. The only place the blue dye will take is where it was photographed blue. The same for the red sheet, and the green sheet, until you have a perfect print. They had wonderful color control with that process and were able to make great prints. There's a print of the movie *Robin Hood* that is exquisite even today.

For a long time that's the way color pictures were made. Now we have a three-color process all in one film. Eastman Kodak has it, so we no longer use Technicolor. The Kodak company obviated the necessity of having all three negatives.

You can't talk about light without talking about the picture. Let's say that you put a certain amount of light on to get a proper picture, and that negative is developed by, say, time and temperature. You haven't had enough light on there to get what they call a printing density. That should be printed up at light number 21 or 22, but yours is only printing about 16 or 17. It's weak and thin, and when you put it on the screen you will see that light effects are all grayish.

I had an interesting experience with Richard Boleslawski, a very good director and a very good man to work with. He did many pictures, including *Operator 13* with Marion Davies. He asked me to make a light effect for him one day. We had a dark mahogany office in the scene. He said, "Folsey, we like dark."

Okay. I put on a thing called a junior, a 2,000-watt bulb, from a platform down across the wall. He said, "No, no, Folsey, no light."

I said to myself, "I guess he doesn't like the direction of it," so I put it from the other side.

Again he says, "No, no light."

So, in my exasperation, I said to him, "Boley, why don't you take a piece of black leader and put it between this scene and that scene, and you'll have no light."

"Oh," he says, "I've got to see something."

I explained to him, "That's what I've got that light for. Now, look, go back there and sit down and leave me alone. When you know what you want I'll get it."

You have to have a printing density to begin with, and that's what I was trying to do there. If the scene is fully lit, and it reads a printing density of about 26 or 27 (which is where we like it), you have to have that amount of printing density somewhere in the light effect or you won't get a printing density, and they can't print it at 26. They have to print it at 21, or 20, or 18, and then you've got nothing. There's nothing to keep the projection light out of the screen; it grays it up and it doesn't look dark—it looks black and gray. You increase the contrast.

You don't make a light effect by removing light. The solution is to increase the contrast. Put a strong light on one side of the scene, put no light on the other side, and the printing density prints it at 27 or 28 on that bright side, which gives me a wonderful quality of skin texture and everything, and I can see it. You can put breaks in it, a little shadow here and there to break it up. But on the other side you put nothing, or you silhouette the blackness against a little glow of light on the wall behind. Now you've got something strong and sharp. The projection light can't get through there and light up your screen.

When I finally did this for Boley, he didn't understand what I was doing. But when he saw it the next day he said, "Folsey, that is perfect, that is exactly what I wanted."

The cinematographer's job is to photograph the picture in the manner that he and the director discuss, and what the script calls for, to create the various moods. The light is used to show the mood of the scene. I remember a long time ago I was shooting a scene with a man named Chester Franklin. He taught me more about photography than anybody I have met in the business. He was an artist. We were doing a scene with a woman dying in a circus wagon. She was lying on a little cot. The director says to me, "I'd like to have some kind of an effect emphasizing her dying."

Remember, these were the arc light days, not incandescent light. I said, "All right," and got a piece of barber net. I stretched it across behind her, about five feet back of her, and I pulled it this way tightly, and I pulled it that way tightly. You couldn't see it because there was nothing on it, and I put two little lights on it, from different directions.

Then I put an ordinary room light on her. As she died, I opened the spotlight above her head—I opened that little iris and had one of those gel diffusers on it, bringing that light down on her like an ethereal light from heaven. At the same time I brought up the lights on the back of this stretched barber net, and it formed a silk highlight. Each of those pulled places showed a highlight, and a little cross appeared just above her head as she lay dying. When she finally died, that ethereal light came up on her and the cross in the back appeared. It was absolutely sensational!

Boley jumped up and down, he was so pleased. But you could only do that with somebody like him because he was so receptive and helpful; he cooperated with you, and he was enthusiastic about it. So this is how I tried to create a mood.

I worked on another picture with Boleslawski called *Men in White*, starring Clark Gable. Here, too, the leading lady, Elizabeth Allan, was dying, and again Boley wanted some unusual effect on her. There was a black floor and a white bed in the hospital room. In Allan's death scene the light was on her, and her bed looked like it was hung in mid air over this black floor. I had taken a big sheet of glass and covered the whole lens in front, then took thick gobs of vaseline and rubbed it all over the glass, all around, underneath the bed, running along the edge, making it thick so you couldn't see anything except what the light would pick up. It took the light and changed it in all kinds of ways. There was no bottom to anything. So you see the whole mood was created by the lights. The cameraman's job is to make his photography never obtrude upon the scene, but to make it embellish the mood and create an atmosphere.

Arthur C. Miller was, I think, one of the greatest people I've ever met in this business. I worked with him as an assistant for a couple of years, but I knew him when I was a kid office boy. I knew him around the studio as a great cameraman, and then eventually I got to work with him a little bit here and there. Just working with him, knowledge rubbed off on you, sort of like osmosis. There was no particular, specific thing that he actually taught me, but I could see how he did things, and I'd understand, and learn.

One time he really embarrassed me. Now here's a guy that I had worked with as an assistant, that I've learned so much from. He called one night because he was going to photograph Irene Dunne, and he knew I had been photographing her. "Can you tell me something that you do with Irene Dunne?" he asked.

I was so embarrassed. "Arthur," I said. "I can't talk to you about that. It would be an offense; I couldn't do it." Well, he convinced me that I should tell him, so I did, to the best of my ability.

I told him how I would get the scene lit with Irene Dunne, and she would look just lovely, smooth as a baby. We'd put her in the scene, and she'd start to play it, when a little black mark would appear on her chin. I'd think, "What the hell is that?" We'd have to let it go while she'd continue the scene with the black mark. So I began to think about it and decided that it had to be some kind of muscle; it had to be something that appeared as a result of her talking.

So the next time, I took a small spotlight with a snoot on it, and put it on a swivel. I told the electrician who was working with me, "You keep that pointed on her chin whether the light's on or off. Just keep it on there."

Then I put that light on a dimmer. I had a man on the dimmer, and I said to him, "You watch me; don't watch anybody else but me." I then stood by the camera and watched Irene with my hands behind me. As she played a scene and I began to see that thing, I'd bring my hand up and the light would come on, and that little mark would disappear. I'd kill it before it became visible.

When she saw the film she cried, "George, the little spot is gone!" She couldn't believe it. Today she still says, "He's the man who took my black spot away."

Along with creating the moods, the cinematographer has to keep it going, and moving quickly, because it's very expensive. That stopwatch will drive you crazy. He works very closely with two people: the gaffer and the head grip. The grip is extremely important. The grip sets up the dolly, and sets the camera on the tripods, and puts them on the dolly, and he gets the cutters and the gobos and the grilles.

Speaking of grilles, I have to tell you a story about a special grille with a special name. *[He produces a large piece of perforated wood resembling a tropical leaf. It is hinged at the bottom so it can open like a fan.]*

This is known as a cokuloris, and it was invented out of my desire to break up background light. This is how it works. Now, if you were photographing Joan Crawford, with her big Adrian-designed shoulders, it was always a big expanse of white. I always wanted control of the light on the white. I wanted to control it because if you put the light down below, and you put a solid cutter or nets above, that degraded it and made it gray. I wanted it clean and white, but I wanted it broken up. So I would take this device and put it up in front of the light that hit on Crawford, and it would throw shadows all over her and break it up. I could also vary the amount and the strength of that shadow by putting it closer or further from the light, whichever I felt was called for.

It's made of plywood and can be any size. Before, I used to turn a stepladder upside down to get the shadows. Or, if it was a bigger area, a bigger ladder. I had to think of ways to break up that light subtly. Sometimes I would take a bar, a ladder, and a cutter and mix it all up so that there was a variety of shadows. I would get up on a ladder and hold leaves on top of Crawford's head. Bob Young always used to call me George Foliage because of that.

But my grips got tired of holding all these things up. One day my grip Harry Reid said, "George, I think I can go down to the shop and cut out something for us." He came back with a big piece of cut-out wood.

In *Boom Town,* there's a shot of Colbert in bed. We get up in the air and we shoot down on her. I've got a nice soft key on her, but it lights up the pillowcase, the bed clothing, and all her clothes, and it's the same color as her face. So I don't want that, I want to pick her out, away from all that. Harry Reid had made me a couple of these grilles, so I got one and started using it on one side, with Hal Rosson watching. I threw a little shadow, softly so it wasn't definable, but it was a shadowed area. It reduced that light. Then I brought another one in from the other side, and reduced that light. I brought in still another on the pillow. I surrounded Colbert with soft white light that took your eye away from the pillows. You looked at her instead of the pillows.

Hal said, "Hey, that's pretty good." When it came time for him to shoot an opposite kind of a shot with Hedy Lamarr, he began using it, too. He'd say, "Hey, give me one of those high cokulorises."

He didn't invent the word; he read the same fairy tales I did when I was a little boy. I'll bet you I was the only one on the stage that day who knew what he was talking about. For some reason that word had stuck in my mind all those years. It was out of either Grimm's or Andersen's fairy tales, I think, but I've never been able to find it. Eventually it got reduced from "high cokuloris" to "cokuloris," and then it became simply "kook." Now if you say, "Give me a kook," they know what you mean.

It never occurred to me to have this patented; it was more like inventing a system to make the job easier. All I was trying to do was improve my photography, which it did. You can't patent that.

Another thing I invented was an addition to a ladder. I used to see guys go up on a ladder to fix a light, and they would only go up so far before they would begin to teeter. They were reluctant to go up to the top step because there was nothing up there to hang on to. So I had my grip make me a pole—or a little board—cut into that top step. You could tie it off, tightly. Now when you got up there you had something to hold on to. It got them to climb to the top, so they called it "Folsey's Ladder," and it's still in use at Metro.

Again on *Boom Town* with Hal Rosson, I was photographing Claudette Colbert. Jack Conway was the director. He was a very difficult man to work with. He wanted to tell me where Tracy was going to be. Tracy has to show me where Tracy was going to be and what he was going to do. And he never did what Jack told me he was going to do. I'd always find out that I had the keys (the main source of direct light) and learn I should have had them from the other side.

So I'd say, "Don't tell me, show me." Then he'd get mad at me. So he didn't want me on *Boom Town,* and he put Hal Rosson on it.

But now Hal comes to me and asks, "How do you photograph Colbert?" I told him exactly what to do. Not only did I tell him where to put the light and how to use the broads (three instead of one), but what diffusion to use, what f-stop, what light to use, and how to get the camera in the air.

Anyway, I told Hal what to do, but she never was satisfied, and she didn't like the way she looked. This is the irony of this business. He's there doing a big picture with my star, and I'm shooting second unit of his picture, which consists of a little jackass in a little circus. I'm shooting a jackass and he's shooting Colbert.

Anyway, he came down and said, "Hey, pal, come on down and show me how to do this. Take a look at this."

I went down. I had told him before not to have Colbert look squarely into the camera, that he should always have her look at it from the side. He had a marker (to show where the star is supposed to stand) right in front of the camera—that's where it was when I came on the set. I watched the scene and I said, "Hal, she's looking too square into the camera. Move the marker over." So he moved it over, but while he was doing that Conway was doing something else.

Conway came back, sat down, started the scene, saw that they were looking to the side, reached over, pulled the marker back over to the wrong place, and I looked over at Hal. It's not *my* place to tell him. After all, I'm down there shooting a jackass.

The next day I met the two of them coming back from the projection room. Conway says to me, "Now, George, you'll have to tell Hal what to do about this girl, because she's not looking well."

I said, "Mr. Conway, she's looking too squarely into the camera."

He says, "I've got nothing but profiles in the whole picture."

They eventually decided that I should come on the picture and photograph only Colbert's scenes, which was the most asinine decision I ever heard of.

So I said, "Hal, look, let's do this. You photograph everything. I'll stand behind you and tell you what to do with Colbert. Then you shoot everything, Colbert will look all right, and that will be that."

We came to a close-up. We had a shot of Colbert standing at the mantle of a fireplace, and over the top of her head is what we call a five-light strip. It's five 1,000-watt bulbs, with a solid glass frame in front of it, which diffuses it some. But here is this predominant light coming down on her, and he's also got a strong spotlight hitting her. It's axiomatic that you don't need as strong a key light on a brunette as you do on a blonde, because she's got the contrast with her already. So here she is with all this strong light on her, and I said, "Hal, let me read it." It was way hotter than I would have wanted, so I cut it. I knocked it down a great deal, and the scene was fine. We lit the fireplace from the left, put cutters (gobos) in front to keep the light off, and we solved the problem.

I always preferred photographing women to men. With a man you put character and quality into the picture, but with women you can't do that. You have to get softness and gentleness across.

I don't think of cinematography as an art. When I'm doing it I think of it as a job, my primary purpose being to project the people away from the walls and get it as stereoscopic as I can in one dimension. I feel that when you look at something it should stand out.

So I guess I think of cinematography as a craft, though you have to be somewhat artistic, you have to have some feeling for painting in your life. You have to have an understanding of light and shade, and balance.

There used to be almost no planning ahead of time with the director before we started shooting. I remember working at Metro and I'd finish shooting one picture, and a man was shooting another picture that I'd started two days before, which was my picture. When I finished this picture, I walked on to that other picture—he left, and I took over. In cases like this I'd have no chance to talk to the director, except as we went along, and I'd find out what went on and catch up. I had had a chance to read the script so I had some idea what it was about. At Metro they sometimes had twenty-seven companies working. You were just a number. Imagine getting twenty-seven cameras out of the camera department, with twenty-seven second cameramen and assistants, and having all the equipment trucked to the stage where you were working. Plus the fact that they had to have twenty-seven grip equipments, twenty-seven grips, assistant grips, second grips, and best boys. And maybe fifty-five or sixty electricians, gaffers, and best boys. Trucks going in all directions, bringing the cameras in at 7:30 in the morning, and getting them to the stage, operating, and everybody ready to work by nine. That's quite a bit of organization. That camera department was a beehive of activity!

Cameramen never had the authority to say something should be reshot; that was up to the director and the producer. If they didn't like what they saw in the dailies, we would reshoot. Generally there was a give-and-take relationship with the director. It was my understanding that the director was always the boss. I never felt that the director wasn't in charge, even if he was inexperienced. It was his picture and he got what he wanted. He told me what he would like to have, and I would try either to give it to him or make suggestions if I thought there was a better way—but always bearing in mind that he was the one who ultimately made the decisions.

≡

I don't know any other business I would like to have been in. My family wanted me to quit this business before I was a cameraman, to become an insurance agent and work with my cousin, who was getting a dollar more than I was. But I refused. It was the first time I ever denied my family anything. I stayed where I was, and I'm so glad. It was the greatest thing in the world that I walked into the very thing that I loved to do.

September 1985
February 1986
Brentwood

Editors' Note: George Folsey died in November 1988.

FILMOGRAPHY (partial)

1929	*Applause* (dir. Rouben Mamoulian, Paramount)
	The Coconuts (dir. Robert Florey, Paramount)
	The Hole in the Wall (dir. Robert Florey, Paramount)
1930	*Laughter* (dir. Harry d'Arrast, Paramount)
	The Big Pond (dir. Hobart Henley, Paramount)
	Animal Crackers (dir. Victor Heerman, Paramount)
1931	*The Smiling Lieutenant* (dir. Ernst Lubitsch, Paramount)
	Secrets of a Secretary (dir. George Abbott, Paramount)
	My Sin (dir. George Abbott, Paramount)
	The Cheat (dir. George Abbott, Paramount)
1932	*The Big Broadcast* (dir. Frank Tuttle, Paramount)
	Storm at Daybreak (dir. Richard Boleslawski, MGM)
1933	*Reunion in Vienna* (dir. Sidney Franklin, MGM)
	Going Hollywood (dir. Raoul Walsh, MGM)

1934	*Operator 13* (dir. Richard Boleslawski, MGM)
	Men in White (dir. Richard Boleslawski, MGM)
	Chained (dir. Clarence Brown, MGM)
1935	*Reckless* (dir. Victor Fleming, MGM)
	I Live My Life (dir. W. S. Van Dyke, MGM)
	Page Miss Glory (dir. Mervyn Le Roy, MGM)
	Kind Lady (dir. John Sturges, MGM)
1936	*The Gorgeous Hussy* (dir. Clarence Brown, MGM)
	The Great Ziegfeld (dir. Robert Leonard, MGM)
1937	*Mannequin* (dir. Frank Borzage, MGM)
1938	*The Shining Hour* (dir. Frank Borzage, MGM)
1939	*Lady of the Tropics* (dir. Jack Conway, MGM)
	Remember? (dir. Norman McLeod, MGM)
1940	*Third Finger Left Hand* (dir. Robert Leonard, MGM)
	Boom Town (with Harold Rosson, dir. Jack Conway, MGM)
1941	*Come Live with Me* (dir. Clarence Brown, MGM)
	Lady Be Good (dir. Norman McLeod, MGM)
1942	*Panama Hattie* (dir. Norman McLeod, MGM)
	Seven Sweethearts (dir. Frank Borzage, MGM)
	Rio Rita (dir. S. Sylvan Simon, MGM)
	Dr. Gillespie's New Assistant (dir. Willis Goldbeck, MGM)
1943	*Thousands Cheer* (dir. George Sidney, MGM)
	Three Hearts for Julia (dir. Richard Thorpe, MGM)
1944	*Meet Me in St. Louis* (dir. Vincente Minelli, MGM)
	The White Cliffs of Dover (dir. Clarence Brown, MGM)
	A Guy Named Joe (dir. Victor Fleming, MGM)

1945   *The Clock* (dir. Vincente Minelli, MGM)

1946   *The Green Years* (dir. Victor Saville, MGM)

          The Harvey Girls (dir. George Sidney, MGM)

          The Secret Heart (dir. Robert Leonard, MGM)

          Till the Clouds Roll By (co-cameraman, with Harry Stradling, dir. Richard Whorf, MGM)

          Ziegfeld Follies (co-cameraman, with Charles Rosher, dir. Vincente Minelli, MGM)

1947   *Green Dolphin Street* (dir. Victor Saville, MGM)

1948   *State of the Union* (dir. Frank Capra, MGM)

          If Winter Comes (dir. Victor Saville, MGM)

1949   *Adam's Rib* (dir. George Cukor, MGM)

          The Great Sinner (dir. Robert Siodmak, MGM)

          Take Me Out to the Ball Game (dir. Busby Berkeley, MGM)

          Malaya (dir. Richard Thorpe, MGM)

1950   *A Life of Her Own* (dir. George Cukor, MGM)

1951   *The Man with a Cloak* (dir. Fletcher Markle, MGM)

          Night into Morning (dir. Fletcher Markle, MGM)

          Vengeance Valley (dir. Richard Thorpe, MGM)

          Shadow in the Sky (dir. Fred Wilcox, MGM)

          Mr. Imperium (dir. Don Hartman, MGM)

          Law and the Lady (dir. Edwin Knopf, MGM)

1952   *Million Dollar Mermaid* (dir. Mervyn Le Roy, MGM)

          Lovely to Look At (dir. Mervyn Le Roy, MGM)

1953   *All the Brothers Were Valiant* (dir. Richard Thorpe, MGM)

1954   *Executive Suite* (dir. Robert Wise, MGM)

       Seven Brides for Seven Brothers (dir. Stanley Donen, MGM)

       Deep in My Heart (dir. Stanley Donen, MGM)

       Tennessee Champ (dir. Fred Wilcox, MGM)

       Hit the Deck (dir. Roy Rowland, MGM)

1955   *The Cobweb* (dir. Vincente Minelli, MGM)

1956   *Forbidden Planet* (dir. Fred Wilcox, MGM)

       The Fastest Gun Alive (dir. Russell Rouse, MGM)

1957   *Tip on a Dead Jockey* (dir. Richard Thorpe, MGM)

       House of Numbers (dir. Russell Rouse, MGM)

1958   *Saddle the Wind* (dir. Robert Parrish, MGM)

       Imitation General (dir. George Marshall, MGM)

       The High Cost of Loving (dir. José Ferrer, MGM)

       Torpedo Run (dir. Joseph Pevney, MGM)

1960   *Cash McCall* (dir. Joseph Pevney, MGM)

       I Passed for White (dir. Fred Wilcox, Allied Artists)

1963   *The Balcony* (dir. Joseph Strick, Walter Reade-Sterling-Continental)

Linwood Gale Dunn with his custom-built special effects optical printer, at RKO
Radio Pictures in the 1930s.

LINWOOD
GALE DUNN

Visual Effects Director
of Photography

===

Linwood G. Dunn was born in Brooklyn, New York, in December 1904. Moving to Hollywood in the middle twenties, he worked for several movie studios and independent production companies before settling at RKO Studios, better known as RKO Radio Pictures. During World War II, Dunn and his associate, Cecil Love, designed the Acme-Dunn special effects optical printer for U.S. government photographic units, which had a great impact on the field of special visual effects as it was the first commercial machine of its kind.

We meet Dunn at the offices of the American Society of Cinematographers. He is a compact, energetic man, justifiably proud of his work and abilities, and well aware of the significance of his contributions to visual effects cinematography.

I graduated from Manual Training High School in Brooklyn, and worked for a summer at Hamilton S. Gordon, a music publisher in New York City. I always loved music and had played in dance bands, so I sought a job in that atmosphere, even though all I did was mail out sheet music—mostly copies of "Silver Threads Among the Gold," the only title that I'd ever heard of before. (It must have kept them going!) Because of that connection it was possible for me to buy my first high-grade alto saxophone at wholesale, thus enabling me to get into a higher level with the dance bands that hired me.

From there I got a job as a projectionist at American Motion Picture Corporation (also in New York), running movies for rental by churches and schools. That's where I saw so many of the wonderful early silent classics, particularly all the Charlie Chaplins. That company went out of business, so to keep busy, my brother and I furnished a jazz band for Ferndale, a summer vacation resort in the Catskill Mountains. I loved this job because I could sneak next door to Grossinger's and see many of the great comedians in their early days.

Before leaving for Ferndale, I had applied for a job as assistant cameraman for a Pathé serial, *The Green Archer,* to be directed by my uncle, Spencer G. Bennet, at Astoria Studios, Long Island. When the wire came telling me to show up, I had to quit in a hurry, as there would be two others waiting to take my place if I didn't show up on time. That was my start in the movie business. I came to Hollywood when Pathé moved its operations here in order to get a variety of weather conditions to suit the series they would be making in 1927 and 1928, just before the advent of sound movies.

I began my career in special visual effects when I joined RKO Radio Pictures. I was employed steadily there from 1929 to 1957 and learned about the vast scope of optical printing. Now, an optical printer is a film effects–creating device, and they were all custom built in the studios by hand, every one different. Each studio designed its own. They were really Rube Goldbergs, with levers, knobs, and controls hanging all over them.

The optical printer is nothing more than a movie camera photographing a section of film in a projector. In the early silent days we did our trick photography directly in the production camera. We'd shoot a scene, say for a double exposure, and wind the raw film back to the start and shoot the second scene over it.

That was very hazardous, as it was quite difficult to get just the results you wanted, because once you shot the film with your best guess at exposure balance and positioning, that was it—the film was exposed, never to be changed.

The effects optical printer made it possible in a superimposure to shoot each scene separately and, in a duplicate negative, expose the one over the other. Then, if you didn't like the way it looked, you just made it over again. You could do that because the elements were separate films. So the optical printer is basically a film projector, with a camera in front of it, photographing that film in the projector, both units in synchronized motion. That's all it really is. From there on, the extra gadgets are added to increase its capabilities.

Now, when you make a duplicate movie film you can also do it by the contact method, just sandwichlike, and print it the way you would a still picture in a printing frame. When volume release prints for theaters are made in the lab, the raw stock and negatives are sandwiched together and run off at a thousand or more feet a minute. That's called "in contact" printing. Optical printing, although much slower, gives the same results, except that by the two films being separated, you can move them independently, to make zooms, superimpose clouds, titles, skip frames, add frames to slow down action—in fact, the effects that you can create are now limited only by the imagination, the skills of the operator, and the scope of his particular equipment.

The sophisticated optical printer is the backbone of special visual effects. There are other effects categories, like miniatures, matte paintings (where you combine paintings with live action), background projection (where you have foreground action in front of a screen showing the background), animation, and special full-scale mechanical devices. And today we have added electronics and computers in a variety of applications. Those various techniques are all used separately at various times. Sometimes even one scene will require all categories to obtain the results wanted. And sometimes a scene will be entirely a painting. In *It's a Mad, Mad, Mad, Mad World,* for example, for the long shot of the plaza with the ladder swaying, the upper eight stories of the building were entirely a painting. This scene required twenty-one optical printing and matte camera exposures to complete—seven scene elements times three color separations passes.

At RKO I used the optical printer, a little or a lot, on almost every picture, hundreds of them over the years. I was given screen credit on the historic classic *Flying Down to Rio,* Astaire and Rogers's first film. It was the first time such sophisticated transitional optical effects were used in a major feature. In the distance shots of the girls on top of the biplane, we used model planes with miniature girl models, with the sky and ground in back of them on a movie screen. In those long shots, you would never know whether or not the plane and girls were real. In the close shots, we used real girls, wired safely onto the top of the plane, with a wind machine blasting at them, and a background screen showing projected clouds behind them, also. Those shots were, of course, full scale.

When I did the optical effects on *Flying Down to Rio* and, earlier, *Melody Cruise* and *So This Is Harris!,* they gave me an absolutely free hand to do anything I wanted for the transitional effects. A great opportunity for me! So if it was a band musical number, then I'd bring in assorted music notes, kind of punching in the new scene with them. I had screen roll-ups, action-related matte wipes, page-turns, and many other such optical effects that were never done before.

Now, foreground and background composite process shots are made in different ways, and the effects specialist often has to determine which of several technologies is the best to use for that occasion. The more conventional method is with a screen behind the actors, projecting the background from rear or front. Blue screen is another compositing process, and that's similar to chroma-key on television, where you see the newscaster in the studio talking about a foreign land, and there it appears behind him. We use this blue screen process often where we cannot have the background available on the set, for various reasons. Suppose you have a situation like the ship in the storm sequence in the major production *Hawaii*. Now, how would they know what the backgrounds should be until they've shot and edited the foregrounds? And what are the camera angles? They'll shoot stage scenes on the ship off the stern, off the middle, and off the bow, as required. As the eighty-foot ship is in a wild storm, the bow, mechanically controlled, will rise up, so the background must accordingly go down, and so forth. So we couldn't possibly create the matching backgrounds until the foreground scenes were shot and final editing was approved. Obviously, background film screen projection could not be used.

I did all the composite effects work on *Bringing Up Baby*. The leopard was never in the scenes with the actors. I shot the leopard separately, then I shot Hepburn and Grant. There's a typical scene where Cary Grant walks across a hallway and steps into an elevator. Following close behind him is the leopard. As Grant closes the elevator door, the leopard goes down the stairs. Hepburn enters from her room at the same time, and she sees them both. At one point, the three of them are on the screen at once, but they were all shot separately. The three scenes were put together on the optical printer, using traveling matte moving split screens. These mattes both follow and precede the action, precisely blending together the three scenes into one realistic composite.

Orson Welles was one of the few so-called geniuses I observed in my whole movie career. I worked with him the first time he ever shot anything in a movie studio, as far as I know. He came to RKO to make tests for a production they planned to produce called *Heart of Darkness,* a Joseph Conrad story. I became involved because Welles wanted to have sequences with no scene cuts, meaning that when one scene ended it blended somehow into the next one. There were to be no direct film cuts within a series of related scenes. My job was to find a way in postproduction to get from one scene smoothly to the next one without cuts, when they had been shot separately. Also, he used the camera as the first person, so that you'd always see just a shadow of that actor. If he sat down, you'd see just his shadow on the wall do so. I will say, for a man who had never worked in movies before, Welles seemed very capable in making camera setups. I remember we had a shot of Robert Coote playing a piano in a bar in the hot tropics. Someone entered the scene, and there was a little tricky business to play. The cameraman was trying to get the best angle when Welles quickly said, "Now let's move the piano over here and have him come in from this angle instead. We'll get it." Boy, I'll tell you, I soon became impressed with the man. He really had a gift for staging tricky action, among his other talents, soon to be recognized.

I think, though, that for *Citizen Kane* I did some of my most involved optical effects work of my career. I seldom received screen credit for my work in my earlier RKO days. Although I did all the studio's optical printing effects in that period, the head of our photographic effects department at the time usually got overall credit for all visual effects. And Vernon Walker was that man, another true genius.

Welles didn't know at first what an optical printer was. When he was finally introduced to it and learned that there was a tool that could alter scenes after they were shot, then he used it like a paint brush. Boy, he'd come in and want work done that I would say was impossible—but he'd persevere. He'd take a scene that was already shot, like the one with a girl sitting in a library on a bench. Nearby there's just the bottom of a statue that says

"Thatcher." You see a scene in the show with the camera panning down the statue and pulling back to a long shot. That's the scene as shown in the picture. Well, they had shot that scene with no statue on the set, just the girl on the bench, and you saw only the base of a statue.

Now he's editing his show, and says, "I want to start up on the statue and pan down to the base." Just like we can wave a wand and have it!

I said, "You didn't have a statue to shoot, only the base of one."

"Well," he said, "can't you fix it?"

In such a situation I would say, "No, it's not practical." Because I'm working for the studio on a steady, responsible job, I'm thinking of its value for what it would cost to do this.

Then he'd politely say, "Well, you mean it's impossible?"

I'd say, "No, nothing is impossible. It's just a matter of time and money, and how good is it going to look to take such a scene and alter it so much."

So he'd go to the front office to check and come back and say, "Well, I've got the money okayed, and you've been allowed the extra time." Of course I would double-check on this to be sure. And they'd tell me to give him what he wanted, and that they would step in when he went over his budget.

So to change that statue scene I had a small scale model made, and shot it stationary, so I could then make a motorized pan-down off the printer aperture, blending a split-screen matte into a pan-down onto the master scene frame with the base only.

Then there was the scene where the camera raises up the side of the nightclub building in a storm, over the roof, and through the skylight. The camera never did go through the skylight. The filming had stopped right at it. But now Welles is editing and he says, "I don't want to stop there; I want to go on through the skylight and into the nightclub below." So, on the optical printer,

I made a zoom into the skylight, and then matched it to another zoom inside, moving up to the table. So this tied the two scenes together. In order to smooth out this transition, I added extra lightning flashes on the skylight by overexposing frames on the optical printer.

This kind of postproduction conversion work was a wonderful experience for me because I got into visual optical effects areas that I normally would never have otherwise attempted. So the picture became loaded with all kinds of such scene modifications that were created after production filming was finished.

I got on the team that did those wonderful visual effects for *King Kong* by observation, really. The *King Kong* special visual effects operation was set up at RKO, where one whole stage was turned over to Willis O'Brien and his crew exclusively. Because setups for this type of work were so critical and precise, they wanted to lock the stage doors at night and know there would be no unauthorized entry. To operate efficiently, they often had four camera setups, so that the animation work could continue, by moving from one to the other while waiting for the film to be processed from each one as photographed. They had an array of fine special effects equipment, but they did not have an optical printer. I was not then working as part of the *Kong* crew, but I knew them all and was familiar with the work. I was on RKO's regular payroll, doing the optical printing for all the studio's productions. By observing the *Kong* operation, I could see that some of the animation composites were being done the hard way, without benefit of an optical effects printer. For example, they'd animate model figures and composite them into a previously filmed background scene at the same time, by bipack printing in the camera. When that scene came back from the lab next day, the animation would be okay, but the composite part sometimes wasn't good because the background and foreground contrast or density balance didn't match. Well, after they had done all this good animation work, they'd have to do it all over just to correct that balance. So I said, "Go ahead and just animate the foreground action as a scene on a separate piece of film, and I'll take your background and composite the two together on the optical printer." Then, if they wanted to remake it to change the background in any way, the animation scene was still good to composite on the printer again.

In special photographic effects you have two major categories: reality and fantasy. It's either the depicting of lifelike scenes, like the statue in the library scene in *Citizen Kane*, or a painting added to extend stories to a building, or it's the *King Kong* model monster, which is truly "fantasy."

In "reality" we include the altering of scenes so that they would still appear normal (as previously described in those *Citizen Kane* scenes) and salvaging ruined scenes, where something went wrong in production photography. A very simple example is in the early days of sound when the microphone would accidentally drop down into the picture. Well, we'd just make a blowup on the optical printer and crop out the mike, like you would in a still picture enlargement.

There were other ways we could save scenes that were absolutely ruined. In *It's a Mad, Mad, Mad, Mad World* there was a scene where a truck backed into a water tower. The tower was then to fall over from the impact and knock down an outhouse. Well, that shot was no good the way they shot it. The truck had backed into the tower, the tower fell over, and before the tower actually hit the outhouse, they pulled it down prematurely. See, they had wires on it, as they wanted to make sure it came down. So they got trigger-happy, and here's the tower going over and the outhouse falling down before the tower had actually hit it.

So they called me and asked, "Do we have to shoot it over?" They would have had to build the whole set again, because a service station building complex was also collapsed. This would have cost well over fifty thousand dollars to rebuild the set and shoot the scene over. So they hopefully asked, "Can you fix it?"

I said, "I'd have to see it, but from what you say I think we can if they didn't pan the camera with the collapse."

Well, when I looked at it I saw that they did pan the camera as the outhouse fell over. We were still able to save the scene, but it was now much more difficult. I made a hard-edge split screen, matted the edge of the outhouse right where the tower was going to hit it. I ran one side of the scene through the optical printer, then printed the other side next to it, but I put the two halves about sixteen frames out of sync, staggered enough to hold the outhouse in position until the tower hit it. Think of the time and thousands of dollars this saved, and the salvaging achievement known to so few!

Visual effects optical printing was mostly done after the production shooting was completed. When new film editors came to RKO, I tried to educate them about the optical printer's capabilities, because they could be my best salesmen. They always viewed the daily filming, and if there were problem scenes they'd usually say, "Oh, Lin can fix it up on his optical printer." Sometimes this put me in very tough spots where I just had to come through. But I had always said nothing is impossible.

I was always looking to promote our effects department and solicit business, so I found several film editors who wanted to get more educated about the value of the optical effects printer. I also had a few that didn't want to even look at this complex device. Elmo Williams, Robert Wise, Mark Robson, and John Sturges were among those who really wanted to learn everything they could about its importance to their work. It was a special creative tool they could really use, and they all did so freely, to great advantage.

At RKO, I'd occasionally get a call from a writer who would ask me if he could freely write in scenes that would require certain expensive visual effects. I could then tell him at the story's very creation how to play his action so it could likely save thousands without affecting his story line. Or we'd get into this discussion in early production meetings, with the art department then at hand, still in the early planning stages, which was so important. So we had that big advantage in the early studio days. We were like a big family, all the talents in departments, readily available for consultation.

There were seven major studios then, and RKO was the smallest. And because of this we did all the various visual effects categories in one department—great for me to learn them all. The big studios like Fox, Universal, and MGM had the optical effects department, the background projection department, matte paintings, miniatures, animation—all separate studio departments. At RKO we did all these visual effects in one department, and thus operated more like a close family, a tight team. It was much more efficient, and very cost effective, too. We had a full staff as we needed enough skilled help on hand to handle the surges of work that could suddenly pile in. But when the work load was not that heavy, we had that staff on hand with not that much to do. So that's when we could do our R & D and exciting experimental work. I'd work on developing new tricks in between production assignments, many of which paid off well for the studio over the years.

Regarding the Acme-Dunn optical effects printer. About 1942, when World War II came along, the U.S. government needed optical effects printers for the armed forces' photographic units all over the world. So I was commissioned by our government, through Eastman Kodak, to furnish this specialized equipment, as none were on the open market. They gave me a contract for several, and I found the right company to manufacture them properly and on time. Cecil Love, my valued associate of many years, and I designed and supervised the construction. After the war, the printer went out on the worldwide market, and it became the first machine of its kind that was a manufactured stock item, so anyone could buy it. The U.S. government had ordered many of them, and from then on, they soon became the standard all over the world. In 1946 I received a Commendation Award from the Motion Picture Academy for that new, unique special effects machine. Then, in 1981, this award was upgraded to an Oscar statuette, because that equipment was still in use, and for the great impact it had made on the movie industry as a whole, well beyond just its field of photographic effects. This made it possible for many independent optical effects houses to go into business without having to design and custom build their own equipment.

In 1946 I started my own company, Film Effects of Holly-wood, while I was still at RKO. I became the pioneer in 16mm special optical effects, which was not done commercially before. I made the first 16mm blowup to 35mm single-strip color negative for theatrical use; and that's one of the reasons I was given the Gordon E. Sawyer Award, the Academy's highest honor for film technology, in 1984. My work was also my hobby. As well as running the RKO optical effects printer all day, I'd go home at night and work in my garage developing a 16mm commercial optical effects printer. My wife is saying, "You work all day at RKO on the optical printer, and then you come home and go out in the garage and do more of this work!"

I'd say, "Well, dearest, someday this thing might amount to something." And this really did come true. I was certainly a lucky man because, difficult and highly responsible as it was, I loved the creativity of my work and the wonderful associates it has brought me over the years, and to whom I owe so much of my success.

September 1985
Hollywood

FILMOGRAPHY (partial)

1926   Eight silent Pathé serials

1929   *Flight* (dir. Frank Capra, Columbia)

(At RKO Radio Pictures, except where noted)

1930   *The Case of Sergeant Grischa* (dir. Herbert Brenon)

            Danger Lights (dir. George Seitz)

1931   *Cimarron* (dir. Wesley Ruggles)

1932   *The Most Dangerous Game* (co-dirs. Ernest Schoedsack, Irving Pichel)

            Bird of Paradise (dir. King Vidor)

1933   *So This Is Harris!* (award-winning short, dir. Mark Sandrich)

            Melody Cruise (dir. Mark Sandrich)

            Flying Down to Rio (dir. Thornton Freeland)

            King Kong (co-dirs. Merian C. Cooper, Ernest Schoedsack)

1934   *Anne of Green Gables* (dir. George Nicholls, Jr.)

            Hips, Hips, Hooray! (dir. Mark Sandrich)

1935   *The Last Days of Pompeii* (co-dirs. Merian C. Cooper, Ernest Schoedsack)

            She (co-dirs. Irving Pichel, Lansing Holden)

1938   *Bringing Up Baby* (dir. Howard Hawks)

1939   *Gunga Din* (dir. George Stevens)

            The Hunchback of Notre Dame (dir. William Dieterle)

1941   *Citizen Kane* (dir. Orson Welles)

1943	*The Outlaw* (dir. Howard Hughes)
	Bombardier (dir. Richard Wallace)
1944	*Days of Glory* (dir. Jacques Tourneur)
	Experiment Perilous (dir. Jacques Tourneur)
1945	*Back to Bataan* (dir. Edward Dmytryk)
1946	*It's a Wonderful Life* (dir. Frank Capra)
1949	*Mighty Joe Young* (dir. Ernest Schoedsack)
1951	*The African Queen* (dir. John Huston, United Artists)
	The Thing (dir. Christian Nyby)
1952	*Androcles and the Lion* (dir. Chester Erskine)
1956	*War and Peace* (dir. King Vidor, Paramount)

(At Film Effects of Hollywood)

1959	*On the Beach* (dir. Stanley Kramer, United Artists)
1960	*Inherit the Wind* (dir. Stanley Kramer, United Artists)
1961	*West Side Story* (co-dirs. Robert Wise, Jerome Robbins, United Artists)
1963	*It's a Mad, Mad, Mad, Mad World* (dir. Stanley Kramer, United Artists)
1964	*My Fair Lady* (dir. George Cukor, Warner Bros.)
	Kiss Me, Stupid (dir. Billy Wilder, United Artists)
1965	*The Great Race* (dir. Blake Edwards, Warner Bros.)
	The Satan Bug (dir. John Sturges, United Artists)
	The Hallelujah Trail (dir. John Sturges, United Artists)
	In Harm's Way (dir. Otto Preminger, Paramount)
	Ship of Fools (dir. Stanley Kramer, Columbia)
1966	*Hawaii* (dir. George Roy Hill, United Artists)
	The Bible (dir. John Huston, Twentieth Century–Fox)

The Russians Are Coming, The Russians Are Coming
(dir. Norman Jewison, United Artists)

What Did You Do in the War, Daddy? (dir. Blake Edwards, United Artists)

Murderer's Row (dir. Henry Levin, Columbia)

1969   *Airport* (dir. George Seaton, Universal)

Gaily, Gaily (dir. Norman Jewison, United Artists)

1970   *Darling Lili* (dir. Blake Edwards, Paramount)

Song of Norway (dir. Andrew Stone, ABC)

Expo 70 (Japan)

1979   *Star Trek* (TV series)

≡ HEARING THE PINS DROP ≡

Ralph Butler, soundman (right).

RALPH BUTLER

Soundman

≡

Ralph Butler is a rugged man in his early seventies, who looks like an actor in the westerns he loved to make. A private man, he enjoys observing his cohabitants at the Motion Picture and Television Fund retirement home, where he has lived the last five years.

A sound technician records on-production sound when a picture is shooting. I was more involved in on-production shooting than in re-recording and dubbing, which I always found too confining and repetitious. I was a boom man for about twenty-five years, and a mixer for about fifteen. A mixer is in charge of sound recording, on-the-set recording.

My mother had to work to support my brother and me, here in California, and we had to work summer vacations to augment her income. One summer we got jobs together as laborers in the Hal Roach Studio. There were no unions in those days, so there was an open pool for laborers. You helped the carpenters, you carried paint for the painters, you washed windows for the prop department, you drove cars, you did whatever had to be done, and that was everything.

The following summer, 1928, I went back to see the man in charge of the labor pool. He told me that sound was coming in and that the studio was building a large excavation on one of the stages to install the new equipment. It would be the first permanent installation.

The studio wasn't doing anything except construction on the sound equipment installation, but my boss sent me over to talk to a man at the Victor Talking Machine Company. He had just come out from their headquarters in Camden, New Jersey. They needed personnel from the coast in addition to the technicians they had brought out.

The people they brought were mostly engineers from places like MIT, and they were getting big money—$300 to $400 a week under contract. It was a lot more than Hollywood was paying. They had no idea what a soundman should be paid.

The man who interviewed me asked a few questions about basic electricity, and we talked for about an hour. I told him I had monkeyed around with cat-whisker crystal radios and one-tube radios. I guess he thought I had adequate knowledge, because he hired me.

"Will twenty-five dollars a week be enough?" he asked.

That was a lot of money then, so I said, "Of course."

He described the job. "We need someone to work on our soundstage here, and I think you'll work out and fit right in. I'll probably ask you to do everything and anything, because we have a lot of work to do. We have to record orchestras, and that means setting up the stages, the easels, the music racks, everything."

Well, I was happy as a jaybird. I started on April 3, 1929. I remember the date because it was a very big day for me, the day I started a steady job.

In the very beginning, I started by sweeping out the stages and setting up for the orchestras—hanging the microphones, getting the communication systems working. We didn't record the orchestras over at the recording studios. We did it live from theaters and nightclubs, after they'd signed their deals with Victor.

Roach couldn't afford to pay for all the necessary sound equipment, so the studio signed a leasing contract with Victor, and Victor supplied the services and the recording. By that time,

Roach had built two sound trucks under his name, but we still got paid by the Victor Talking Machine Company.

Roach's studio was the laugh studio. You had to have a sense of humor to work there; you had to be able to take a joke and put up with a fair number of practical jokes as well. Mr. Roach himself liked funny things, and anything that was tolerable was funny. Expense didn't mean a thing. Some disaster would happen that would tie up the picture for two or three days, but he didn't mind as long as everybody had fun.

He was a wonderful man who made a point of knowing everybody in the studio by their first names. It was like a great big family. And there were no lines of demarcation. There was no such thing as directors not talking to this guy or that guy.

Roach used to make the *Our Gang* comedies along with Laurel and Hardy, Patsy Kelly, Charley Chase, and God knows how many others. I worked on the first Laurel and Hardy sound picture (a two-reeler), and I worked on the first *Our Gang* talkie.

Back then they didn't have microphone booths, as we were to know them later. We had to hang everything by ropes. So we were called "mike monkeys" because we were always dropping and pulling up ropes with mikes on the ends. We'd do two or three or even five at a time. The actors weren't supposed to say their lines until we were all set up.

When I first started we had to coordinate closely with the cameramen. The sound had to mesh with the movement and acting, but the actors also had to cooperate with us.

With the companies that really cared about sound our orders were to stop shooting when a plane or train went by—we couldn't obliterate that sound. They used to try to pick locations that were away from plane routes, checking with the airports for flight patterns. Way out in the valley, south and east of Los Angeles, used to be a prime location for westerns. We could shoot all day long with no problems out there.

No one was yet used to sound, and we'd have big soundproof booths for the cameras. They were about four feet wide and about six feet long, double glass, insulated on the inside and out. They were a mess to move around.

In 1939 I went to Universal to work with Charles Lamont. He was the director for the Abbott and Costello comedies, and I went there for that reason. I had been working with comics all my life, and I knew the difference between a "feed it" line and a "snapper" line. They wanted me because they'd been missing dialogue in the Abbott and Costello pictures. The microphone was in the wrong place, and the guys would say a line where you couldn't hear it. Then they'd have to come back to loop the dialogue, a practice which later became fashionable.

I liked working with them because I'd heard all the jokes, knew all the routines. I was fast and alert and used to comedy. Universal even paid me over scale.

There was a big difference between Abbott and Costello and Laurel and Hardy. Laurel and Hardy were very unselfish about who got the laugh. Laurel would say that Hardy should get the fade-out scene, and he would insist that they do it that way. If he thought that his cry would be the topper, then they'd end with that. Abbott and Costello were not so generous. Costello always got the laughs. He was always the winner because he was boister-ous and loud and would act up.

When I first went there it was for five weeks. Once the picture was over I thought I'd be through. But just before it was finished they asked if I would stay a couple more days and do some additional scenes on another picture. Before that was up they asked if I would stay on and do still another picture. When they did *Hellzapoppin,* with Olsen and Johnson, they signed me before anybody else. They knew that I'd heard all the jokes and knew when the punchlines were coming. There's a pattern to all that stuff. When you get to know comedians and how they work, you can anticipate their lines. You learn their timing and what it means when they look at each other a certain way, so you can get there just in time.

At that time, the studios were busy because the war had started in Europe, and they were preparing for it. Audiences were hungry for entertainment, so movies were the only real outlet. People went every night that they could afford to go. It was two bits then, and the loges were sixty-five cents.

When the war ended and I got out of the army, I went back to Universal, where I was guaranteed at least a year of employment under the G.I. Bill. It was 1946 by then, and I'd lost all my contacts as an independent. Roach had gone into the air force and had closed down his studio. All the people I had known had moved around, and techniques had changed, so I thought I'd go back to Universal for a year until I could make some new connections and find some of the old contacts. I did my year there, and then quit to go to Fox.

At Fox I worked on *Two Flags West* and *Jackpot,* with Jimmy Stewart, and then I went to Germany for nine months to work on a picture called *Decision Before Dawn,* directed by Anatole Litvak. When I came back I quit Fox and went over to Monogram.

Fox couldn't understand my leaving, but I'd made a handshake deal years back with a fellow boom man, that if one of us became a mixer the other guy would quit whatever he was doing and go with him. You need help when you start out on a new job.

Another reason was I hadn't been too happy with the way I was treated over in Germany. I had worked my tail off there, working night and day and Saturday and Sunday. I lost seventeen pounds. We'd work all day and travel all night. And they never reimbursed me for all the new winter clothing they told me to buy—overcoats and jackets and boots and socks and caps and gloves. They would pay me when we got back. I still have the receipts. I spent $300 on clothing. They refused to pay.

A guy at Fox asked me if I had gotten another job when I quit. When I told him I was going to Monogram he looked at me like I was crazy. He said, "You mean you'd quit Twentieth Century–Fox to go to work for Monogram?"

I said, "Well, I'll tell you the truth. I'm going to Monogram for one reason. It's a very, very small studio run by a bunch of little people, but they have big hearts and they're really big thinkers. Twentieth Century–Fox is a big goddamn studio run by a bunch of fucking little people." Excuse my language. "Good-bye, thank you very much." Out the door. And they didn't hire me back till I was a mixer years later. Then they had to pay me through the nose.

By the time I got back from the war, things had really advanced technically. Boom mikes and crab dollies were very much in use by then. But as far as procedure for getting the job done, it was still the same. Every camera was different, every director had his own style. You learn adaptability very early in the picture business.

We had no job protection until after the war, so whatever seniority you had, you'd lose when you moved. You had to keep starting over. The seniority system didn't really come in until about the mid-fifties. The union had a seniority system, and the studios also had their versions. The unions started about 1930, but there was no sound technicians' local until later. I joined a sort of general crafts union, Local 37. Electricians, prop men, grips—everybody except the painters and carpenters—belonged to it. Later on, unions became more specialized. Salaries changed as different unions were formed, and our hourly work week changed, too. We never had a forty-hour week in the studios—the closest we ever came to that was a fifty-four-hour week. It was nine hours a day, six days a week. Eventually we got to a five-day week.

Monogram changed its name to Allied after the war, because Monogram had become a lousy name on the screen. Universal changed their image on the screen, too. They changed their symbol, their emblem, because they were associated with garbage. Monogram was associated with sewerage. After Monogram became Allied it got a shot in the arm. New money came in and they started making better pictures with higher budgets. We made some good pictures there. I worked on *Friendly Persuasion*—in fact, we got an Academy nomination for sound for that picture.

I used to get the tough jobs. One of them was for a picture that was being shot in a newspaper office. The actor went down a long hallway, from one office to another, stopping at different desks, talking to different people. We used a plywood crab dolly to track him the whole way. Well, the thing was popping and crackling like you wouldn't believe, so the director panicked and asked me, "Holy Christ, how can we use it?"

I said, "We'll use the sounds of all the typewriters clacking— one at this desk, one at that—all going at the same time." And that sound was underneath the whole track, and we never heard the pops and cracks.

After that, the director, Joe Newman, said to me, "You're going to be on every picture I do." It's an example of one of those things you just learn—how to get yourself out of a hole.

February 1985
Woodland Hills

Editors' Note: Ralph Butler died in April 1987.

Edward Bernds, soundman and director (right), with Walter Mirisch (left) at Allied Artists Studio, 1956.

EDWARD
BERNDS

Soundman

═══

We are introduced to him by Al Keller, his longtime cinematographer friend from the Frank Capra days at Columbia Pictures, the glory days for both of them. We meet at the offices of the American Society of Cinematographers, where Bernds recalls events with the clearest detail, choosing his words carefully. Only occasionally does a note of bitterness creep into his speech. If he is disappointed with his lack of recognition in the film community, he has long since made his peace with it.

I was working at WLS and WCFL in Chicago, where my boss was a man named Howard Campbell. He was offered a job as chief engineer of the sound department at United Artists Studio in Hollywood. The first thing he had to do was recruit a thirty- or forty-man sound crew, and he offered me a job to come to Hollywood. I grabbed it, my wife and I jumped into my old car and made the journey, and I went on salary at United Artists in October 1928 as a soundman.

I stayed there for only nine months. Campbell turned out to be so arrogant he made a lot of enemies. He operated on a "give 'em an inch, they'll take a mile" premise. He encouraged us to be belligerent toward the directors and writers—to insist on our rights, which was a lot of nonsense.

When I got a chance to go to Columbia I grabbed it, and I was never sorry, even though I worked those typical Columbia sixteen- to eighteen-hour days. Harry Cohn was already there. When I went there in August 1929 they were just a cut above Poverty Row.

By the time I left UA, I had developed an interest in pictures as such, even in those few months, and I realized that credits are the lifeblood of pictures. At UA, I had only gotten three partial credits on pictures—though for the benefit of the interviewers at Columbia, they became whole credits. And by the time I had been at Columbia a few months, I had about six full credits. Though they were for B-pictures, they were still credits.

Columbia ground movies out like sausages. That's why they had to finish on schedule. We had to work all night Saturday night, even if it meant going well into Sunday morning, because another picture was starting on Monday and the stages and equipment were needed, even if we weren't. Saturday nights were crazy.

The soundmen didn't have a union then. There was a spontaneous strike in 1933. All of us nonunion people were so badly mistreated that this thing just erupted, but it didn't have a chance. The soundmen's strike was broken by the IBW. A union came in and broke the strike, and their reward was jurisdiction. We were forced to join the union that had broken our strike, and it was controlled by a Chicago mobster called "Umbrella Mike" Boyle. For a number of years we paid our tribute to Umbrella Mike, but conditions didn't improve at all. They didn't give a damn about us; they were rewarded by the producers for breaking the strike. I imagine they shook them down for a lot. Later, Willie Bioff and George Brown, also a couple of Chicago racketeers, shook down Joseph Schenck for a million dollars, but were caught and convicted for it. Joe Schenck was sent to prison, not for paying the bribe but for perjury. Still, the result was the same, we were then in thrall to George Brown and Willie Bioff. Our experience with unions was not a happy one. We workers got nothing but a thoroughly rotten contract.

Until the National Labor Relations Board declared that you had to get overtime after forty hours, our basic contract was for a work week of fifty-four hours, which was traditional in those days. It was a six-day week, nine hours a day, though we frequently worked more than that. We had Sunday to recuperate.

As a radio man I used a volume indicator and a volume control to monitor sound, which is what a movie mixer does, but there is a vast difference. In radio, you placed the mike where you wanted it, then you placed the announcer, the singer, or the orchestra where *you* wanted them to be. Radio, easy. Movies, at times very difficult.

The mixer is the top of the operating sound crew. He corresponds in a way to the first cameraman, for the director of cinematography. He's the boss of the crew; usually it was a four-man crew made up of the mixer; the mike man, who moved the mike around; the cable man, who assisted the mike man; and the man who ran the recorder. I was the mixer from the time I came to Columbia, on the strength of my inflated UA credits.

This is how the actual mechanics worked: On a typical Capra picture, you might shoot thirty separate scenes in a day, each one with its one, two, or three cameras and one sound track. Music is scored to the picture later. The sound effects are either created or taken from a sound effects library and cut in sync. The sync machine is very interesting—it brings together picture, dialogue, music, and as many as three sound effects tracks.

After shooting, the dubbing mixer, who is a highly-skilled technician, puts them all together in the proper proportion. In the old days nobody seemed to realize how important that job was. Production mixers used to do it to fill in between pictures, which was ridiculous.

It's an interesting process. When the film is shot and the director says, "Print that," the assistant cameraman circles the take number on the picture, and the recorder circles the take number. Then they're developed and printed, and then they are sent to the sync room together. An assistant editor works in the sync room as a sort of apprentice. He takes the sound track of, say, Take 56. Each take or scene has a start mark—in the old days it was the clapper—and he puts the start marks together, attaches them to the preceding scene with paper clips, winds the film through until he finds the next scene, which might be Take 59, and so on, until, together, they become the dailies.

Dailies are not necessarily in any sequence at all (relative to the final picture) except that in which they were shot. The assistant editor takes the scenes and puts them on a rack in more or less the order in which they'll be used. Then the editor takes them, runs them, and begins the process of editing.

The sync machine ensures that the film still stays in sync even after it is cut up. There are edge numbers, and even if you cut a six-inch slice out of the middle of a scene you can sync it up by matching those edge numbers.

Now, before the film was even shot, the mixer and the cinematographer always read the script. I always read the script, though some mixers didn't. It always helped to know what the story was about.

When I first came to Columbia a mixer named Winfield Scott Hancock got into trouble. They were working on one of those terrible tropical melodramas. He was insisting they pull a thatched roof off, when the cameraman protested. It was a total impasse between the two of them. They called me to come in and take over from Hancock. The problem was how to get the mike in close enough to record the people on the porch.

Well, I don't claim to be a genius, but the solution was utterly simple. All you had to do was pull out enough thatch to drop the mike through. The hole didn't show because the camera angle was end-on to the roof. As the camera moved forward, the mike dropped through the hole and you got the scene.

At Columbia I was lucky enough to hitch up with, to my mind, probably the best mike man that I ever saw in action, Bus Libott. I used to say that he was probably the only guy who could tell from the back of an actor's neck when he was going to make an unscheduled turn, which would double-cross the average mike man. Bus worked effortlessly. His reactions were tremendous. The mike man not only had to be skillful and have a tremendous instinct for what actors were going to do, but he had to be gentle with the mike. If he jerked it, the mike would clunk. I worked with Buster on all the Capra pictures.

My first Capra picture was *Ladies of Leisure*. A mixer, Harry Blanchard, had talked his way onto the picture, and he started it, working on interiors. Then they were scheduled to go out to Lake Malibu to shoot the night stuff. Blanchard didn't want to go on location, so I was assigned to do the job at the night locations at Malibu Lake. I was the newest mixer there, and Blanchard probably thought I was the least likely to threaten him. I didn't make any particular effort to impress Capra; I just did the best I could. When he was laying out the scene to Joe Walker, I'd listen in and get my information that way. When we came back, I prepared to go back on those crummy Columbia B's, but to my surprise and gratification Capra said he wanted me to finish the picture, and that was it. I did every one of Capra's pictures after that, except *The Miracle Woman*.

I got very close to Capra; he was always a very accessible man. I could tell him—if I did so discreetly and unobtrusively—if I thought a scene was not right, and he would listen. He was secure enough not to feel he had to bite the head off of anybody that made a suggestion.

In *Ladies of Leisure,* as Capra recalls in his autobiography, Barbara Stanwyck was dynamite to handle. He claims that he never let her put it all out in a rehearsal. He says that he learned this early in working with her. She always had one great performance in her, and if she expended it in a rehearsal, it was wasted. That was certainly true when we made those first few pictures with her. It was a hardship on the camera and sound people because Capra would walk through the paces with a stand-in; we sound people got no rehearsal and it was tough, but that was what he wanted. His thesis was that she did it in one take, and I think it was true.

When he finally brought her on the set, it was like bringing on a ticking time bomb—you had to be ready. That's where Buster came in handy. No matter what she did, that son-of-a-gun would follow it. Lots of the time it wasn't just a question of getting the mike in front of a person. On certain high-pitched scenes he'd have to take the mike away a little bit, especially those old mikes. So, on his own, he would take away the mike when she really let loose. And, by God, we got those scenes in one take. It put us on our mettle, but we were a good crew.

Capra was very dependent on the competence of the crew, and there was tremendous morale on a Capra picture. I'm kind of an inveterate diary keeper, and in 1939 when we finished *Mr. Smith Goes to Washington* I wrote down something he said to me. He said, "I want you to know that you've been more help to me than anybody. I mean that." I've always treasured that.

We always worked very hard. I used to lie awake nights thinking how I could do my job better and maybe get a little edge on the other guys. It was Depression times, and there was no unemployment insurance, no Social Security, no Medicare. If you lost your job, you could damn well starve. But I did have an edge. Because I was Capra's man I was often carried. But they wouldn't let me stay at home and pay me; I'd have to come in and maybe sit in the dubbing room and help out, be available for tests if necessary. But I wasn't ever laid off.

There were injustices in the system, for sure. One I especially remember. On westerns we'd start out before daybreak and come back long after dark. After a weary bus ride in from location the sound crew would all go to the bulletin board outside the department office, where our fate was awaiting us. It was the last day of the picture. Three men—my recorder, my mike man, and my cable man—and I looked at the board. I was to report to the dubbing room, and the rest of them were laid off. Just like that.

September 1985
Los Angeles

FILMOGRAPHY (partial)

1929	*Bulldog Drummond* (dir. F. Richard Jones, Samuel Goldwyn)
	The Iron Mask (dir. Allan Dwan, United Artists)
	Coquette (dir. Sam Taylor, United Artists)
	The Taming of the Shrew (dir. Sam Taylor, United Artists)
	Lady of the Pavements (dir. D. W. Griffith, United Artists)
1930	*Rain or Shine* (dir. Frank Capra, Columbia)
	Ladies of Leisure (dir. Frank Capra, Columbia)
1931	*Dirigible* (dir. Frank Capra, Columbia)
	Forbidden (dir. Frank Capra, Columbia)
1932	*American Madness* (dir. Frank Capra, Columbia)
	Platinum Blonde (dir. Frank Capra, Columbia)

1933   *The Bitter Tea of General Yen* (dir. Frank Capra, Columbia)

Lady for a Day (dir. Frank Capra, Columbia)

The Lady Is Willing (dir. Mitchell Leisen, Columbia)

1934   *It Happened One Night* (dir. Frank Capra, Columbia)

Broadway Bill (dir. Frank Capra, Columbia)

Twentieth Century (dir. Howard Hawks, Columbia)

1936   *Mr. Deeds Goes to Town* (dir. Frank Capra, Columbia)

1937   *Lost Horizon* (dir. Frank Capra, Columbia)

The Awful Truth (dir. Leo McCarey, Columbia)

1938   *You Can't Take It With You* (dir. Frank Capra, Columbia)

1939   *Mr. Smith Goes to Washington* (dir. Frank Capra, Columbia)

≡ WORDS AND MUSIC ≡

Jule Styne, composer.

JULE STYNE

Composer

≡

Jule Styne was born in London in 1905. After his family moved to Chicago he began to study piano. By the age of nine he was an accomplished concert pianist, performing with the Chicago Symphony. Coming to Hollywood in the thirties as a voice coach, he was soon writing music, collaborating with top lyricists like Frank Loesser and Sammy Cahn.

We meet in Styne's cramped office in the Mark Hellinger Building on Broadway. A small, dark man with a dead cigar in his mouth, he shows his reluctance to do the interview by giving short, clipped answers to our questions. Despite the terseness of his responses, Styne nevertheless conveys a largeness of spirit, one that fueled an undeniable (and still viable) talent.

In the mid-thirties I was asked to come to Hollywood by Joe Schenck, president of Twentieth Century–Fox, to coach people how to sing. I was a voice coach—and more than a voice coach. I made musical arrangements, put everything in shape to present a song in a movie.

A voice coach teaches a person who *can* sing *how* to sing a particular song to the best effect. The director tells him how to sell it. I coached Alice Faye, Tony Martin, Shirley Temple, Tyrone Power, Arlene Whelan, Mary Healey, Leah Ray, Judy Canova, and virtually all the Fox stars until I left in 1941.

I wrote songs for pictures, and later in my career I also scored some films. One reason I left Hollywood was that the producers would dictate to you what they wanted. It wasn't like the theater, where you read the script and created something yourself. They would just tell you where they wanted the songs, and you would then write them to fit. The songwriter had no say about placement or writing for the story.

Songs in the movies hardly ever advanced the plot. The producers just wanted a song that would win an Academy Award nomination. By contrast, on the musical stage songs are integral to the plot. Composers from New York, like Rodgers and Hammerstein, would carry a little more clout in Hollywood. When I went back, after I was established on Broadway, things had changed for me.

There's a big difference between writing songs for the stage and writing songs for the movies. Not many people can do both. When a scorer scores a movie, the movie has already been dramatized by the director. All the scorer contributes is the mood for the picture. In the theater you start with a blank page and you make the drama, both musically and lyrically. You don't do the show and then write music for it.

My first success wasn't at Fox, but at Republic Studios, where I wrote songs for westerns. I left Hollywood in 1946 and came back to Broadway to write *High Button Shoes*. For a few years then I went back and forth, as many people did, and in 1953 I came out to do *Three Coins in the Fountain*. I was surprised when I finally got the Academy Award for the title song, because I had lost seven times before—and I had been nominated for better songs.

It often happens to songwriters that a song they write isn't used in the film. It happens on the stage, too; but there, as the script progresses and changes, the songwriter tries to change his songs. When they did *Gypsy*—a dreadful movie—they didn't use seven of our songs. For *Funny Girl* I wrote a couple of extra songs and they interpolated a few old songs, and that was the fatal mistake that caused the destruction of that movie. They destroyed its drama; that's why it didn't win an Academy Award. They made the leading character self-pitying, whereas on the stage she was a strong woman. At the end of the movie, she sang "My Man" and cried, full of self-pity. On the stage she sang "Don't Rain On My Parade." It was a completely different tone. The same thing happens to 90 percent of the movies made from Broadway plays.

I made good friends during my Hollywood days, and that's very important. I learned the values by seeing the nonvalues. I got good taste by watching bad taste. But I really learned by working in the theater, with people like Jerome Robbins, Arthur Laurents, Stephen Sondheim, and George Abbott, people who really understood drama and understood what constituted musical theater. They didn't sit down and teach me, but I watched them. And they'd ask for my suggestions, I suppose, because they thought I had something to offer them.

Robbins understood my talent more than anyone else. He understood everything I was doing. When I wrote "Rose's Turn" for *Gypsy,* he knew that my stuff was really far ahead of anything he had heard in the theater up to that time. I worked with him on his big "cops and robbers" ballet, and actually got into a big argument with him because I didn't immediately understand what he wanted. So I told him to get Lennie Bernstein or somebody, but he said, "No, I want your kind of music." We ironed it all out, and I wrote one of the best ballets he ever did, as a result.

At times, when I teach at schools, the first thing I tell students is that I can't teach them how to write a song. You can't learn that. You are either born with a feeling for it or you aren't. You can teach someone how to play the piano, or how to orchestrate.

You can have a thorough musical education and still not be a songwriter. It's a very special thing. Irving Berlin had no training. Cole Porter had no training. Dick Rodgers and Harold Arlen had minimal training. But these were real songwriters, unlike the people who win the awards today. Everyone still remembers "Over the Rainbow." There is a lot to remember in the songs from the past.

Great songwriters write what they feel, and they are not influenced by the latest vogue. Dick Rodgers never changed. Gershwin never changed. Thank God!

March 1985
New York

FILMOGRAPHY (partial)

1938   *Hold That Co-ed* (dir. George Marshall, Twentieth Century–Fox)

           Kentucky Moonshine (dir. David Butler, Twentieth Century–Fox)

           Straight, Place and Show (dir. David Butler, Twentieth Century–Fox)

1940   *Hit Parade of 1941* (with Walter Bullock, "Who Am I?," dir. John Aver, Republic)

1941   *Angels with Broken Wings* (with Eddie Cherkose, dir. Bernard Vorhaus, Republic)

           Sis Hopkins (with Frank Loesser, dir. Joseph Santley, Republic)

1942   *Hi, Neighbor* (dir. Roy Mack, Republic)

           Ice-Capades Revue (dir. Bernard Vorhaus, Republic)

The Powers Girl (with Kim Gannon, dir. Norman McLeod, United Artists)

Sweater Girl (with Frank Loesser, "I Don't Want to Walk Without You," dir. William Clemens, Paramount)

Youth on Parade (with Sammy Cahn, "I've Heard That Song Before," dir. Albert S. Rogell, Republic)

1943   *Here Comes Elmer* (dir. Joseph Santley, Republic)

Hit Parade of 1943 (with Harold Adamson, "Change of Heart," dir. Albert S. Rogell, Republic)

Larceny with Music (dir. Edward Lilley, Universal)

Salute for Three (dir. Ralph Murphy, Paramount)

1944   *Carolina Blues* (with Sammy Cahn, dir. Leigh Jason, Columbia)

Follow the Boys (with Sammy Cahn, "I'll Walk Alone," dir. Edward Sutherland, Universal)

Knickerbocker Holiday (with Sammy Cahn, dir. Harry Joe Brown, United Artists)

Step Lively (with Sammy Cahn, "Come Out Come Out Wherever You Are," dir. Tim Whelan, RKO)

1945   *Anchors Aweigh* (with Sammy Cahn, "I Fall in Love Too Easily," dir. George Sidney, MGM)

Tonight and Every Night (with Sammy Cahn, "Anywhere," dir. Victor Saville, Columbia)

The Stork Club (with Sammy Cahn, "Love Me," dir. Hal Walker, Paramount)

1946   *Earl Carroll Sketch Book* (with Sammy Cahn, dir. Albert S. Rogell, Republic)

The Kid from Brooklyn (with Sammy Cahn, dir. Norman McLeod, RKO)

The Sweetheart of Sigma Chi (with Sammy Cahn, "Five Minutes More," dir. Jack Bernhard, Monogram)

1947   *It Happened in Brooklyn* (with Sammy Cahn, "Time After Time," dir. Richard Whorf, MGM)

Ladies' Man (with Sammy Cahn, dir. William Russell, Paramount)

1948   *Glamour Girl* (with Sammy Cahn, dir. Arthur Dreifuss, Columbia)

Romance on the High Seas (with Sammy Cahn, "It's Magic," dir. Michael Curtiz, Warner Bros.)

Two Guys from Texas (with Sammy Cahn, dir. David Butler, Warner Bros.)

1949   *It's a Great Feeling* (with Sammy Cahn, title song, dir. David Butler, Warner Bros.)

1950   *I'll Get By* (with Sammy Cahn, "It's Been a Long, Long Time," dir. Richard Sale, Twentieth Century–Fox)

The West Point Story (with Sammy Cahn, dir. Roy del Ruth, Warner Bros.)

1951   *Meet Me After the Show* (with Leo Robin, dir. Richard Sale, Twentieth Century–Fox)

Two Tickets to Broadway (with Leo Robin, "It Began in Yucatan," "Let's Do," dir. James Kern, RKO)

1952   *With a Song in My Heart* (with Sammy Cahn, dir. Walter Lang, Twentieth Century–Fox)

1953   *Gentlemen Prefer Blondes* (with Leo Robin, "Diamonds Are a Girl's Best Friend," dir. Howard Hawks, Twentieth Century–Fox)

1954   *Living It Up* (with Bob Hilliard, "Champagne and Wedding Cake," dir. Norman Taurog, Paramount)

Three Coins in the Fountain (with Sammy Cahn, title
    song, dir. Jean Negulesco, Twentieth Century–Fox)

1955   *My Sister Eileen* (with Leo Robin, dir. Alexander Hall,
    Columbia)

1960   *Bells Are Ringing* (dir. Vincente Minelli, MGM)

1962   *Gypsy* (with Stephen Sondheim, "Everything's Coming
    Up Roses," "If Mama Was Married," "Rose's
    Turn," dir. Mervyn Le Roy, Warner Bros.)

1963   *What a Way to Go* (with Betty Comden and Adolph
    Green, dir. J. Lee Thompson, Twentieth Century–
    Fox)

1968   *Funny Girl* (with Bob Merrill, title song, "People,"
    "My Man," "Don't Rain on My Parade," dir. Wil-
    liam Wyler, Columbia)

Sammy Cahn, lyricist, in the 1940s.

SAMMY CAHN

Lyricist

Sammy Cahn was born in what he calls a "one-syllable neighborhood" on New York's Lower East Side in 1913. From the Catskills, with Saul Chaplin and the Pals of Harmony, to Broadway and Hollywood, with Jule Styne, Nicholas Brodszky, Gene de Paul and Jimmy Van Heusen, Sammy Cahn has been writing memorable songs for more than fifty years.

We meet in his suite at the Clift Hotel in San Francisco, where Cahn is performing in his revue Words and Music. *He is relaxed and welcoming, and instantly begins telling stories. With four Oscars to his credit he reached the pinnacle of success long ago, but at seventy-three still finds enormous satisfaction in his work.*

When I write songs I am not a mimic. If you said to me, "Imitate somebody," I couldn't do it. But people tell me when I sing a Lanza song, I sound like Mario Lanza; when I sing a Sinatra song, I sound like Sinatra. You know the song "Call Me Irresponsible"? It was originally written for Fred Astaire. He was supposed to do it in a film. One of my highest goals was to write for Fred Astaire. But I had kind of accepted that I was never going to do that. Because I thought if I ever got to Hollywood, if I ever got to a movie studio, if I ever got successful . . . he would be long gone.

But one day I was in the hospital on account of my ulcers, and the phone rings, and it's a woman called Lillian Schary Small, my agent and Dore Schary's sister. She said, "Sammy, I've got some good news. I just got a call from Paramount, and they want you to do the score for a Fred Astaire movie called *Papa's Delicate Condition*."

I said, "Pay them whatever they want."

She started laughing. "No, they want you."

I said, "You don't understand. Hear me carefully. I must do this. I *must* do this!"

She says, "They want you, they want you. But there's a problem. You're over at MGM working for Lanza."

I said, "Well, your brother is the head of MGM, right? Fix it."

So I was working part-time for Lanza, and at night I'm working with Jimmy Van Heusen. I read the script, and the script is replete with the word irresponsible. So I turn to Jimmy Van Heusen one night and I ask him, "Do you like the title 'Call Me Irresponsible'"? Jimmy was lying on the couch with his hands under his head. Finally, he went over to the piano, and as I was giving him some lyrics he started playing a tune. *[Sings the tune.]* So we started writing the song. We finished it that night and I said to Jimmy, "We've got to do this for Astaire."

Well, as much as I *like* to demonstrate songs, that's how much Jimmy *hated* it. He said, "What's the hurry? We've only been working on this picture one day." But I couldn't explain to him in so many words that I'd been waiting twenty-five years to write a song for Astaire.

I said, "This song is the heart of the picture. If this song is wrong, then we're wrong." I kept insisting.

Finally, he said, "Okay, tomorrow."

So I called the studio and they said they'd see us at two o'clock. Van Heusen said, "We'll meet there at twelve."

I said, "Why meet so early?"

He said, "I want to go over it." He wanted to rehearse it over and over. He wanted us to be impeccably correct.

Comes the moment, I was standing in front of Fred Astaire. I can't explain the emotion for me. I explained to him that this song was for a scene after he'd done an irresponsible thing. So I started to sing it for him.

Suddenly, Fred said, "Stop . . ." (Well, Van Heusen almost fell off the piano bench.) ". . . that's one of the best songs I've ever heard."

I said to him, "Mr. Astaire, that's one of the best *half*-songs you've ever heard. May we finish it?"

When it was over he repeated, "That's still one of the best songs I've ever heard." Then he said, "Would you like to know how you got this assignment?"

I said, "Yes, I would."

"Well," he said, "you got this assignment because Johnny Mercer wasn't available."

I said, "That's a great compliment."

He said, "That's not the compliment. I'll give you the compliment. The next time Mercer leaves town I won't worry about it." We wrote "Walking Happy" for him, too.

It wasn't to be, though. I never had the fulfillment of seeing Fred Astaire do one of my songs. He was called away to a prior commitment at MGM, and that was that. It wasn't until some seven years later that *Papa's Delicate Condition* was on the boards again at Paramount, this time with Jack Rose producing and Jackie Gleason in the lead.

I'll tell you an interesting statistic. If any songwriter during his career has written six hits, then he's had a good career. I've had so many more, songs that people react to. You see, every song that Sinatra has recorded, because of the fact that he's recorded it, is special. And I've written dozens of them. I've had twenty-six Oscar nominations, and four of them won: "Three Coins in the Fountain," "All the Way," "Call Me Irresponsible," and "High Hopes."

The presentation of the song is a key element. The first time I played a song for Bing Crosby he said, "You're pretty good."

I said, "Pretty good? I'm the best!"

He said, "Yeah? What about Mack Gordon?"

Now Mack Gordon was a huge man. He must have weighed about 300 pounds. He was great; he was one of my idols. One of his lyrics inspired me. *[Sings.]* So then I wrote a song that sustained me for a while called "You're a Lucky Guy." *[Sings.]*

So here's Mack Gordon, this huge guy, and he used to stand in front of Darryl Zanuck and sing. *[Sings.]* He could even throw in a trombone chorus, with his throat. So I would say to Crosby, "Mack Gordon is disqualified from demonstrating a song because he *sings!*" He really did sing.

A funny thing about writing a song is that people don't realize when they're telling you something, *they're* writing it. And with a proper composer, I can write as many songs as he can play. Music speaks to me. A word is only as good as the note it sits under. Now, sometimes music says a certain thing to me. The notes say certain words. For example, notes might sound like rain.

In my songwriting column for a magazine called *Sheet Music* I tell every young person who wants to learn how to write: if he's a lyric writer, let him take Jerome Kern's music and put new lyrics to it—he's writing with Jerome Kern. If he's a tune writer, let him take Oscar Hammerstein's lyrics—he's collaborating with Oscar Hammerstein. That's the truth.

My favorite story of writing a song is when I wrote "I Should Care." I had just written a song with Jule Styne, "I've Heard That Song Before," which was a big hit. I come into my apartment and there are Paul Weston and Axel Stordahl, who were arranging for Tommy Dorsey. I come dancing in and one of them says, "There he is, look at him. It takes him five minutes to write a song, and it takes us hours to make it sound good."

They asked me what kind of introduction I wanted, and I said, "Who cares about an introduction? Who walks down the street humming an introduction?" Anyway, then they go over to the piano and start playing some notes. The minute they start playing, I say to myself, I'll call it "I Should Care." That's what I mean when I say that the music talks to me.

So I start out on this particular song. *[Sings two lines.]* Well, once you say this much, the song is finished. It's the architecture of the song. The main thing is that they have written a song which is ready for a lyric. It's not quirky, it's not irregular. It nearly writes itself. You can't rhyme *weeping* with *creeping, leaping,* or *peeping,* so you have to say *sleeping.*

I didn't write it; it wrote me. That's what I tell people, and they don't quite understand what I'm saying. Certain songs just write themselves. I wrote "Thoroughly Modern Millie" in just one time at bat. "The Tender Trap," one time at bat.

When Sol Siegel asked me and Jule Styne to write "Three Coins in the Fountain" we asked him what the picture was about, and could we see it. The answer was no. Film not available, script not available, book not available. So he tells us exactly this much story: three girls go to Rome, throw money in the fountain, hope to fall in love. Exit Sol Siegel. So I wrote the first four lines and gave it to Jule; that lyric was ready for music. It was ready for notes. I was having a hard time figuring out what else to write in the damn song, but I used everything I was given.

Finally, we had a song. Sinatra recorded it and it became the title theme and the number one song in the world in the number one picture, *and* it won us our first Academy Award.

I liked writing with everyone I wrote with. Jimmy Van Heusen would rather write a song than do anything. Jule Styne would rather write a song than do anything. It was easy for me to write with them.

I have, in a sense, realized as many goals as anyone is entitled to realize. I'm not sure if I caused these things to happen. I know that I act on things, which brings reactions. I think that today I am the most recognized songwriter in the world.

April 1987

San Francisco

Editors' Note: Sammy Cahn died in January 1993.

FILMOGRAPHY (partial)

1940	*Argentine Nights* (dir. Albert S. Rogell, Universal)
1941	*Go West Young Lady* (with Saul Chaplin, dir. Frank Strayer, Columbia)
	Time Out for Rhythm (with Saul Chaplin, dir. Sidney Salkow, Columbia)
1942	*Youth on Parade* (with Jule Styne, "I've Heard That Song Before," dir. Albert S. Rogell, Republic)
1943	*Crazy House* (dir. Eddie Cline, Universal)
	Lady of Burlesque (dir. William Wellman, United Artists)
1944	*Carolina Blues* (with Jule Styne, dir. Leigh Jason, Columbia)
	Follow the Boys (with Jule Styne, "I'll Walk Alone," dir. Edward Sutherland, Universal)
	Step Lively (with Jule Styne, "Come Out Come Out Wherever You Are," dir. Tim Whelan, RKO)
	Knickerbocker Holiday (with Jule Styne, dir. Harry Joe Brown, United Artists)
1945	*Anchors Aweigh* (with Jule Styne, "I Fall in Love Too Easily," dir. George Sidney, MGM)

Tonight and Every Night (with Jule Styne, "Anywhere,"
dir. Victor Saville, Columbia)

The Stork Club (with Jule Styne, "Love Me," dir. Hal
Walker, Paramount)

1946   *Cinderella Jones* (dir. Busby Berkeley, Warner Bros.)

Earl Carroll Sketch Book (with Jule Styne, dir. Albert S.
Rogell, Republic)

The Kid from Brooklyn (with Jule Styne, dir. Norman
McLeod, RKO)

The Sweetheart of Sigma Chi (with Jule Styne, "Five
Minutes More," dir. Jack Bernhard, Monogram)

1947   *It Happened in Brooklyn* (with Jule Styne, "Time After
Time," dir. Richard Whorf, MGM)

Ladies' Man (with Jule Styne, dir. William Russell,
Paramount)

1948   *Glamour Girl* (with Jule Styne, dir. Arthur Dreifuss,
Columbia)

Romance on the High Seas (with Jule Styne, "It's Magic,"
dir. Michael Curtiz, Warner Bros.)

Two Guys from Texas (with Jule Styne, dir. David Butler, Warner Bros.)

1949   *Always Leave Them Laughing* (dir. Roy del Ruth,
Warner Bros.)

It's a Great Feeling (with Jule Styne, title song, dir.
David Butler, Warner Bros.)

1950   *I'll Get By* (with Jule Styne, "It's Been a Long, Long
Time," dir. Richard Sale, Twentieth Century–Fox)

The Toast of New Orleans (with Nicholas Brodszky,
"Be My Love," dir. Norman Taurog, MGM)

The West Point Story (with Jule Styne, dir. Roy del
Ruth, Warner Bros.)

1951   *Rich, Young and Pretty* (with Nicholas Brodszky, "We Never Talk Much," "Wonder Why," dir. Norman Taurog, MGM)

                Two Tickets to Broadway (story only, dir. James Kern, RKO)

1952   *April in Paris* (with Vernon Duke, E. Y. Harburg, dir. David Butler, Warner Bros.)

                Because You're Mine (with Nicholas Brodszky, title song, dir. Alexander Hall, MGM)

                With a Song in My Heart (with Jule Styne, dir. Walter Lang, Twentieth Century–Fox)

1953   *Three Sailors and a Girl* (with Sammy Fain, dir. Roy del Ruth, Warner Bros.)

1954   *Three Coins in the Fountain* (with Jule Styne, title song, dir. Jean Negulesco, Twentieth Century–Fox)

1955   *Ain't Misbehavin'* (with Johnnie Scott, "I Love That Rickey Tickey Tickey," dir. Edward Buzzell, Universal)

                Love Me or Leave Me (with Nicholas Brodszky, "I'll Never Stop Loving You," dir. Charles Vidor, MGM)

                Pete Kelly's Blues (with Ray Heindorf, title song, dir. Jack Webb, Warner Bros.)

                The Tender Trap (with James Van Heusen, title song, dir. Charles Walters, MGM)

1956   *The Court Jester* (with Sylvia Fine, dir. Norman Panama, Paramount)

                Anything Goes (with James Van Heusen, "You Can Bounce Right Back," dir. Robert Lewis, Paramount)

                Meet Me in Las Vegas (with Georgie Stoll, Johnny Green, dir. Roy Rowland, MGM)

                The Opposite Sex (with Nicholas Brodszky, dir. David Miller, MGM)

Pardners (with James Van Heusen, dir. Norman
Taurog, Paramount)

Written on the Wind (with Victor Young, title song,
dir. Douglas Sirk, Universal)

1957 *The Joker Is Wild* (with James Van Heusen, "All the
Way," dir. Charles Vidor, Paramount)

1958 *Rock-a-Bye Baby* (with Harry Warren, dir. Frank
Tashlin, Paramount)

1959 *A Hole in the Head* (with James Van Heusen, "High
Hopes," dir. Frank Capra, United Artists)

1960 *High Time* (with James Van Heusen, "A Second Time
Around," dir. Blake Edwards, Twentieth Century–
Fox)

1961 *Pocketful of Miracles* (with James Van Heusen, title
song, dir. Frank Capra, United Artists)

1962 *The Road to Hong Kong* (with James Van Heusen, dir.
Melvin Frank, United Artists)

Boys' Night Out (dir. Michael Gordon, MGM)

How the West Was Won (dir. Henry Hathaway, MGM)

1963 *Papa's Delicate Condition* (with James Van Heusen,
"Call Me Irresponsible," dir. George Marshall,
Paramount)

Come Blow Your Horn (dir. Bud Yorkin, Paramount)

1964 *Robin and the Seven Hoods* (with James Van Heusen,
"My Kind of Town," dir. Gordon Douglas, Warner
Bros.)

1966 *The Oscar* (dir. Russell Rouse, Paramount)

1967 *Thoroughly Modern Millie* (with James Van Heusen,
title song, "The Tapioca," dir. George Roy Hill,
Universal)

1968   *Star!* (with James Van Heusen, title song, dir. Robert
         Wise, Twentieth Century–Fox)

1973   *A Touch of Class* (with George Barrie, "All That Love
         Went to Waste," dir. Melvin Frank, UK)

1975   *Paper Tiger* (dir. Ken Annakin, UK)

1976   *The Duchess and the Dirtwater Fox* (dir. Melvin Frank,
         Twentieth Century–Fox)

1978   *The Stud* (dir. Quentin Masters, UK)

≡ THE LOOK ≡

BOB FLATLEY

Carpenter

≡

Bob Flatley grew up in New York at the turn of the century. He came to Hollywood in the thirties, beginning as a laborer at Columbia.

He lives in a cottage on the grounds of the Motion Picture and Television Fund. We ask him about his work as a carpenter, but it's clear he would rather talk about his singing and dancing days. His heart was not in building sets, and the disappointment shows.

I came to Hollywood by way of China. I was in show business all my life, from the time I was eighteen or nineteen. In 1934 I had a chance to go to China to be a chorus boy with a revue. Well, the show closed when some of the chorus girls "went native," and when we got back to Shanghai we found that the owner had left us stranded there.

It was somehow finally arranged to send us back steerage to Seattle, then on to New York by way of Hollywood. I had never been west of Chicago before then, in sixteen years of show business, so I thought, "By God, I'm going to see Hollywood now."

I kind of liked it there and decided to stay. I don't have to tell you how tough it was. But being a dancer, I got a few jobs in musicals; they made a lot of them in those days. Those jobs really saved my life. I was in the chorus of *Gold Diggers of 1935,* the Busby Berkeley musical. Then I did a lot of stand-in work. And I did bits here and there.

After the war, I came back here and I started to get back in the Actors Guild again but I couldn't swing it and finally said, "To hell with it."

I called a friend of mine in the property department at Columbia, who got me started as a laborer. I had to make a living since I was married by then, and it was more certain than extra work. They had a regular eight-hour day and a lot of overtime. I was really pretty lucky. I worked steady there. Then the labor boss asked me if I'd like to grip and I did that for a while. Our job was building the scaffolds up high and then placing all the lights for the electricians. Then, when they were finished with a set, we would tear it down.

I was gripping when the strike came, in 1945, I think it was. They gave all the grips the chance to become carpenters, since all the carpenters had walked out. That was a wonderful opportunity for me, so I took it. I became a regular carpenter or set erector and stayed with it from 1945 till 1965. I worked at Columbia four or five years, then got laid off. After that I worked at every studio. I'd call up the local and they'd send me to wherever the job was.

We carpenters built the sets. The plans for the sets came from the art director. By the time we got them they were all cut up into sections, and we'd follow the instructions. There was a foreman who was our boss. Then a "pusher" would have charge of certain groups, and there would be several groups building the sets.

I worked on *My Fair Lady.* I was in the prop shop in that picture. We were called prop makers, though we weren't, really. We built the sets, but in the prop shop. And we made all these little gadgets. It's funny . . . you don't really pay that much attention to the pictures you work on. I don't even remember some of them.

I remember *Cheyenne Autumn,* John Ford's picture. We went up to Utah for that one. We made lots of bows and arrows and guns. They had a certain number of real guns, but most of them were made out of wood and just looked like guns. But the bows and arrows were real. We turned those out by the hundreds. The arrows were dull, of course, so nobody would get hurt. We made all kinds of things. Naturally, you had to learn as you went along. There was a foreman there who would show you how to do things. So I worked mostly in the mill and on the sets. You would do a lot of the work in the mill, and then they would assemble the stuff on the sets.

Lots of times we had pressure to work quickly. Time was money. Sometimes the budget was tight and other times they would just throw the money away like drunken sailors. They'd give you a deadline and you had to have the set built by that time. We'd get overtime quite often, especially in the prop shop. Ten-hour days weren't unusual. That's where a lot of the work was.

I had my lean days, though. I wasn't a real good carpenter. But I was very fortunate to be able to get the card after the strike. I learned an awful lot and I did work fairly steady. I learned the way to make the money last. We did all right.

I retired in 1965, when I was 66. The pension was $90 a week for a long time. I didn't get a big Social Security check, either. I was still doing free-lance work, but when the pension went up to $200 I just quit one day, after lunch. I had waited for that all my life. I didn't even wait until quitting time. Just said, "Give me the check." Honest to God. I walked right out and went on home. That's how much I liked being a carpenter.

February 1986
Woodland Hills

Editors' Note: Bob Flatley died in May 1991.

Tommie Hawkins, property master, completing the "glass shot" (the last shot of the day) by offering John Wayne his customary Wild Turkey.

TOMMIE
HAWKINS

Property Master

Tommie Hawkins began his movie career first in the labor gang and then as a grip for Universal in the early forties. After serving in the army during the war, he returned to Hollywood and became a prop man, a job he enjoyed enormously over the next thirty-five years.

We are lucky enough to encounter Hawkins on the day he is volunteering at the Motion Picture and Television Fund. A large, easygoing man now in his seventies, he radiates the kind of decency and utter dependability that must have made him indispensable on the set. His prop box was always full of surprises, and he could probably still pull out a few.

You get to be a property master after you have perhaps as many as eight to twelve thousand hours in the business, which works out to about a thousand days. You take a written test and an oral test. The tests have questions like: What are action props? When does a hat become a prop? What kind of medicine are you allowed to give your stars? Are you allowed to have aspirin in your prop box?

You take the tests, and then a board of four or five property masters reviews them and pass on you. If all goes well, you become a property master. The property master works the show with the stars and with the director.

If you two were stars and I was the prop man and we were going to set up this little scene, I would have to make sure that these three chairs are here. And your bag, which you take something out of, is no longer wardrobe; it is a prop. The breakdown in the script would say: "Marion took her pencil and pad out of her duffel bag." We have to have the bag listed so that it comes out if it's part of the story. And the director has to have okayed that color of pad for her to be taking notes on, that color of pen or pencil. If you're a married lady and you have a wedding ring on your finger, that's a prop. That your glasses are the type that tip and don't reflect the light over there—the prop man takes care of all that kind of stuff.

This is all done in preparation, when you get the script. You break it down, and that tells you everything you'll need for each particular scene. Then you make a list and you go out and shop. You either buy it or you go to a prop house and rent it. Then you take it all back to the studio and make an appointment with the director, and you show him what you have, scene by scene. You say, "Now this is for page fifty-one, where the girl comes out with her bag so she can do the interview." The director will okay everything. He might say, "That's fine, but let's don't have it yellow; make it a white bag." Then I might say, "The cameraman likes yellow." You know your cameraman, and you know that whites are bad for the camera because they reflect. They make a person's face "hot." So the director might then say, "You're right."

On the hierarchy of the job: after the set is dressed, the prop man is only responsible to the star and the director. While the picture is shooting, the first assistant director is your immediate superior. He'll check with you and say, "We're going to do this scene next," regardless of what order you have them in. He'll say, "We're going to skip over the next two scenes and go on to this one." So you have to be ready for anything.

Probably the closest contact an actor has on the set, other than with the director, is with the prop man. Because you're the one that hands him his prop; you're the one that's taught him how to use it if it's foreign to him. You have told him if the gun is loaded, told him not to point it at anybody, told him to be at least ten feet away before he fires it, told him to be aiming it because those caps explode side by side and might destroy his eyes. You've told him everything he needs to know about that gun.

With a machine gun, you have to get a license, a permit to use it, to control it, so that you can teach an actor to use it. You've got to be sure that you know how to operate it, and how to keep it working. You've got to know where you're going to store it at night, always under lock and key. When you're through with it, you're ordered to take it to a police station and check it in, unless you have a guard on a truck and the truck itself is locked. The guard has to be responsible to you.

You have to teach people how to use the props. In a card game, for instance. Some of the meanest-looking guys playing gamblers never played a card game in their lives. They don't know how to hold the cards, how to shuffle them; how to use the chips.

On the average movie, there would be a property master and perhaps three prop men—a first assistant and two other guys who might change the set over, move things that need moving. Chairs have to be marked so that they're in a certain position at all times.

On location it was more difficult because you had to take everything you needed with you, and make sure you had it. It was very seldom that you could find what you needed on location, unless it was something like food. The food on a set is real, by the way. We asked the stars what they liked to eat. For rehearsals you'd just give them a plate and knife and fork. The prop men do the cooking, too; it's part of the job. We had our own little kitchen offstage, with a refrigerator and everything we needed. I would even get real dough for a bread-baking scene.

It could be real wine, depending on whether the actor could handle it, but sometimes for liquor we used colored water. I always used real champagne, though, because you need the authentic "pop."

I used to keep aspirin in my prop box. There's supposed to be a medic on the set, and the prop man is not supposed to dispense medicine. But, just like when you go out on a boat, when you're not supposed to have the Dramamine for sea sickness, you'd better have it. You just give it out beforehand, unofficially.

My prop box had thirty-eight drawers in it, on two sides. It had everything from glue to safety pins, needles, thread, hand mirrors, make-up, hairnets, hair spray, bobby pins, shoe polish, extra socks, pantyhose—you name it. The request might come from the actor, who probably ruined the original object. He may have gotten his feet wet and didn't want to catch a cold, that sort of thing. If the actor felt closer to the wardrobe gal, he might ask her; but if she didn't have it, she'd ask the prop man. It was our job to think of everything that might be needed at any time.

September 1985
Woodland Hills

ANNA HILL
JOHNSTONE
Costume Designer

≡

Anna Hill Johnstone began design work in the theater in the early thirties and for many years shuttled between Broadway and Hollywood, managing to sustain a long and happy marriage all the while. She was nominated for Academy Awards for The Godfather *and* Ragtime.

Now in her seventies, she still has a slender, almost boyish figure. For the interview, she is punctual and impeccably dressed, looking every inch a successful costume designer.

The first movie job I got was *Portrait of Jennie*. Lucinda Ballard and I had been working together; I was sort of her assistant and partner. We had done a lot of things together, mostly big musicals on Broadway. Suddenly Selznick called her from California to find out if she would be available to do *Portrait of Jennie*. Lucinda was the second designer to get the job because Selznick had not been satisfied with the original designer's work. He was arriving in New York in time to shoot a particular sequence, with snow in Central Park and ice on the lake. We laughed, but don't think the day he came it didn't snow.

We did the sequence on the lake in Central Park, and Lucinda rushed around and got Jennifer's costume for the ice skating sequence. We also did the white dress with the blue sash that the portrait was painted in. Nobody knew who I was. There was no such category as assistant to Lucinda. I wasn't a dresser or wardrobe mistress, but they were paying me well. We batted around on *Portrait of Jennie* for three or four weeks, I guess, and then Selznick closed down to rewrite the script. That shutdown lasted six weeks. By then they couldn't get Lucinda to come back, so they invited me.

I came back with no title; I don't know what I was. We were shooting up at the Cloisters in the white dress with the blue sash, which had never been tried on even after it was finished. I think Jennifer finally got into the dress for Selznick to look at about six o'clock one evening, and it didn't fit. They had to get on with the picture, so, being completely innocent about how things worked, I took it off her to fix. I took it home to work on it, and it kept me up till about two o'clock in the morning. It was a tricky job; I wasn't trying to make any overtime.

The next day I showed up with the dress altered and ready to wear. I think that's why Selznick invited me to California to finish up the picture. I went. I think I had one more dress to do for Jennifer. It was a very fascinating experience, going out to Culver City and getting to know how they did movies. I still had no title or deal, but he did give me credit. I was the third designer listed, though I was the only one left on the picture.

Portrait of Jennie was a unique experience because it was a Selznick picture. He had been on his own for a long time, and his pictures were special. He knew the studio system and made it work. He was very daring and spent a lot of money to make his pictures unique and of high quality. He was a perfectionist and his pictures reflected that.

The studio system was really very well run when I started. We had marvelous wardrobe departments, and we had good help in the workrooms. I came back to New York thinking that there was nobody on the East Coast who could do a certain kind of smocking or other very fine work. One girl was from Russia, and she'd been trained in smocking and was wonderful at it.

Selznick even sent me one of his famous memos, a horrible memo. We were going to do a scene with Joe Cotten and his landlady. That was here in New York. I had brought a ragged sweater and kind of a smock, just because it looked so right for the landlady. The apartment was supposed to be on 38th Street, between Ninth and Tenth Avenue. We knew what those people were wearing. I put it on the actress when we got to Hollywood, and did I get a blast from Selznick! He was furious. I wrote back saying I thought he was doing a realistic scene and this is the way those people would look.

I had worked on *Tea and Sympathy* for Elia Kazan on Broadway, as well as *Flight into Egypt*. Then I went to the coast with him to work on *East of Eden*. *On the Waterfront* was completely shot in New York. There was actually very little to do on it, except for the men's stuff. I had Marlon Brando and the rest of the actors to dress.

I do remember Eva Marie Saint was hired at about two in the morning, and she went in front of the cameras at about noon the next day. She was in a play that was running at the Henry Miller Theater at the time.

Sam Spiegel, the producer, had told me to go and see her in the play so that I would know what was needed for her. He was meeting her after the theater to get the contract settled. I was to go home and wait for his call, which came to me at 2:00 A.M. So at least I had some idea what she looked like, though I didn't have a chance to speak to her. They got me her dress size, and I went to Saks the next day and bought a dress and a coat for her.

I wasn't allowed to wake her up, as she needed her beauty sleep. A limo took her to Hoboken at noon. We met out there, and I put the dress on her and it fit well enough to go in front of the camera. They wanted her right in the shot with the pigeons.

I said, "Her petticoat's showing." They wouldn't believe me, but it's still showing on the film. Every time I see the film I notice it.

Costume designers were and still are hired picture to picture. It's not a contract situation. The big names, like Adrian at MGM and Edith Head at Paramount, may have had contracts. The studios made so many films in those days there was always work for them.

I always got a script early on, so I could do a lot of research in advance. Usually you meet the director very early, sometimes even before you agree to do the picture. Usually the director makes the final choice, though the producer may be involved as well.

The costume designer works closely with the production designer. They don't actually design together, but they certainly confer. And a lot of the time, the costume designer is recommended by the production designer. That's a relationship that has to be comfortable; those two have to like the way each one works, because they're sort of a team.

It's the production manager who actually makes the deal, but the director has the final say. The production manager is in charge of all of the business end. I would report to the director. If I had any problems he would be the one I would talk to. As far as I'm concerned, the director is the dictator. And has to be. Otherwise nothing works. If you have a weak director who can't make up his mind, it's a disaster.

My first few movies were shot in black and white. The first color film I worked on was *East of Eden*. It was also Kazan's first color film. In black and white you don't have to do as much planning as you do for a color film. You have to think in different terms. You don't put reds together, for example. If two people are in the same scene, you have to watch their colors. We had to work with a color expert, and we had to test extensively. We had to test navy blues to see if they went purple. I remember we were using Eastman Kodak film, and that was one of the great problems. Green seemed to be a very safe color; it would stay green. Brown was good, too, but navy was a problem. The two brothers in *East of Eden* both had navy blue suits, and we wanted a little difference between them.

Make-up had to be tested, too, to make sure that the lipstick didn't go purple. You had to make your tests with the production designer. You had to work things out together.

When I worked on *East of Eden* it was the first time I had a contract. A deal was really made for this one picture. But it just took care of salary; we never even thought about working conditions. You used to get your per diem, of course. You'd always be hired for ten weeks, period, then they'd automatically renew. They never knew how long the picture would take, and they didn't want to be paying you after the picture was finished.

The designer has the choice of planning and choosing the key wardrobe people. There's a head of men's wardrobe and a head of ladies' wardrobe. You get so you're comfortable working with certain people.

I learned a lot from Irene Sharaff and Lucinda Ballard, and I learned how to work from another designer's sketches, what fabric to use, what kind of lace and ribbons and detailing, and so on. I've had people do the same thing for me. I just don't have time to get the designs done and get them through the workroom. Samples are picked and people go shopping, and then you okay what they've bought. I would say I spent over two years learning how to make a workroom function, and it has been invaluable to me.

You have to see what's available to use. It's like dressing the army—and sometimes it *is* the army! Thank God for these wardrobe departments and wardrobe people, because they can handle this kind of scale. The designers couldn't do it alone. The designer gets the background on the wardrobe, then looks at the stuff and okays it. Designers also have to know all the details on armor or guns, which are really props, but are still part of the job.

The studios also had very good research libraries. It's a very important facet of this work. The staff would dig up stuff for you, but actually it's preferable to do some of the research on your own. You can't take it for granted that you're going to get what you need. You have to steep yourself in an era.

I was brought up in the realistic school. I haven't done much of the fancy, creative side of designing. Most of my work, I think, has been in character, and trying to tell something about the part. If you've got Mary Jones, you do it one way, and if you have Celia Smith, you do it another. The clothes do deliver a message.

February 1986
New York

Editors' Note: Anna Hill Johnstone died in October 1992.

FILMOGRAPHY (partial)

1948	*Portrait of Jennie* (dir. William Dieterle, Selznick)
1951	*A Streetcar Named Desire* (dir. Elia Kazan, Warner Bros.)
1954	*East of Eden* (dir. Elia Kazan, Warner Bros.)
	On the Waterfront (dir. Elia Kazan, Columbia)
1956	*Baby Doll* (dir. Elia Kazan, Warner Bros.)
1957	*Edge of the City* (dir. Martin Ritt, MGM)
	A Face in the Crowd (dir. Elia Kazan, Warner Bros.)
	Stage Struck (dir. Sidney Lumet, RKO)
1959	*Odds Against Tomorrow* (dir. Robert Wise, United Artists)
1960	*Wild River* (dir. Elia Kazan, Twentieth Century–Fox)
1961	*Splendor in the Grass* (dir. Elia Kazan, Warner Bros.)

1962   *David and Lisa* (dir. Frank Perry, Continental)

1963   *America, America* (dir. Elia Kazan, Warner Bros.)

1964   *The Pawnbroker* (dir. Sidney Lumet, Landau-Unger)

1965   *Harvey Middleman, Fireman* (dir. Ernest Pintoff, Columbia)

1966   *The Group* (dir. Sidney Lumet, United Artists)

1968   *Bye Bye Braverman* (dir. Sidney Lumet, Warner Bros.)
        The Swimmer (dir. Frank Perry, Columbia)
        The Night They Raided Minsky's (dir. William Friedkin, United Artists)

1969   *Alice's Restaurant* (dir. Arthur Penn, United Artists)

1970   *There Was a Crooked Man* (dir. Stuart Burge, United Artists)
        Cotton Comes to Harlem (dir. Ossie Davis, United Artists)

1971   *The Godfather* (dir. Francis Ford Coppola, Paramount)

1972   *Play It Again, Sam* (dir. Herbert Ross, Paramount)
        Come Back, Charleston Blue (dir. Mark Warren, Warner Bros.)

1973   *Summer Wishes, Winter Dreams* (dir. Gilbert Cates, Columbia)

1975   *The Taking of Pelham One Two Three* (dir. Joseph Sargent, United Artists)

1976   *The Last Tycoon* (dir. Elia Kazan, Paramount)

1981   *Ragtime* (dir. Milos Forman, Paramount)

Arthur Lonergan, art director, holding a preproduction sketch.

ARTHUR
LONERGAN
Art Director

≡

Arthur Lonergan was born in New York in 1906. He moved to Hollywood in the thirties at the invitation of David Selznick. For the following forty years he worked for several major studios, including several years at MGM under the direction of the legendary Cedric Gibbons.

Lonergan is a gentle man of obvious good taste, a gracious host who shows us around the magnificent house he designed and built high on a cliff overlooking the Pacific. Decorated in serene shades of green and blue, the interior is a testament to his practiced eye.

To put it easily and simply, an art director is responsible for everything behind the actors: the sets, the backgrounds, the colors, the locations—of course with the approval of the director and producer. The art director is responsible for the overall look of the film. It's a big contribution. I used to make a tape of the various colors on the set, and make just a few strips out of it. That told me what the rhythm of the color was—were we going from a cool color to a hot color, for instance—and how that rhythm would work out for the entire picture. It's not just a matter of picking a color for a particular set; it's a matter of coordinating the entire picture. It affected the continuity of the film.

We got to see the shooting script before we started. As a matter of fact, on a big picture we would often do a month of research with the shooting script before we even started to design it. If it was a period picture we would have to immerse ourselves in everything about that period: the costumes, the architecture, the colors. I'm an architect myself, and I taught the history of architecture at New York University before I went to work in Hollywood.

I believe a knowledge of architecture is a requirement for an art director, because 90 percent of our work is architecture. A number of art directors in my day weren't architects, but they understood architecture. We were responsible for the design and building of the sets and the color scheme of the picture, which we worked out with the costume department, of course. The art director would set the color scheme, and the costume department would follow through. But every once in a while an actress would want a particular color, and in those cases Edith Head (or whoever was doing the costumes) would call me and say we had to use a certain color, and then we would work the other way. Joan Crawford and Bette Davis, for example, used to request their favorite colors. Generally, the costume designer got involved right from the beginning. Costumes had to be made while the sets were being built, and we usually worked together pretty closely.

I did both sketches and models of the sets. We tried not to make the sketches too detailed. Years ago at MGM, Cedric Gibbons, the head of the art department there, had a saying about sketches. He said, "I don't want to see the doorknobs."

We consulted with the director, of course, but every once in a while we'd consult with the screenwriter, too. It depended on the type of film it was. But most of our work was done with the director and producer. Some directors relied more on art directors than others. Some didn't care one way or the other—you'd give them a set and they'd shoot it. Other directors, like George Cukor, cared about every detail. He was a marvelous director to work with. We used to get together in his office with a lot of books for research, and we'd pore over them and discuss each individual set. By the time we were finished with that conversation I knew exactly what we were going to do with the set, and he knew exactly how he was going to shoot it.

I started out working only in black and white. I don't know if it was any simpler, really, but working in color took some getting used to. But a long time before they shot in color, we did the sets in color. There was a time when we did them in series of grays, but then we went into color for more realism for the performers. We did a lot of things that didn't appear on the screen, just to help the performers. If you had a Victorian room, say, with fancy cornices, we'd put the cornices on the set even though we wouldn't actually shoot high enough to see them on the screen. It was done just to create a mood.

Some of the model sets we made, and the sets themselves, were destroyed after the picture was finished. On a single picture at MGM, I could hardly move in my office because models were stacked four to five feet high. I didn't keep any of the models myself, nor any of the sketches that we made. We weren't allowed to. There was a time when the studios didn't want the public to know what went into making a picture, and so they would take every single sketch and model and store them. Contractually, they owned everything because they were paying for it.

Naturally, budget considerations did constrain us, depending on the picture. If the director and producer were willing to back you up in what you'd like to do, you could get away with a lot. But if they didn't care one way or another, then the production department could cut the hell out of your budget.

MGM was generous with *Forbidden Planet,* the first science fiction picture that was ever made at the studio. Buddy Gillespie was doing the special effects, and he and I decided that since this was the first science fiction picture they'd ever made, why not do it right? So we went ahead and designed the sets, and they were costing a fortune. By the time they caught up with us the sets were half built and all the designing was done. When they discovered we were spending that much money they called in Dore Schary. Schary looked over the situation, saw that we weren't paying any big stars a lot of money, and said, "Why not put it somewhere?" So he approved it, and that's why it came out looking as good as it did.

That was probably the most difficult movie I ever worked on, because it was science fiction and no research could be done. We just dragged it out of the sky and ran with it. I remember going over to Cal Tech for several meetings with some of the professors over there on the latest scientific discoveries. I got a lot of ideas from what they were developing. We had to design and build a robot, and it was quite a job because a man had to be inside it. It took a very small but very strong person, because it was heavy and awkward and full of electronic equipment.

In general, our continuity sketches had a lot to do with what the cameramen would set up. We did a lot of those because directors liked to work with them. They didn't like to admit it, but they liked to have them in their back pocket. You practically directed the picture when you made those sketches. You'd lay the picture out shot for shot. Of course, they didn't always follow it, but it gave them a starting point, something to take off from, instead of coming on the stage cold and having everybody waiting around for an order on how to shoot.

Working on period films was just about the same as working on contemporary stories. You would need more research, of course, for period movies, and we had marvelous researchers. At Twentieth Century–Fox they used to go through all the books even before we did. They would photograph the particular pieces they thought might be useful and put them into looseleaf folders for us so we didn't have to look through everything ourselves. So by the time I started a picture there would be a tall stack of looseleaf folders for me to work with. I would take them and make hundreds of sketches and notes to try to absorb the atmosphere of whatever period I was working in.

I worked for MGM, Twentieth Century–Fox, Paramount, Universal, Warner Brothers, all the big ones. Then I went out and free-lanced.

At MGM there were nineteen art directors at one time. Each one worked as an individual under Cedric Gibbons, who was the supervising art director. He only supervised in the sense that he assigned the pictures. He had nothing to do with the actual design. He hired us, and we had to show him what we were doing and get his okay, but he left us pretty much alone.

We made a budget for our part of the picture. As soon as I got a script, the first thing I did was make a breakdown, all the scenes, how many, on the set. Also the number of scenes on location, and then figure out how much that should cost. Then we would submit that to the budget department. After that first phase we'd have a budget meeting, and all the departments would sit in and we would all discuss our different budgets. Then if the total budget for that picture came to more than the studio wanted to spend, cuts were made and the money was allotted accordingly. We had to trim our budget to fit.

Preparation time would vary, depending on the picture. I worked on pictures as short a time as six weeks, including preparation, and I worked on single pictures for over a year. One of the Gene Kelly musicals took us over a year because we shot the book first, then we stopped production. Then each musical number was written and designed and produced individually. We had about ten numbers, and that took months.

I actually started out as an illustrator, a special designer working for an art director. The very first picture I did was *A Star Is Born*, the original 1937 version, for David Selznick. Selznick didn't worry about the budget at all. It was Selznick who brought me out to Hollywood in late 1934. Right after *A Star Is Born* I went over to MGM.

I was almost ideally suited to be an art director because I was trained not only as an architect, but also as an illustrator. I had also taught interior design at the New York School of Interior Decoration. When I first came to MGM, Gibbons told me that even with that background it would be five years before I'd have enough experience in the business to become an art director. There were a lot of technical things that you had to understand.

In the very early days of the industry we did very little location work, but that changed over the years. Then, if we needed a street in Paris, we built a street in Paris. The trouble was they would use the sets for everything, and the sets began to get familiar.

Since movies are not shot in sequence, we would work on a set at a time, according to the shooting schedule. They had a board with strips on it, and on those strips they would have every scene. Each strip would show the amount of time that scene would take. The strips can be arranged so they get a setup they like. Then the production department goes over it with the director, and the director might decide that he can't shoot that sequence in that amount of time. If he says he needs more time, they'll put another strip on there for him. That's the way they work out the shooting schedule. The strips are made of plastic, and the boards are curved so the strips fit in tightly, and they can be moved any way you want. After that board is made up, and after they get the director's approval, then it's typed into a regular schedule.

Sometimes when we saw the dailies, we would see that there was something wrong with the set. Something just wouldn't look right. Maybe a color was wrong, or the aging was too heavy, something like that. And we'd have to correct it.

We mostly never had that problem at MGM because they used to test the sets before shooting them. They'd light the set and shoot some footage on it; then they'd run it and we could see how it looked. That made sense, but of course it cost money, and after a while they decided to cut it out.

It's pretty hard to anticipate what can go wrong, because there are so many different conditions. On an Esther Williams picture at MGM once, there was a set for an underwater ballet. The art director had to build a set underwater. They made a tank with portholes at the side, and they had to figure out how to get the cameras in. He built the sets first and filled them full of water, and they shot a test and discovered that the refraction of the water was changing the shapes of things. They then had to empty the tank and correct the shapes to make them work with the refraction. Then they shot another test and found that the color wasn't staying. So they had to empty the tank a second time and work on improving the color's staying power. After that, they emptied the tank two more times to correct various things before they could begin shooting.

It was also a tough lighting job, as you can imagine. They made two more lighting tests and finally agreed on the way the set was to be lit. Now the company moves in on the set. All the regular cameraman has to do is sit down and say, "Light it." The thing on the screen with Esther Williams was a glorious shot, a masterful shot. In the projection room when they ran the dailies that night, the art director, Randall Duell, happened to be in there, too. The shot was so good that the actors and the technicians watching gave the *cameraman* a standing ovation. He got up and took a bow. Randall walked out the door of that projection room and never went inside a studio again!

One of the interesting things about my career was that every picture was a different idea, a different challenge. You really couldn't be bored. I'm glad I never went into architecture.

September 1985

San Pedro

Editors' Note: Arthur Lonergan died in January 1989.

FILMOGRAPHY (partial)

1937	*A Star Is Born* (illustrator, dir. William Wellman, United Artists)
1948	*Man-Eater of Kumaon* (dir. Byron Haskin, Universal)
	Pitfall (dir. André de Toth, United Artists)
1949	*Outpost in Morocco* (dir. Robert Florey, United Artists)
1953	*Ride, Vaquero!* (dir. John Farrow, MGM)
	The Actress (dir. George Cukor, MGM)
1955	*It's Always Fair Weather* (dir. Stanley Donen, MGM)
	The Tender Trap (dir. Charles Walters, MGM)
	Ransom! (dir. Alex Segal, MGM)
1956	*Forbidden Planet* (dir. Fred Wilcox, MGM)
1961	*On the Double* (dir. Melville Shavelson, Paramount)
1962	*My Geisha* (dir. Jack Cardiff, Paramount)
	Who's Got the Action? (dir. Daniel Mann, Paramount)
1963	*Papa's Delicate Condition* (dir. George Marshall, Paramount)
	A New Kind of Love (dir. Melville Shavelson, Paramount)
	Who's Been Sleeping in My Bed? (dir. Daniel Mann, Paramount)
1964	*Robinson Crusoe on Mars* (dir. Byron Haskin, Paramount)
1965	*Tickle Me* (dir. Norman Taurog, Allied Artists)
	Red Line 7000 (dir. Howard Hawks, Paramount)
1966	*The Caper of the Golden Bulls* (dir. Russell Rouse, Embassy)
	The Oscar (dir. Russell Rouse, Paramount)

1968   *Yours, Mine and Ours* (dir. Melville Shavelson, United Artists)

        How Sweet It Is (dir. Jerry Paris, Warner Bros.)

1969   *Che!* (dir. Richard Fleischer, Twentieth Century–Fox)

1970   *M.A.S.H.* (dir. Robert Altman, Twentieth Century–Fox)

1971   *Plaza Suite* (dir. Arthur Hiller, Paramount)

Harry Horner, production designer.

HARRY HORNER

Production Designer

≡

Harry Horner was born in Czechoslovakia in 1910. After studying acting and architecture in Vienna he went to work for Max Reinhardt, accompanying him to the United States in 1935.

He now lives in a beautifully appointed house nestled among the tall trees of Pacific Palisades, California. The room where we talk is lined with books in French, German, and English; also with records, paintings (some by him), sculpture, family photographs, a piano, and two Oscars, won for The Heiress *and* The Hustler. *The scene resembles a movie set: the central character is Horner, with his attractive dark-haired wife and the faithful if somewhat mischievous dogs Pablo and Lulu in the background.*

It is obvious from a limp and a weak arm that Horner has suffered a stroke, but his memory is mostly clear and his sense of humor is intact. He is a gentle soul, thoughtful and sensitive, with impeccable, old-world manners. One wonders how he survived in the jungles of Hollywood.

I came to America to do *The Eternal Road* with Max Reinhardt. It was very fortunate for me because if I had stayed in Vienna . . . one doesn't know what would have happened. It wasn't a matter of being a refugee yet, it was still a matter of choice. Very soon it was not a choice.

After *The Eternal Road* was done, there were times of great hardship for me because I sometimes had no work. I was a young foreigner; what could I do? I couldn't be an actor in America, because I couldn't speak the language well. So I did all kinds of things.

When I first came to Hollywood in 1940, I knew Thornton Wilder very well. He asked me if I wouldn't try to do a film design job. He liked my designs on the stage. By that time I had done several things in New York. So I worked on the film version of *Our Town*. Unfortunately, the director, Sam Wood, was not very sympathetic to the play, which shocked me very much. I never in my life knew of a director who didn't like the material and directed it anyway. Anyway, I designed the sets for the movie. I wanted to do it with very little scenery and discussed that with Wilder. I just wanted props that were necessary for the action. That was the way it was done in New York. But they didn't like it, and they wanted more and more scenery. In the end, we did it the way the director wanted it, but very reluctantly.

At that time I had also befriended a gentleman called Sol Lesser, a producer. I designed two Tarzan pictures for him. Those were the films he did primarily. It so happened I liked them. I designed an awful lot of jungles, since they were not shot on location. They had caves and a treehouse; it was a real fantasy.

Because I didn't have enough to do at Sol Lesser's studio, he loaned me out, and I had a chance to work on *The Little Foxes* with Bette Davis, a marvelous play and also very interesting as a film. After *The Little Foxes* I became a little more well known, and finally did *The Heiress*, which was a great opportunity for me. The preparation for that picture lasted quite a long time, and I built a whole house for the set. It was a necessary step. There was a staircase, the famous staircase, which made me famous. I wanted to focus on some object which would dramatize the different callings, or the different appeals, that had to be made to Olivia de Havilland, the heroine. First of all, those houses in New York City at that time had three or four floors, each floor with a different use. The first floor was the living area, and the floor below was the kitchen. We decided that the doctor, Olivia's father, would have his office on the floor below as well. On the second floor the doctor and his daughter had their rooms. The third floor was for guests, and also for the maids and Olivia's aunt, played by Miriam Hopkins.

For all four floors the staircases were built so that one could shoot certain scenes in continuity, going up and down. There were scenes where the heiress was very gay because she had a new lover, and because she felt successful she would run up and down.

Then, when she had the scene at the end where she is so disappointed because the man she loves doesn't come to take her away when he is supposed to, she has to drag herself up the stairs to her own floor. All these different emotions could be expressed through the use of the staircase. The director, William Wyler, liked the idea very much and enjoyed shooting around these different floors.

We researched the house in New York. At that time, there were still certain areas of New York that were unchanged from the way they were a hundred years ago, like Washington Square. The best part of building the house just for the picture was that it had all the features that we wanted and needed for each room. It would have been too much to expect from a real house. We could take the whole thing apart and move walls, and then put it together again. Rooms which looked like solid rooms were not solid at all. You could take a wall out and shoot behind it. That was very helpful and very important; it actually saved a lot of shooting time. We used the house in a symbolic way, with the logic of fantasy.

In 1961 I designed *The Hustler* with Paul Newman and Jackie Gleason. I remember we went around looking at locations, primarily in and around New York. There are some marvelous and ugly places in New York. Robert Rossen and I got along very well. He often told me about the tragedies in his life and his political difficulties, which pained him very much. We finally shot the film in New York because we had found these marvelous locations (miserable and marvelous) in existing pool halls, in black areas. But ultimately Rossen decided not to shoot in those locations because he wanted to be free to move the camera in and out. So I built all these sets of pool halls, which turned out to be just as authentic as the ones we were going to use. The only real pool hall we did use was one that had a marvelous view of the Times Square area.

I enjoyed working with our cinematographer, who was a very well-known German photographer, Eugene Schuftan. The scene that took place in the bathroom, where Paul Newman's thumbs were broken, was a set. That scene was actually my contribution to the film. We had built that old pool hall with that men's room. The original plan was to go in there, shoot, and show the whole scene. I was squeamish about it, so I decided that we would only see the scene from the outside, through the glass door.

The only time that Rossen became difficult was after the end of the picture. What happened was I won an Oscar and Rossen was very hurt because he didn't get one. For some reason he took it out on me. The day after the awards ceremony I walked into his office to thank him for giving me the opportunity, and he said something like, "I don't want to talk about it because I should have won." He was an unhappy man. But I must say, during the picture he was very generous.

I was very fortunate most of the time, because I worked with directors who let me do what I wanted. So I was more or less independent of them, yet at the same time I did depend on their moods. George Cukor was a marvelous person and a wonderful director. For instance, on *Born Yesterday* he said to me, "You do the setups, and I will shoot with them once you have worked out where you want them to sit or stand and act." Cukor involved himself in every aspect, but he let certain things slide when he knew he had people he could trust. We were shooting at the time that Senator McCarthy was in Washington, and we sort of became part of that historical event. We built the sets for the hotel room because it was more easily conceived and easier to shoot.

When I started a movie, I usually made sketches. Then, when the costume designer was engaged, I would show them to her and tell her what my feelings were, and then she could make her own sketches, keeping in mind my general ideas. On *The Heiress* I worked with Edith Head. We were very good friends. She was marvelous at her work and was a brilliant businesswoman, too. That worked very well, and I made some suggestions that she used.

There was a time in Hollywood when they thought that the designer was no more than a draftsman. I did my own drawings because for me it was the most fun. I used to make models at one time, but it took so long, and a good drawing would do the job.

Very often I had the first opportunity to talk to the director about the design of the picture and the sets, only because I was there. The costume designer came into the picture a little later. In New York I had designed my own costumes because it was very convenient for a stage designer to do that. But in Hollywood I would never presume to do that. Sometimes I would have some ideas which would bring out the general character of the role.

I always thought a film shouldn't have too much locale. It should not be the locale that one is attracted to primarily, but the characters and how they fit into the landscape of the action. It would work best if the designer and the costume designer thought alike and also liked each other. It's very important to get along with one another, to be empathetic.

I actually enjoyed my career very, very much. I never really had too much trouble working with people. What I suspect is that I was so "civilized" that they never had the opportunity to do anything about me. I didn't give them the chance. Now life for me is really a different season.

September 1985
Pacific Palisades

FILMOGRAPHY (partial)

1940	*Our Town* (dir. Sam Wood, United Artists)
1941	*The Little Foxes* (dir. William Wyler, RKO)
1943	*Stage Door Canteen* (dir. Frank Borzage, United Artists)
1944	*Winged Victory* (dir. George Cukor, Twentieth Century–Fox)
1947	*A Double Life* (dir. George Cukor, Universal)
1949	*The Heiress* (dir. William Wyler, Paramount)
1950	*Born Yesterday* (co-designer, dir. George Cukor, Columbia)
	Outrage (dir. Ida Lupino, RKO)
1951	*He Ran All the Way* (dir. John Berry, United Artists)
1952	*Beware, My Lovely* (dir. Harry Horner, RKO)
	Red Planet Mars (dir. Harry Horner, United Artists)
	Androcles and the Lion (dir. Chester Erskine, RKO)
1953	*Vicki* (dir. Harry Horner, Twentieth Century–Fox)
1954	*New Faces* (dir. Harry Horner, Twentieth Century–Fox)
1955	*A Life in the Balance* (dir. Harry Horner, Twentieth Century–Fox)
1956	*Man from Del Rio* (dir. Harry Horner, United Artists)
	The Wild Party (dir. Harry Horner, United Artists)

1958	*Separate Tables* (dir. Delbert Mann, United Artists)
1959	*The Wonderful Country* (dir. Robert Parrish, United Artists)
	Step Down to Terror (dir. Harry Keller, Universal)
1961	*The Hustler* (dir. Robert Rossen, Twentieth Century–Fox)
1964	*The Luck of Ginger Coffey* (dir. Irvin Kershner, UK)
1969	*They Shoot Horses, Don't They?* (dir. Sydney Pollack, Twentieth Century–Fox)
1971	*Who Is Harry Kellerman?* (dir. Ulu Grosbard, National General)
1972	*Lady Sings the Blues* (dir. Sidney Furie, Paramount)
1975	*The Black Bird* (dir. David Giler, Columbia)
1976	*Harry and Walter Go to New York* (dir. Mark Rydell, Columbia)
1978	*The Driver* (co-director, with Walter Hill, Twentieth Century Fox)
1979	*Moment by Moment* (dir. Jane Wagner, Universal)
1980	*The Jazz Singer* (dir. Richard Fleischer, EMI)

≡ THE SUPPORTING PLAYERS ≡

Eve Ellman Boyden (à la Clara Bow) in a photo she used for the Central
Casting Agency in the 1920s.

EVE ELLMAN BOYDEN

Extra

Eve Boyden is a remarkably young and still beautiful woman of about eighty. She lives alone in a highrise in downtown San Francisco, where she leads a quiet life. She loves to paint and does so every morning. Much of her own work adorns the walls of her small apartment.

I got a job as an extra because I hadn't been trained for anything. Once or twice I did small bits during the silent days, around 1926 and 1927. I remember working at Paramount, RKO, David Selznick, Warner Brothers, and a couple of the independents.

Central Casting was really a small operation at that time. You took a couple of your photographs over, and they got a little record of your background. Then you'd check in with them every afternoon at about four o'clock, and if they had an assignment, the next morning you'd go to work. Sometimes you'd have to get up at four in the morning to be on the set at seven, all made up and ready to go.

Being an extra, you met a lot of wacky people. Once in a while you'd meet a star like Ronald Colman, who was the lead in *The Night of Love* with Vilma Banky. They had such passionate titles then. I was an extra in a harem scene. It seems to me I was lying around all day on cushions, wearing voluminous chiffon harem pants and a gold lamé jacket. Mr. Colman was very democratic, and we had a little conversation on the set, but nothing really intimate. I remember Vilma Banky as more standoffish. I guess the men were more friendly, especially to the girls in harem pants.

I worked in some pictures that were produced on a shoestring. Once we went to Balboa for four days. The producers had chartered a yacht for four days, and I remember we were in bathing suits all the time. I remember vividly having to climb up and down the side of the yacht. In those days, of course, we wore brassieres (you didn't go out on the street without your hat and gloves), and they insisted I take mine off. Well, I didn't have any support, and I was kind of busty.

It was strictly fun. I never had any ambition; besides, I never saw many extras becoming stars.

Though it was a long time ago, I still miss the movie business because I got so involved in it when I was so young. It spoiled me for real life.

February 1985
San Francisco

CYNTHIA LINDSAY

Stunt Woman

When we arrive at Cynthia Lindsay's Malibu home, we are greeted by two protective chihuahuas. Lindsay's daughter is in the kitchen creating a beautiful salad for our lunch, her husband is on the phone, and two Englishmen sit out on the deck, making notes for a project they are working on with her.

Our hostess is a warm and welcoming presence, unfazed by the chaos that surrounds her. Still beautiful in her mid seventies, it is easy to imagine her as a young swimmer and diver. Her hair, though white, looks blonde, adding a touch of glamour to her appearance.

She is articulate and intelligent. After she quit stunt work, she was a junior writer at MGM for a short while, and went on to write many books and magazine pieces. She has also co-written autobiographies of famous stars.

When we inform her that our next visit is a follow-up with legendary assistant director Artie Jacobson, she exclaims, "But I worked with him!" We encourage her to join us and she immediately accepts, game for the adventure.

Although Jacobson (now ninety-two) doesn't immediately recognize her ("You weren't blonde"), she gives him clues and eventually they have a hilarious reunion, recalling Sun Valley ski scenes from I Met Him in Paris, made in 1937.

Cynthia Lindsay (right), stunt woman, with Laurie Lane on the set of *I Met Him in Paris* (Paramount, 1937). Temperature was 40 below.

I was seventeen. So *you* figure out when I started. *[1933.]* I was still at Girls' Collegiate, a very good girls school in Glendora, California. I adored the school; I was just about to be the president of the student body—but my father lost all his money. I had to go to school, so I landed in Hollywood High, which to me, coming from Girls' Collegiate, was something. I was rather pompous and given to unwanted opinions: "You may think of Noel Coward as a comedy writer, but you can't deny the impact of *The Vortex*," I said to my teacher one day. This poor man just looked at me. I received a "D" for my class contribution.

One day, a friend of mine from Girls' Collegiate came by and she said, "They're having a call for swimmers at the Hollywood Athletic Club for this big aquacade number in a Warner Brothers movie. We can swim free today."

I said, "Let's go."

We were fooling around in the pool, and I did this perfect swan dive off the high board. I surfaced and this man was leaning over the side and said, "Be on the set at seven o'clock tomorrow morning." To my complete surprise, I had been hired for that enormous waterfall number in *Footlight Parade,* which Busby Berkeley directed. *[Sings line from "By a Waterfall."]*

Being gung ho as always and ready to try anything, even all the dangerous things, I was Berkeley's "tryout" girl. I was dispensable but was having such a good time that I never realized I was being exploited.

Then another stunt job came up, then another, and then I joined the Sonja Henie ballet, and I put my talents on ice. I was desperate for work, so when anybody asked if I could do anything, I just said yes. I went to the skating rink and taught myself to skate. I had skated as a child in Greenwich, Connecticut (where I came from), but on double runners. But I learned fast. The first ballet was the Borodin "Prince Igor" suite. We had to be able to skate backwards fast, and that was not easy to learn. The company didn't have skates to fit me—they were too big. I was the last one in the crack-the-whip. This was nightmare time, but I stumbled through it.

I went from skating to falling off horses—you know, *real* stunt work. I had one scene in *Under Your Spell* where I had to wrestle with a Great Dane which was supposedly trying to drown me. I was doubling for Wendy Barrie, who was starring opposite Lawrence Tibbett. Then I doubled for all four of the Yacht Club Boys in another film, then dived with Buster Crabbe in something called *Thrill of a Lifetime.* Then came an offer to go to Japan in a girls' swimming act, actually a seal act. That's when my father said no.

There were many dangerous things, very dangerous things. I worked in the Thorne Smith story, *The Night Life of the Gods,* at Universal. Smith was a very funny writer; the movie wasn't. I was supposed to be a mermaid chased by Neptune. The more I swam away, the more he would stick me with his trident. I couldn't swim very well because I had on this long fish tail and my legs were tied together. The tail was covered with sequins; it was like a long stocking. I think I just had a bra on top, and the rest was bare.

This was all done in a forty-foot tower, and the top was all wide open and had electrical cords. One couldn't get anywhere near them when wet—and of course we were always wet. This was an Olympic swimmer and I, and when we went below water we had to be very careful not to hit the underwater lights. It was just terrifying, because all the grips were saying, "Don't touch those lights—you'll get electrocuted."

So we did the scene, and the director, Lowell Sherman, was forty feet below, applauding, and as I came down he looked at me and said, "Good God, girl, you're Henry Hobart's daughter!"

I said, "Yes."

"Does your father know what you're doing?" he asked.

I said, "No."

He said, "You could have been killed."

I said, "Well, suppose it was somebody else. Would you have cared? Would you have cared if you had killed another swimmer?"

He said, "I suppose so, but not as much as a friend's daughter."

So the Olympic swimmer and I went to the front office and said, "Don't you think $7.50 a day and no overtime (and we worked twenty-four hours straight on this one) is kind of low?"

The guy said, "Do you want to work in pictures again?"

We said, "Sure."

Then he said, "Then $7.50 is just right."

And that's the way it was, generally, before the Screen Actors Guild. There was no protection for the stunt people. There was one skiing scene in a picture called *I Met Him in Paris*. We were in Sun Valley for six weeks. Boy, was I a happy kid. I adored it. It was a Wesley Ruggles–directed picture, with Claudette Colbert, Melvyn Douglas, and Robert Young. It was a lovely movie, written by Claude Binyon, who was a wonderful writer. I just had a great time, and the girls and I became chums.

Paramount had a contract with Union Pacific, which had just built the Sun Valley Lodge. We girls were put up in a little hotel in Haley, a nearby small town, heated by sulphur springs. It smelled quite a lot until you got used to it. The stars stayed at the lodge.

All the girls had one line in the picture and had to ski. I said, yes, of course I could ski. I'd never been on a pair of skis.

I kept waiting for my big line while we were having a fabulous time. Wesley Ruggles called me over one day and said, "Cynthia, you're on." I didn't need any make-up because I was so tan; all I needed was lipstick. I looked great. I saw my name in lights. He said, "What I want you to do is just go to the top of that mountain over there. See where that one tree is? Go up there. Do you see those cows that are just standing there?"

I said yes.

He said, "The studio is complaining that everything is so beautiful that people will think it's a glass *[fake]* shot. So what I want you to do is, when I yell on this loudspeaker system, I want you to poke the cows, and I want you to make them move down the mountain."

I thought I might get a chance to say, "Hi, there," or something. Not at all. He just called, "Okay, Cynthia! Start your cows!" So I started my cows—I poked them with my ski pole—and followed them down, and that was the end of the scene. I never got in. I was never even photographed.

One day on another picture I was doubling for Mary Astor. The film starred Mary Astor and Robert Young. They had hired some of the Olympic kids. I was friends with this one boy before, because we had worked together. In the scene, I was supposed to fall, he was supposed to ski down and then pick me up. Well, we looked at this setup and what the studio had provided was plate glass, so we'd be sure and fall. It was covered with bleached corn flakes and some gypsum over the corn flakes.

I said to the director, "Look, I'm really scared. If we fall on this, we're going to get sliced."

So they called in the producer and he said, "Are you the troublemaker?"

I said, "I'm not being a troublemaker, I'm just afraid, sir. I'm afraid to fall on this glass."

He said, "Well, you know, you can drown in your own bathtub."

I said, "I don't think that's particularly apropos." Unfortunately, I always spoke better English than some of the executives.

This one didn't like that. He just said, "Huh? What are you? French or something?"

At any rate, they took the glass away, and then they brought in more corn flakes and then put oil under the cornflakes so that we would slip, but at least we weren't going to fall on glass.

Bob Young came on the set to watch this being shot, and he looked at me and said, "Oh, my God, Little Greensleeves." I was learning to ski on the set, and naturally fell down all the time, and I usually wore a green sweater. Bob said, "My God, are you still falling down?"

Well, we did the scene. Then they wanted to put the glass back, but I was smart. I called Boris Karloff at home. He was a beloved friend of the James Gleasons (my future in-laws) and therefore of mine. Boris always loved me. I was kind of a second child to him. At that time Boris was one of the heads of the Screen Actors Guild, and I told him what they were doing. Forty minutes later a person came on the set from the guild. It was just the day the guild started, which made a real union member out of me. The guild representative said, "You can't do this. Guild rules. Number one: give them a raise. Number two: make this safe for them."

We people who did all these things were very snobbish about extras because they got twice as much money as we did and all they did was sit. I always proudly said I never did extra work.

But we stunt people were expendable. One of the girls I worked with broke her nose in the waterfall number in *Footlight Parade.* We had to dive from ten-foot diving boards into three and a half feet of water. That was not easy, because you had to break immediately on hitting the water. This was so the Berkeley beauties would have their breasts show above the water in the close-ups. I missed one day and scraped my nose on a Berkeley girl's rhinestone-studded cap. These caps were molded to look like hair, blonde and brunette, to come down and go across our breasts. They were quite sexy-looking, and I was a little brown mouse and terribly shy. When I first looked in a mirror with my "nymph" outfit on, I was agreeably surprised. I hadn't even been out with a gentleman or ever been kissed, for that matter. I was really young and very, very innocent. But I was just so gung ho—oh, anything for the movie and Mr. Berkeley. It took a lot of make-up to cover my nose so that I could keep on working. They put medicine on it first, then make-up, and I wasn't in any close-ups anyway.

One day some important visitors from abroad came to the set and Berkeley brought them over. They were royalty or of some great importance, and the heads of the studio brought them to see the already famous water ballet. Berkeley called me over and said, "Kid" (he always called me "kid" because the other girls were a lot older and more experienced in every way), "I want you to try that slide." I tried it, and it threw me off the side.

When I came up from the water I said, "Mr. Berkeley, it's too fast. They're going to get hurt. I'm hurt now." That didn't matter. I was still healing from the skinned nose, and I was still kind of battered.

He said, "Well, we're going to have to slow it down. Okay, lunch, everybody." He hoped the royalty would come back after lunch to see the scene. So after they slowed the slide down he said, "Okay, kid, try it now."

I was easily disposed of. So I got on the slide again. Well, they had slowed it down with raw cement. I hit the water and my poor bottom was raw. The cement had ripped off the back of my suit, though I didn't know it. I pulled up out of the water and everybody was giggling. Somebody came with a towel. I was stark naked in the back, and raw. I said, "It's not going to work, Mr. Berkeley."

He was very good about it, very comforting, and sorry I was hurt. He was nice to the girls. I liked him. But we were disposable. I have trouble with my back to this day. I never thought about the connection till this minute. I never went to a doctor, just went home. My mother used something called Unguentine, and the scrape gradually healed, though it hurt a lot to sit down.

We had to take care of ourselves. I suppose if you broke a limb, they would have sent you to the hospital. When the girl broke her nose she went to the hospital, but I don't know if the studio paid for it or not.

If we had an accident, the first person to come over was the assistant director. We went to him for everything. There may have been a doctor or a nurse around, but I don't remember any. And there should have been on those movies. The guilds did an incredible job; everything's changed now.

I dived with Buster Crabbe, and I swam with Weissmuller in a film of which I don't remember the name. This is all pre–Esther Williams. It's what gave Esther Williams the idea, or gave the studio the idea about Esther Williams. Buster was an Olympic star himself and he once played one of the Tarzans. I wasn't in any of them. I'm surprised they didn't have me wear a monkey suit and swing from a tree, considering the other things I had to do. I might have been good at it, and my father wouldn't have recognized me.

August 1993
Malibu

Fayard (right) and Harold Nicholas, tap dancers, in *Sun Valley Serenade* (Twentieth Century–Fox), 1941.

≡

FAYARD NICHOLAS

Tap Dancer

≡

*On our first visit we find Fayard Nicholas, of the fabulous Nicholas
Brothers dance duo, seated in the library of the Motion Picture and
Television Fund. A small, dapper man who is all smiles, he looks entirely
too young and full of the devil to be living in a retirement home. But
the presence of an elegant cane leaning against the couch gives a
clue as to why he is no longer dancing.*

*Several years later, we return to check in on Nicholas, who is now
seventy-nine. He is dressed in a colorful jogging suit, low black boots,
and a baseball cap that says "Let's Tap!" The intervening years have
been kind to him; he looks unchanged. But one important thing has
changed, and he demonstrates it for us in the hall: he can dance
again, thanks to a hip replacement.*

*The years have also brought him and his brother, Harold, many
honors, including a Kennedy Center Award, and soon an award from
the French government, and he is now much more aware of the
success and recognition that the Nicholas Brothers have enjoyed.
What he is reluctant to acknowledge, however, is the racial prejudice
that marked the era we are talking about. Occasionally an edge of
bitterness cuts into his uproarious laughter, but he quickly recovers
and reverts to accentuating the positive. By the end of the interview
he has danced all around the issue with his trademark grace and
agility.*

My mother and father were musicians, and they had an orchestra that played at the Standard Theater on South Street in Philadelphia. My father played the drums and my mother played the piano. Their act was called "The Collegians."

Every day after school I would go to the theater where my parents were playing. They played for such artists as Louis Armstrong, Buck and Bubbles, Adelaide Hall, and many others—all the big stars. I would get as close as possible to my dad as he was playing the drums, and I'd watch the performers on the stage. He was playing in the pit and I was watching these entertainers. I'd think to myself, "Jeepers, they're having fun up there! I'd like to be doing something like that."

So just by watching I taught myself how to dance, and I taught myself how to sing, and I picked up the drums just by seeing what my father did. I tried to imitate him. But I never took a lesson in anything. Then I taught my younger brother, Harold, and my little sister.

My brother and I had these little routines that we had created. I choreographed them. One evening when my parents came home from the theater they saw all the lights on and asked us, "What are you doing up? You should be in bed. You have school tomorrow."

I said to them, "Sit down. We want to show you something." So we started doing all these different routines, and after we finished, my parents looked at each other and said, "Hey, we've got something here."

They gave up their orchestra to manage us. My brother was seven and I was eleven. Eventually my sister couldn't take the late hours and had to drop out. We worked every theater in Philadelphia.

New York came later. We were working at a theater in Philadelphia called the Pearl. The biggest acts worked there: Cab Calloway, the Mills Brothers, Earl "Fatha" Hines, Count Basie.

In those days they called us the "show-stoppers." Everywhere we went we stopped the show. Nobody ever wanted to follow our act, so they always put us in the closing spot.

We played all over the East: Baltimore, Philadelphia, New York, and as far west as Chicago. Everybody was hearing about the Nicholas Kids. New York started to hear about us. We started in 1930, I think. This was vaudeville, remember? We started to get a reputation, and we heard soon that the manager of the Lafayette Theater in New York was asking around, "Who the hell are these Nicholas Kids?" Finally, he made a special trip to Philadelphia to see us.

The night he saw us we stopped the show like we always did. He came backstage to talk to our parents. "I just saw your two sons and I think they're pretty good, and the folks really like them. I'm the manager of the Lafayette Theater in New York City and I'd like to book them there."

My dad said, "If the price is right, we'll be there." Dad and Mother, they took care of all the business. All we wanted to do was get up on that stage and perform. We didn't know anything about money. They always kept us sharp, dressed us alike, like twins.

We opened in New York at the Lafayette Theater. Another sensation. We just stopped the show. All the agents from all over Manhattan were trying to sign us up. But my daddy was wise, he wouldn't sign with anybody. At that time, the manager of the Cotton Club and the manager of Connie's Inn (those were big nightclubs in New York), both of them wanted us. Some friends told us, "Your best bet is the Cotton Club." Connie's Inn was a good place, too, but Cab Calloway and Duke Ellington played at the Cotton Club, so that was for us.

During that time we made a short two-reeler for Warner Brothers called *Pie, Pie, Blackbird,* with Eubie Blake. That's back when Warner Brothers was called Vitaphone. It was our very first film and such a thrill for us. The producer had seen us at the Lafayette Theater and had spoken to our parents about our doing the movie. When we saw it in the theater I watched myself and thought, "I didn't know I looked that good!" And I was watching my little brother tapping away, thinking what a little thing he still was.

Well, right after that we went into the Cotton Club, the world-famous Cotton Club. We opened with Cab Calloway and his orchestra. They put on such a beautiful show, with these lovely showgirls, great dancing, and marvelous comedy acts. They decided to close with the Nicholas Brothers. Now we were the Nicholas Brothers, because we were growing up. It was a black show, but black people couldn't come in. It's really unbelievable.

Well, we stopped the show every night. Everybody came to see us—the Broadway stars, the movie stars. But here's a strange thing that happened. When we were working with Duke Ellington, they wanted the whole show to appear downtown on Broadway, at the Paramount Theater, which showed a movie and a stage show. Well, we opened and stopped the show. Our first time on Broadway and what a big thrill for us! After our number we went to our dressing room to shower and rest, and all of a sudden there was a knock at the door. My mother opened it and a woman said to her, "Oh, Mrs. Nicholas, your boys are wonderful. What a show they put on."

My mother thanked her and the woman said, "But they can't work here."

"Why not?" Mother asked.

The woman explained that she was with the organization that prevented cruelty to children. Working five shows a day was regarded as cruelty to children. She didn't know how much energy we had. We could have done ten shows a day. So we couldn't work downtown anymore.

But uptown we could work till the wee hours of the morning. Do you know why? Because the gangsters were running the

Cotton Club. They were paying off the law, that's why. We stayed there for two years and didn't work anyplace else.

We'd sleep all day, or at least until three in the afternoon, then our tutor would come to the apartment and we'd have a few hours with her. We didn't have to rehearse because we'd get a routine down once and didn't need to practice it again. I worked out the routines with my father. He had a great influence on me. He couldn't dance, but he knew what looked good. He'd say, "Don't do what other dancers do, even though you might do it better. Do your own routines. Another thing: Don't look at your feet. You're not entertaining yourself, you're entertaining those people in the audience. They're the ones looking at your feet, not you."

I always liked to dance on a wooden floor, but I never asked anybody for a special floor or had one made. Whatever the floor was, I tried to perform on that floor. If it was too slippery, I would ask them to kind of tone it down; I didn't want to be slipping all over the place. If it was a glass floor, I would ask them to work on it. I know that Eleanor Powell had a special dance mat that she traveled with wherever she appeared, whether it was Las Vegas or London. Maybe I should have taken my own floor.

We were really mixing it up with the Hollywood stars who came to the Cotton Club: Charlie Chaplin, Harold Lloyd, Al Jolson, Fanny Brice, Gloria Swanson, the Marx Brothers. We'd sit with them and order orange juice. The other entertainers would be watching us from backstage. The manager gave us special permission only because we were kids. Remember, black people weren't allowed out there. They didn't like colored people sitting there with the white people.

We were so young then that we never did think about discrimination. There's really not much discrimination in show business. Everywhere we went, we were welcome. We were among the first blacks to work at the Coconut Grove. We were the first to work in many places. We went to places where blacks couldn't go. I'm not proud of that. When I found out about it, I didn't like it and would not go anymore. Who needs it? Maybe we opened some doors. I am proud of that.

Sam Goldwyn saw us one night at the Cotton Club and wanted us for a film called *Kid Millions,* starring Eddie Cantor, Ethel Merman, George Murphy, Ann Sothern. That was our first and it was 1934. By then we were with the William Morris Agency.

When Mr. Goldwyn signed us he didn't want us to do the same routines as the ones he saw, so we worked with the studio choreographer. I remember working with Seymour Felix, but we did most of the work. My brother was my best pupil, the very best, number one. He worked so hard that I'd say, "Brother, let's rest. We'll do it tomorrow." But he'd insist we keep on working. A lot of dancers don't know what hard work it was.

The steps would just come to me while I was fooling around. Then my brother would copy it. If he had any trouble I'd break down the steps and then let him try again. When I teach I don't count; I never did. *[Snaps fingers and taps feet.]* When I hear the music I get the beat—yeah!

We made over forty movies. I liked them all. My brother's favorite is *Stormy Weather,* with Lena Horne and Cab Calloway. Remember how we danced down these big stairs and jumped over each other's heads? We mostly made our pictures on the back lot. You know Hollywood in those days—they made their own Argentina. We didn't have to go, for *Down Argentine Way.*

We played the Coconut Grove here in Hollywood; we also played some theaters in San Francisco. But the Cotton Club was kind of like home. We could always go back there whenever we finished a job somewhere else.

I think if I had a chance to do it all over I would have done it the same, but been a little wiser. There are a few things I would have changed. I think I would have tried to learn more about the business end, gotten more involved. Harold and I just wanted to get on that stage and entertain. That's what we loved. We didn't think about money at all; we just weren't interested.

We should have paid more attention to how we were presented in the movies, too. I think what I would do today, if I started all over again, would be to get more into acting. More versatility, 'cause I had it—we had it—in us. Not just singing and dancing, and not shuffling or being a butler or washing dishes or cleaning up. We wouldn't want that.

I think we're being discovered by a new generation. Maybe they saw us in *That's Entertainment.* Sometimes when they come to see me they say, "Mr. Nicholas, I've never seen anybody dance like that before. How did you do it?"

And I always answer, "Very carefully."

They always come up with that damn question, about being black. I had a fight with some guy who interviewed me a few years ago. It was a nice interview, but he starts off his article and says, "Fayard Nicholas, the black dancer." Why didn't he say just "Fayard Nicholas, the dancer"? You wouldn't say, "Fred Astaire, the white dancer." Why do you have to put that in? Everybody knows I'm black, what the heck? What do you have to keep reminding them for?

I don't recall ever seeing any black guys behind the camera. If there was, there wasn't many. It was hard to get in the unions in those days, I guess. On the set, it was just like a happy family. We were all performers, and we looked at each other as human beings. It wasn't, "He's white, he's black or yellow or red." It wasn't like that on movie sets.

When we came out here to Los Angeles, we stayed at a private house that we were renting. Eddie "Rochester" Anderson, he built this house. Wait, let's see if I have the exact address: 3706 Van Ness Avenue. *[Laughs.]*

My first wife and I, we bought a house. It was in a nice area where we lived, near Exposition. Everybody stayed there—you name it, they were there. It wasn't just a black area. A funny thing, my wife and I were the first ones to have a television in that area. It was that television that was round, black and white. So all of the neighbors would come over and we had a packed house. We had to turn them away every night: "You come tomorrow. You come the next night."

I don't recall that there were any places we couldn't go. I think we were the first black entertainers to play the Coconut Grove, at that time. That was in 1934. Long time. And everything was great. I mean, people just loved us. They loved us for our talent. They didn't look at us as black or white. We were the Nicholas Brothers, not the black Nicholas Brothers or the white Nicholas Brothers. Just the Nicholas Brothers. That's the way they looked at it; that was our identity. When they see us on the stage or in the movies they're looking at the Nicholas Brothers. They're looking at the talent. Not black or white or red—it's the talent.

At the Coconut Grove on opening night, all the celebrities were there. It was *the* place. After we did the show (we stopped the show cold) they couldn't get enough. They wanted more, more, and more, but I was so tired. My brother and I would do dance after dance, dance after dance, and I was getting so tired. I said to my brother, "Something's got to be done. I can't stand this any longer."

He said, "Well, what we gonna do?"

I said, "I'll tell you what. Let's talk to the people. We go out there, we do our first number, then we go to the microphone and say, 'Good evening, ladies and gentlemen, we're glad you came to see us.' We're resting now." I said, "Let's put a little singing in the act, too, to catch our breath. We'll dance for them, but let's take it easy. All this dancing is killing me!" *[Laughs.]*

So now we are entertainers. Before, we was dancers. Now we were entertainers, because we would do everything: we'd sing, dance, talk to the people, tell them jokes. There were times my brother would sing a song and I'd conduct the orchestra. They loved that, they just loved that. When I directed the orchestra, I'd use everything: my hands, my elbows, my head, my feet, my buns. *[Laughs.]* So they're listening to him, but they're watching me!

After we did our act we went to our dressing room, and we're drying off and relaxing. The head waiter comes back and says, "Mr. Nicholas?"

I say, "Yes?"

He says, "There's a wonderful lady out there in the audience would like to see you."

I said, "Yes? Who is it?"

He says, "Bette Davis."

So we went out there and we sat down at her table. She says, "What'll you have?"

I say, "Some orange juice."

She says, "Oh, you guys are so wonderful, I just cried when you did your performance."

I say, "Thank you, Miss Davis, thank you very much." I say, "I cry when I see *your* movies." *[Laughs.]*

Ruby Keeler also came to see us. She took a few lessons from me, right there at the Ambassador Hotel. This was in 1934. And Betty Grable took a few lessons from me. You see? You see how performers are? I think there's less prejudice in show business than in any other business. Less. There is some there, but less. So when performers get together, they appreciate each other, they respect each other for their talent.

We were always class—class and grace. I don't think they would dare ask us to play something like a butler, because they never did ask us. But they never did give us any lines to say in the movies. Only one time they did. It was in a picture called *The Big*

Broadcast of 1936. We were part of this radio station that was run by Jack Oakie and Henry Wadsworth. They were shanghaied somewhere, so we took over the radio station. We did our thing and we had a couple of lines.

We loved that, but in other films they never did write us into the script. They would always have us sing and dance. It was so wonderful, because we were the hit of all those films. Maybe we were on the screen for about five minutes.

I'm not really bitter about it because it made us famous all over the world. There's nowhere in the world you can go that they don't know about the Nicholas Brothers. That's why I'm not so bitter, because we headlined everywhere. In this country, too, we headlined everywhere. It was so wonderful years ago when we would go to Europe. At the airport, people would be waiting there for us. On the television, radio, the newspapers: like they did for the Beatles. Remember when they came to America? That's the way they were for us in Europe. Only on the screen for five minutes, but they remembered.

The first movie we did for Twentieth Century–Fox was *Down Argentine Way.* When they had the preview, the people in the audience were whistling, stomping their feet, clapping their hands. The operator in the projection room had to rewind the film to show it over again. And at some theaters they had to do it twice.

So you see, because of that they should have starred us in movies. But Twentieth Century–Fox did give us a five-year contract because of that sensation of *Down Argentine Way* in the theaters. They would have found a way to star us if we had been two little white guys. We would have been starred, after that sensation—because they did it with the Ritz Brothers. But I say I'm not *too* bitter.

But, like I said, those films made us famous. Let me tell you something else. After *Down Argentine Way,* some of the people who saw the film, they'd go and tell their friends, "Oh, you should see those Nicholas Brothers, they're sensational. Oh, my goodness."

And then the friend would say, "What time do they go on?" They'd find out the time and then come into the theater just at the right time to see us. After they see us, they walk out the door. *[Laughs.]*

Then the manager of one of the theaters, after this happened, changed the marquee from DOWN ARGENTINE WAY: STARRING DON AMECHE, BETTY GRABLE AND CARMEN MIRANDA to DOWN ARGENTINE WAY: STARRING THE NICHOLAS BROTHERS. Only on the screen five minutes. Isn't that amazing?

Back then I knew some of the black actors. I knew Hattie McDaniel and Stepin Fetchit. We never did get on that subject, about prejudice. We had such a good time wherever we'd go. We were always invited out to these marvelous homes in Beverly Hills with all the movie stars. We didn't have *time* to think about prejudice and that stuff. So everything was okay. I mean, we knew it was bad, and we would fight it all the time. But change was coming slowly, it came so slowly. Like now—oh, my goodness, look at Eddie Murphy, look at Bill Cosby, look at everybody. Oh, my goodness.

When Hattie McDaniel won the Academy Award for best supporting actress in *Gone with the Wind,* I was so happy for her. I wasn't there that night, but when I'd go over to her house I'd tell her how proud I was of her.

Eddie "Rochester" Anderson, he didn't talk about it, either. We all knew it was there and that we were fighting to make it better— with our talent, in motion pictures and television, radio, theater, nightclubs. We tried to make it better for everybody, not just for us. Like they say, we are the pioneers. We're the reason Bill Cosby is where he is now. Sammy Davis, Jr., and Harry Belafonte used to say the same thing: that we were the pioneers.

Sammy Davis married a Swedish woman, Mai Britt. But what about that other thing, before Mai Britt? With Kim Novak? There's a little story about Sammy and Kim Novak. First she was going with Frank Sinatra, and then Sammy took her away from him! The president of Columbia Pictures, Harry Cohn—he called them into his office. He says, "Wait a minute. Sammy, I have twenty million dollars wrapped up in this lady. I don't care about you having a little fling and all, but please don't get married. If that's what you're thinking about, don't do it. I'll lose all this money."

I guess they listened to him, because they didn't get married. And then, to get rid of all that publicity, Sammy married a black girl. But he didn't stay married long. It was just for show, to quiet down the whole thing. Nothing like that would happen today. Later, Sammy got a girl who looked as much like Kim Novak as possible.

The last movie I made in Hollywood (it was by myself) was called *The Liberation of L. B. Jones*. It was a dramatic role. I played Benny, the assistant to L. B. Jones. Roscoe Lee Browne played the title role. I was the assistant in this funeral parlor. It was a thing about prejudice. It was a white and black cast. I had a big speaking role in it, a real part. I enjoyed making that. The director, William Wyler—oh, he was crazy about me.

Tallulah Bankhead was wonderful. I loved her. She loved us, and she's from Alabama. But she didn't like this prejudice thing that was going on. There is some show people who are bastards. Right now I can't think of who they are. *[Laughs.]*

There are very few people in show business who are really prejudiced. I've been around them, but how I fight it is with my talent. See, I can be on the stage with this bigot—whoever he might be. I get up there and stop that show. He just stands there, mouth wide open. The people out there, they like what they see of the Nicholas Brothers. Like I told you, they don't see black or white; they see the talent.

And I guess the bigot—whoever he is—doesn't like it that we're a bigger success than he is. Thinking, "Oh, I'm white, I should be better than they are." But an audience, they don't look at it that way. They want to be entertained.

Did you know that three countries—the United States of America, South Africa, and Australia—are three of the most prejudiced countries in the world? Did you know that? Those three. In Australia they have those aborigines. Listen: My brother and I, we did a show in Sydney, Australia. This was in the seventies. We were playing in one of the big hotels. It was our show, nobody but the Nicholas Brothers and a big orchestra. We did an hour show, and sometimes an hour and a half. They had our names in lights outside the hotel, two feet tall.

We made some friends, and this little girl said to me one night, "I want to take you to a nice nightclub."

I said, "Fine, fine."

So we go there, and there's a doorman there. And as we approached, he called us over to the side. He didn't want to let me in. I guess he thought I was an aborigine. But she told him that I was an American and an entertainer. When she said "Nicholas Brothers," he knew right away, because all our movies played down there. I come up there with this blonde, blue-eyed girl. Hey! But she says, "Don't you know who he is?"

Then he says, "Really, well, go right in." Now ain't that terrible? Ain't that bad? That's the same type of thing that's happening in this country.

And South Africa, oh, forget it. Once I was in Paris and my agent there says, "Say, Nicholas, I'd like to book you in South Africa." (See, we played the continent, all over Europe and North Africa and Asia.)

I say, "You can't do that."

He says, "Sure I can. You're very popular down there."

I say, "What do you mean, I'm very popular?"

He says, "All your movies have played down there."

I say, "Well, only the black people go to see them."

He says, "No, the white people go, too."

I said, "Get outta here." Then I say, "You know how it is down there with black people. How are we gonna arrange this? Where we gonna stay?"

He says, "When you go there, they will declare you white."

I say, "What do you mean, they're gonna declare me white?"

He says, "That way, you can stay at the best hotels and you'll be treated royally. Because you are an American. You're not from there."

I said, "I guess I just stay down there a little while and get the hell out of there. I can't stay there too long, being declared white." *[Laughs.]*

He says, "Because of the way you act and the way you handle yourself, they'll know you're not from down there."

I say, "I don't want to go." Being declared white? No, no. What kind of stuff is that? But that's the way a lot of black entertainers have gone down there.

Like I say, South Africa, Australia, and the United States of America. Oh, this country's getting better. It's not perfect, but it's getting better.

February 1985
August 1993
Woodland Hills

FILMOGRAPHY (partial)

1932   *Pie, Pie, Blackbird* (short)
       Barbershop Blues (short)

1934   *Kid Millions* (dir. Roy del Ruth, United Artists)

1935   *The Big Broadcast of 1936* (dir. Norman Taurog, Paramount)
       An All Colored Vaudeville Show (Vitaphone)

1936   *Black Network* (short)

1937   *Calling All Stars* (dir. Herbert Smith, UK)

1940   *Down Argentine Way* (dir. Irving Cummings, Twentieth Century–Fox)
       Tin Pan Alley (dir. Walter Lang, Twentieth Century–Fox)

1941   *The Great American Broadcast* (dir. Archie Mayo, Twentieth Century–Fox)
       Sun Valley Serenade (dir. H. Bruce Humberstone, Twentieth Century–Fox)

1942   *Orchestra Wives* (dir. Archie Mayo, Twentieth Century–Fox)

1943   *Stormy Weather* (dir. Andrew Stone, Twentieth Century–Fox)

1948   *The Pirate* (dir. Vincente Minelli, MGM)

1949   *The Bandit* (dir. Alberto Lattuada, Lux Film Corp.)

1970   *The Liberation of L. B. Jones* (dir. William Wyler, Columbia)

Daniel Selznick, at age 6, with his father, producer David Selznick, in 1942.

DANIEL
SELZNICK

Son and Grandson

═══

Daniel Selznick, son of David O. Selznick and grandson of Louis B. Mayer, was born into the royal family of Hollywood in 1936. Being a crown prince has not been easy for him, and he carries the weight of it to this day.

He is a large, gentle man who seems to be existentially weary. His successes as an independent producer have been modest and his self-confidence is meager.

His office is in a small bungalow on a Beverly Hills sidestreet which he shares with another producer. He is eager to please and quite candid in discussing the dynamics of his family. He speaks lovingly of both his father and grandfather, but at the same time seems to be preoccupied with living up to them.

In a strange way I don't think I was completely aware of my father's and grandfather's positions in Hollywood until after their respective deaths. I mean their historical importance. From a very early age I was aware that my grandfather was the head of one of the major studios—the one that, by its own advertisements (the lion metaphor) was the king of the jungle. My father was obviously a respected producer, but I went to school with the children of a lot of respected producers.

In those days, most kids in Beverly Hills were in a public school. When I was in elementary school there were a lot of references to *Gone with the Wind,* which my father did not allow me to see until I was ten. (He didn't think I'd appreciate it.) When I finally saw it, I was allowed to have my whole class attend. We had a screening at the studio, and it was so awesome. Only then did I realize that he really had made this classic.

I'd traveled with him and I had seen that people were sort of in awe of him. As I got older and moved in wider and wider circles people began asking, "Are you related to David Selznick?" And they said it like, "Are you related to the Maharishi?" Eventually I began to realize his impact.

I went on a lot of MGM sets because I was allowed to go on a soundstage whenever I visited my grandfather for lunch. Of course, I was also allowed to visit sets in my father's studio, which was down on Washington Boulevard. I remember going on the set of *Since You Went Away*—in fact, that's where I first met Jennifer Jones. I remember going on the hacienda set of *Duel in the Sun.* I remember going on the courtroom set of *The Paradine Case.* I remember being there for the flood sequence in *Portrait of Jennie,* watching Jennifer and Joe Cotten being flooded.

My brother Jeffrey and I, as children, mostly saw our father on weekends, because we were up very early to go to school and we went to bed early. He'd come home from the studio and kiss us goodnight when we had already had our dinner and were ready for bed. We had our six o'clock dinner with the governess. The family did a lot of things together on weekends. There was also quite an active social life that we participated in.

After my parents divorced I went east with my mother. She became a theatrical producer. It was not like our huge house in California, where we had a live-in staff of eight. In my mother's New York apartment there was just one person living in, so I was answering the door, helping out. It was a big change and it was wonderful, much more human, much more normal. You know, kids want to be like everybody else, and I ended up having that whole boarding school experience of being picked up in a limo and asking to be dropped off before you got back to school. My parents were sensitive; they knew we wanted to be normal kids. And they "allowed" it, once they got the message. In elementary school, if we were taken to school by the chauffeur, he was not in uniform but wearing khakis, and we were taken in a station wagon.

My parents' divorce was pretty traumatic. They tried not to make it too bad for us. They did what all parents try to do—you know, telling us, "You'll be seeing me, we'll spend more time together." And, in fact, I would have a full Sunday with my father instead of a half Sunday. In a sense, it was more time together. But it still was very painful.

I didn't feel it was my fault, the way some kids do. I'd read the newspaper accounts: "David O. Selznick has fallen in love with his discovery, Jennifer Jones. When is he going to finalize his break with Irene?" But my parents always wanted me to know that it wasn't that simple. It wasn't just another woman. And I think it wasn't.

My grandfather represented a certain lifestyle which was, by its very definition, grander. Even though my father was known to be a very extravagant man, he was, by personality, so funny and warm and human and accessible—emotionally accessible—that I never put him on a pedestal, nor did my brother. My grandfather put himself on his own pedestal. It was not that he was less human, but that he had a little bit of the . . . czar? . . . I'm trying to think of the right image for him. What would be the right metaphor? Maybe in the comic strip, "The Little King."

It wasn't until I was much older, and my mother arranged for me to go out and stay with my grandfather and his second wife, that I began to see him from the perspective of being a grown-up.

I get crazed when I see him portrayed as some sort of Jewish caricature, chasing women around tables and pinching actresses' asses. He did not do that, to my knowledge, in front of me, or even in private. He had a circumspect attitude toward women. He put them on pedestals.

The other thing that people so seldom read was the absolute adoration that the people who worked for him had. People who were just there for years. The secretary, the driver, the cook . . . they just adored him. So dear with him. A secretary, I think, had cancer. And he covered all the bills and took care of everything. He was a complete father figure to them.

I just assumed, always, that I'd be in the movie business. I think we all did. My father clearly wanted me to go into the business. He also thought I might be in the theater. There were times, after his death, when I was working for Universal in a wonderful bicoastal job where I was literally spending twenty-six weeks a year on each coast, that I could imagine him saying, "That's perfect for Danny. I saw him in Hollywood and New York, and this is just perfect for him."

I got mixed messages from my mother. She thought I should pursue whatever I was good at. I spent a lot of time in the sixties in journalism, and she thought that was terrific because I was writing, and she's always been a big fan of my writing. I had studied English and American Lit at Harvard, and I took a lot of creative writing courses.

In college I also studied playwriting. It was a very select and hard-to-get-into group. I actually had a play put on. I sort of figured at that time that I would first get into the theater and then into movies later. (I always thought the movies would be there for me—a mistaken assumption, of course.)

As a child, having a lot of approval from my grandfather was a fabulous thing to have. It is probably not as good a thing to have as one gets older, because if you really think that you know it all and you have the abilities, you don't feel you have to go out and sell yourself (and it's been said of me that I'm not very good at selling myself). I have my own kind of drive. It's just not my mother's or father's.

I think I really don't know how to "play the game." If I knew, I would probably play it. To me, it's handling yourself with a kind of outrageous confidence, which I believe would be unbecoming to me, given my circumstances.

In the silent picture days, when my grandfather started, the rules of the game weren't even set yet. They were inventing them as they went along. My father probably played the game, but those were different times and different games. Actually, he played his own game. He made up his own rules and occasionally even broke some of them.

My grandfather once said to me, "One day all this will be yours." I guess it was when I was about eight. My father never said that. He may have implied it, but, you know, the Selznick studio was never "all this." The Selznick studio was by comparison only a few rinky-dink soundstages down the street in Culver City. My father would never have said, "All this will be yours." My father would have said, "You're going to have your own."

September 1985
Beverly Hills

MAXINE MARX

Daughter

Maxine Marx is the only child of Chico and Betty Marx. She grew up in the rarified atmosphere of the New York and Hollywood entertainment world, attending theater and movie openings the way most children go to birthday parties.

Now in her late sixties, she lives in a large, comfortable apartment on New York's Upper West Side. Until recently, she worked as a casting director in a major advertising agency.

She is quite articulate, and her speech reflects her many years spent in therapy. She has no difficulty revealing intimate details of her life.

In addition to being a skirt chaser, Chico was a compulsive gambler. He started gambling at the age of nine or ten, learning from his father. My father could never be trusted with money. You couldn't give him fifty dollars to go anywhere. I remember when he hit a very bad time in his life, when he and his band were in Chicago. I went out to visit him. Every day we stopped at a cigar store on our way downtown. I would say, "Daddy, is your bookie in there?" And he would laugh and tell me I was beginning to sound like my mother.

Chico's name originated when he and the brothers were in vaudeville. They traveled with a guy who loved to make up nicknames. In those days women were called chicks, so he was known as Chicko *[pronounced CHICK-oh]*, the chick chaser. It was spelled C-H-I-C-K-O originally, but once, in a program, it came out "Chico" *[Cheeko]*, and he never bothered to correct it. And when he hit Hollywood, where there's such a Spanish influence, many people pronounced it in the Latin way. We ended up calling him Chickie, Chicko, or Chico.

I don't think my father actually cared so much for other women; it was the chase that he loved. Harpo once said, very astutely, "Chico will never leave Betty because he loves being followed, he loves having somebody on his tail trying to outwit him." And he was right. Chico never left my mother. But, finally, she just couldn't stand it anymore and she left him.

For all my father's faults, though, he was such a darling. I worshipped the ground he walked on. I was madly in love with him. He was so lovable, particularly if you didn't cross him. And I didn't until I was about seventeen and started to have some political opinions he didn't share. Yet he was bright. Groucho once lamented, "Had I been born with his brains, what I couldn't have done." One of the things that made Groucho so angry at my father was that he felt Chico had wasted his gifts.

Unless you'd seen the brothers on the stage, you had no idea of their talent. The movies showed, I would say, 60 percent of that talent. They needed the spontaneity and the freedom of the stage to unleash that incredible wildness. I saw them on stage in *A Day at the Races, A Night at the Opera,* and *Out West.* Then I saw the movies, and though I think the movies—particularly the first two—were superb, they didn't hold a candle to the impact of those scenes on stage.

Harpo moved in circles that I wished my daddy had moved in. Even Groucho didn't move in those circles, though he was very close to George S. Kaufman. Groucho could write a certain kind of stuff, and he wanted to be a writer more than he wanted to be a comedian. He never really examined that. (The Marxes were the least introspective human beings I have ever known. Maybe that's why they were so funny.)

Harpo got in with that "Round Table" group, first of all, because he was a star. Second of all, he was not verbal, which is why they preferred him to Groucho. They didn't want Groucho around because Groucho was too much competition. Groucho would have been as funny as George Kaufman, as funny as Alexander Woolcott. Harpo brought his zaniness and a physical kind of humor that was totally different. And he had an absolutely engaging personality. He and Chico both had an innate sweetness, though they manifested it differently.

Having a Marx brother in this literary group was a plus. And Harpo learned a lot by listening. He wouldn't always understand, but Woolcott, who adored him, would explain things to him.

There is a famous story about an island they owned (I think it was off the coast of Maine). The whole group owned it, and one day they saw a party in a boat approaching to have a picnic. They were horrified. It was their private retreat and they didn't want anybody else there. Harpo said, "Leave it to me."

He waited until they got the whole picnic spread out and then he came charging out, stark naked, wearing only a red wig and brandishing an axe. He uttered strange Indian whooping sounds, and you never saw a group pack up so fast.

That was Harpo's marvelous zaniness. The Round Table group had its own brand of zaniness, but it was highly verbal. Harpo was also the one who, when some of the group thought of calling their own telephones to give their dogs some exercise, got into one of the apartments and, when the phone rang, picked up the receiver and barked into it. They just loved him.

He once took up painting very seriously, but he wouldn't let anybody see his work. Finally, a few friends prevailed upon him to let them visit his studio. He set it all up so they couldn't see his easel. When they arrived they saw a nude model on the dais, and Harpo behind his easel. They were very impressed, watching his painterly gestures. Eventually he let them come around to see the painting, and on the canvas was a banana!

Following in the family footsteps, I started out as an actress and I think I had some talent. But because of my background I never trusted it. I was extremely timid. My name never really helped me. It opened doors, but no one ever really paid attention to me. I was a fly on the wall. They had Lana to worry about, Judy to worry about, Anne Shirley to worry about. If they passed me in the hall they'd say, "Hi, Maxine. How's Papa?"

In our immediate family we had dinner together every night, and if I wanted to go to the prizefights with Daddy, I could. And once a week we went to the movies together. We had an hour together before dinner almost every night. We would chat and I would rub and tickle his feet, and he would take a little snooze.

I always wanted to write a white paper on what it was like being the daughter of a celebrity. You're royalty while you live in the palace, but once you leave it you're a nobody. Boy, that's something to try to handle. One of my analysts once said to me, "Your mother was your rock that you clung to." My father was a will-o'-the-wisp—you lost him in the fog somewhere. I had an image of him as this utterly enchanting man who was always just beyond my reach.

June 1985
New York

FLORENCE HALEY

Wife

═══

For fifty years of married life Flo Haley acted as manager, straight man, confidante, and moral support for her husband Jack, a man who had difficulty believing in himself and in the staying power of the movies.

A former Ziegfeld girl, she seems to be about eighty, though her energy and enthusiasm don't begin to betray her age. Her Beverly Hills home is a veritable museum of photographs, awards, Tin Man memorabilia, and children's artwork.

Jack didn't actually like pictures. He wanted a reaction. With film he couldn't get a reaction, and that bothered him. He didn't know whether what he was doing was any good or not. He needed that audience. He used to tell me, "Don't unpack the trunk." He figured we might not stay.

My main job with Jack was always trying to convince him that he was good. I'd say, "Didn't you hear the applause? You didn't pay them, you know." He'd admire somebody else and I'd say, "He's not as good as you." But Jack could never see how good he was. So I tried to give him confidence. Jack always had an inferiority—there's no two ways about it. He never thought much of his talents and was always afraid to try what he really could do.

Bert Lahr, Jack Haley, Judy Garland, and Ray Bolger in *The Wizard of Oz*, 1939.

I would help him learn his lines, and he used to try his routines on me to see if I laughed. I think that's why he married me, because I laughed at his jokes.

We didn't have a manager; I was his manager. When there was an argument or a problem, I would take it up.

Jack was under contract to Fox throughout the thirties, but Fox loaned him out to MGM for *The Wizard of Oz* in 1939. He also worked for Paramount, RKO, and Warner Brothers.

When the talkies started, they were bringing people from New York who were trained to speak and project well. They had to be heard up in that balcony. So, when they brought us all out, we were a clique. Like Bob Hope and Dolores, they were part of our group. So were Fred Allen and Portland. Spencer Tracy was another one from the New York theater.

It made it easier to come out here because we already had friends who could tell us all about this new business. It was so different facing that camera.

When Jack went on location I would usually go with him. Occasionally, I would visit him on the set, but not too often. I remember taking my son Jack to *The Wizard of Oz* set. He was hypnotized by the munchkins.

Victor Fleming was the first director of the picture, God love him. He once asked Jack what he thought: "How would you do it? What would be your interpretation?"

Jack said, "I'd like to do it like I tell my kids a bedtime story. And I would do it in that same voice."

Fleming was delighted. "That's just what I want."

The make-up for the Tin Man was a real problem. Jack had to get up at six o'clock to get that stuff on his face—and once he got it in his eyes and had to be in a black room for a week. His costume was so cumbersome he couldn't go into the commissary. He had a slant board to rest on because he couldn't sit down, and he had to eat through a straw.

The days were long, not because he actually worked that many hours, but the make-up took so long to apply, and then so long to get off before he could come home.

The funny thing is, Jack didn't even think *The Wizard of Oz* was going to be a good picture, so he didn't enjoy it at all. He was surprised by its success. But that movie ended up putting them all on the map. I'm glad he did it. It was a good thing to leave behind.

None of the Hollywood stories shows the good side of life here. No one tries to investigate the stable kind of life that we all led. I still have the same friends I made in those days, the ones who are still alive. It was really a community of friends. We'd all go see each other's children in their school plays. It was nice living.

The studios, however, did have a thing about children. They didn't want their actors to be married because it would spoil the illusion of youth and sex. So everybody was hiding their kids—everybody was somebody's "sister."

I enjoyed being a part of this business. I enjoyed the new friends I made, though I kept the old ones too. I'd be happier now if I still had my guy. He left a void. There's no way that will ever be filled. I miss him all the time.

February 1985
Beverly Hills

ANONYMOUS

Assistant

≡

I got my first job in the movie business in the early fifties. I was sent out by an employment agency to be interviewed by the executive assistant to the president of a major film company. Before taking me to meet my future boss, his assistant tried to talk me out of taking the job, saying I was too nice. I didn't know what he meant and, besides, once I saw the big pictures of movie stars on the walls of the executive floor, there was no way I was going to turn the job down.

Of course I had heard of the casting couch, and I had read enough books about the movie industry to be aware of what went on in Hollywood—but this was New York, and I wasn't an actress.

I soon found out that if you were young and not too bad looking, you were fair game, even though you were doing an honest day's work for your dollar. It was a big surprise to me that it was just part of the job. They treated older women in one way and younger ones in another. My boss had two middle-aged women who worked for him. One was his receptionist and appointments secretary. The other one took care of his personal, non-movie business. They were treated with respect and deference, as useful, serious people. It was the young ones who were treated as objects, even though they were working hard and doing a good job. I had been warned, but I didn't get it.

The president had two shifts of people working for him. The early shift started at eight in the morning and left at five in the afternoon. The late shift, which was me, came in at eleven in the morning and stayed until eight (usually even later) at night. I was happy to take the late shift because I never liked getting up early. What I didn't realize was that most of the office personnel left by five-thirty. That left me alone in the office with my boss. He worked through both shifts because he never got tired.

During the day, I spent most of my time with him. We worked in the office, and we worked outside the office. I went along when he went to meetings, to lunches, to the airport, wherever. He hated to waste time, so he always wanted someone in the car with him. That someone was usually me.

At the end of the day, after everybody had gone home, I was still working, of course, trying to finish all the work he had given me. His office was not too close to mine, and he liked to talk to me in person rather than use the interoffice phone. Because he spoke with a heavy accent, the telephone seemed to garble his speech. I would hear his footsteps coming down the hall, and I would have to steel myself. He always had some pretext for giving me a big, wet kiss: it was somebody's birthday, or a national holiday, whatever he could think of. He considered it just a friendly kiss, of course, but I hated being grabbed like that. He was an old man and his breath smelled bad, but I was afraid to say anything. I would just laugh nervously and try to distract him.

When we worked in the car, he liked to grab my thigh—for emphasis, of course. He was so emphatic that I had black and blue marks on my legs the entire time I worked for him. I would try moving away, but he moved with me. He liked to be close.

He had his winning ways, I must say. He could laugh at himself. Once he told me that, before I came to work for him, there had been only one other person who could understand his broken English. When he asked her how come, she answered, "Oh, I used to work for Gregory Ratoff." (He was a Russian director with another famous accent.)

My boss was very warm to the people he liked, and he was also very approachable. You could walk right into his office without standing on ceremony. I don't think he took himself very seriously. I really liked that about him. So there were some good times, too—or at least some good moments.

But the harrassment was relentless, an ongoing "what-else-did-you-expect?" attitude. That was the movie business. There wasn't even a name for sexual harrassment in the fifties so how could it exist? I only knew that I hated it, and I felt uncomfortable most of the time.

Three afternoons a week, at precisely five o'clock, a registered nurse in a white uniform appeared in the outer office to give my boss a shot. We called it his pep shot, although we didn't know what was in it. We only knew it preceded a visit to his mistress's apartment. It was the office joke, and everybody thought it was funny. Everybody but me, because I had to go with him.

We worked in the car on the short ride over to the Upper West Side. When we arrived at the address, he would go upstairs, leaving me and his chauffeur to wait for him. His driver was very sympathetic, and we would spend the time discussing the indignities of our respective jobs.

In less than an hour my boss would reappear, grinning, smelling of perfume, and smeared with lipstick, which he didn't bother to wipe off. We would resume our work and drive back to the office for a few more hours. Of all the things he did to me, this ritual offended me the most. But I never said anything to him about how I felt. I wanted to keep my job.

Many mornings when I was asked to come in early for one reason or another, he would send for me so that we could work in the Turkish bath. He had one in his private office and always spent an hour in there before his daily massage. He told me that this was how he survived on five hours of sleep or less.

There was usually another guest in there, often a producer like Otto Preminger, who liked to smoke cigars while sweating it out. I was fully dressed, of course, but they wore only towels around their waists. I got to see a lot of white chest hair.

I did get up the nerve to protest about this, and they hired a young man to go into the Turkish bath when needed. The trouble was that the man couldn't understand a word my boss said. After a while they started to send me in with him so I could translate. The arrangement didn't last long.

One morning I was told that I would have to accompany my boss to Philadelphia the next day. There was an out-of-town opening of a new play that was being considered for a movie, and we would stay in Philadelphia overnight. I absolutely panicked. I knew what it meant for me. I decided I wouldn't go, no matter what happened. I was ready to quit my job if necessary.

I went in to see the man who had hired me. By then I was in tears. He was very understanding. "I'll do whatever you want," he said. "Just tell me what you want me to say to him."

I thought for a moment. "Just tell him my mother is dying and I can't leave town." I knew these guys all had a thing about their mothers. It was overkill, but I was desperate. It worked, and I was never asked to go out of town with him again.

I guess the general opinion of women in the movie business was pretty low. I once overheard an executive talking about Marilyn Monroe: "She was handed around like an hors d'oeuvre when she first got started, all the way from grips and gaffers to the big shots." He said it in such a pitiless way.

I knew that some actresses were generous with their sexual favors. It worked for them sometimes. One studio head used to put his girlfriends into his films, in starring roles. None of them could act, and eventually it cost him his job. The stockholders didn't like losing money.

I was so naïve I didn't realize there was a lot of hanky-panky going on all around me. A friend of mine was having an affair with her boss. When his wife started making threatening phone calls to my friend, my friend tried to end the relationship, but her boss wouldn't let her go. The secretary of another one of the top executives was also his mistress, enabling her to get a top job for her brother. That was the climate at the time, and it was beginning to sink in.

There was never any talk of getting promoted if you cooperated. In those days there were no big jobs for women, as there are now, with women becoming producers and even studio heads. There were a few women directors, and there were always film editors, but that was it.

After I left I heard that my successor had gotten a fancy apartment, rent free. I guess that was all you could hope for: not a great career, just a great apartment.

My job was considered a plum. No one could understand why I was unhappy. I hardly understood it myself. I was supposed to be flattered by my boss's attentions. He worked me too hard because I was his favorite. He took me everywhere with him because he liked me best. It was a little like being the sultan's favorite in a Turkish harem.

When I finally got up the nerve to leave, I handed in my resignation to the man who had actually hired me. I knew that if I went to my boss he would sweet-talk me out of leaving. He was so wily, so funny and charming. He would know exactly the right thing to say: "How can I do without you? No one else understands my English. You know how I love you, you're like a daughter to me." So I waited until he was out of town.

I had given it plenty of thought. I knew I would probably never have such a glamorous job again. I met movie stars, I went to movie premieres, I conferred with important people. My boss trusted me with his correspondence. I had presigned stationery so I could write to people myself. He let me negotiate with Latin American exhibitors because I spoke Spanish. A lot of it was exciting and fun.

I realized something, though. I was close to power, but I had none of my own. I couldn't even tell my boss to keep his hands to himself.

September 1993
New York

☰ THE
CUTTING
ROOM ☰

MGM messengers, 1935. Herbert Wrench (later, international film editor) is seated at left.

HERBERT
WRENCH

International Film Editor

Herbert Wrench entered into a lifetime love affair with MGM when he joined the messenger fleet in 1930. Moving to the international editing department seven years later, he prepared every MGM feature and short for the foreign market. Since retiring to Sun City, California, he has felt lost.

I left school in 1930 and became an usher at Loew's State in Los Angeles. Then I decided I'd like to go to work in a studio. My boss gave me a letter to MGM.

I didn't hear from them for two weeks, so I went back kind of teed off and asked for my letter back. I was going to go to Fox. But when I walked in I was told a fellow was leaving the following Monday and that I could take his place, for two weeks anyway. It lasted forty-six years.

I worked as a messenger until I heard about an opening in the sound department. They sent me down to the sound union, but nobody would interview me. That afternoon the front office calls to tell me Peggy O'Day needed somebody in the international division of the editing department. She had been an old silent actress who went on to be an assistant to C. B. deMille's cutter, and now she was head of this department. They asked me if I would like to go in as an apprentice. That was back in 1937.

We had a good gang there; we were just so close together—me, Peggy, Scotty Perry, and the others. We had to be; we were in a small cutting room. Three in the daytime and three at night.

Some time after that the editors' union came in, and I became a charter member. I stayed on in the international division, though two or three times I thought I'd like to get out of it and get into the domestic part. But there was so much of a challenge in this. Every day there was something different to be done.

I stayed with MGM because when I was a messenger I broke my leg and Fred Kelton, the studio manager, kept me on the payroll for six weeks. Also, when President Roosevelt shut down all the banks, MGM pulled out their payrolls in cash, so we could go to the cashier and get our money. I became a company man—boom—right then and there.

Everything that I did for MGM was to ensure that their product was tops. If I did a cut, it was to be made so nobody would notice it. When I first went into the department my job was to strip all the dialogue out of the picture. Every time we stripped dialogue out we would also have to take out all the other sounds, like footsteps. Then we had to put it all back together again. We would build up an absolutely complete picture with no dialogue, just effects.

Putting the effects back in was always a challenge. Frank Morgan used to drive me nuts. His hands were always busy; he was always patting somebody, and we had to get all those sounds back in the picture. I had to devise some ingenious ways of reproducing those pats. Sometimes I just took a grease pencil and drew lines on an optical track, for a soft noise. That got through. Sometimes for footsteps I would take a razor blade and scratch right on the film.

Most of the sounds came from a library of effects. We had door closings and horses' hooves, almost everything you could think of. We would break the picture down into loops, taking the reel and going as far as we could go. We'd mark the end of the sections. Then we'd go over to the synchronizing stage and create all the effects you couldn't find in the library. We'd pour Coca-Cola, put ice in it, walk around, whatever was needed. I remember in *Parnell,* Myrna Loy had on a taffeta dress that rustled when she walked. So I'm sitting there with a whole handful of taffeta, watching her fanny. When she walked, I just went with her.

We had a lot of fun doing all the effects in *The Wizard of Oz.* We were borrowed by the domestic department because my teacher, Scott Perry, was better than anybody they had in their sound effects department. We were the Tin Man—he was really cardboard, so we had to make tin noises—we were the Straw Man; we were the Lion.

We worked a lot of conniving. Like one night when we were building some sound effects, I needed some men laughing, and I couldn't find anything just right. So I went down to the library and got some chickens clucking, and ran it backwards. I just thought it might work, and it did. I put it in there and nobody knew. You had to be on your toes.

There were six of us in the department, and we had to deliver a picture every ten days. This work went to Italy, France, and later on, after the war, Germany. Then other work started coming in, where we had to take the film and do censorship for territories. Some of the territories were very picky—like England. They have certain words that they pronounce differently from the way we do. So the script would be checked over before they started shooting, and they would come back and pick up the lines that contained the problem words. If the actor wouldn't do it then we would have to get someone in to dub it for him. That's where we went into a loop.

On one musical, the studio shot the picture using a Canadian girl. Well, the English wouldn't accept this girl because her accent wasn't right. So we had to loop that girl from beginning to end.

After looping we had to synchronize because they often didn't hit everything quite right. Luckily in those days we were working with optical soundtrack, because with that you can see the start of the words and it's easier to line up the patch.

We also took care of all the titling for the countries that didn't want synchronization. Mexico, for instance, didn't want synchronized pictures. They wanted the subtitles on there so they could learn English.

Sometimes, in the late thirties, they would film a movie with different casts for the different languages. They would do the scene, go out, and come back with a different cast to do it in, say, French. Then they would go out again and come back and do it in Spanish.

Each country had its own censorship rules. For instance, in a Judy Garland film she sang a song that had God in the lyrics. For the British release we not only had to find someone else to sing the song, but we had to take the word "God" out.

I was a mixture of everything in there, always trying to come up with solutions to sound effects problems in the remakes. At one point we did a reissue of *Mutiny on the Bounty,* for which we did a lot of sound editing, rebuilding the thing. We had to go to the library for water noises for when the ship has a wreck and water starts pouring through a porthole. Well, it turned out the noise we found was just sort of puny-sounding, so I said, "Go back, redo it, and put a waterfall in there." It worked.

Finally our work became mostly censorship. There were no general rules. Something that was not allowed in one country might be fine for another. I guess the Catholic countries were the strictest. The Irish had the most rules. It was always, "Tone down dancing. Tone down legs." Countries would usually screen the stuff and then tell us their objections. We'd do one, put it away, and then, shucks, in a few weeks somebody would be asking for the same darned thing. So we started making up these books of what was allowed and not allowed in the different countries. Later on they'd send these books out by teletype to the various offices so they could do their own cuts.

Here are some examples. *[Shows us a large black binder.]* Now, here's one of the Tarzan movies for India. Pages of prohibitions like: "No scenes with drinking"; "eliminate thigh exposure"; "delete objectionable dialogue"; "delete fight between women"; "delete scenes of kissing."

Night Diggers for South Africa: "Eliminate the seduction and rape of Mary." An Andy Hardy movie in Ireland: "Delete scene where Mickey Rooney and Judy Garland are in bathing suits by a pool." In *The Postman Always Rings Twice* we couldn't show exactly how the man gets killed.

If the scene was integral to the story we would have to do a replacement for it. That usually meant going into the outtakes of the feature, trying to find something that would get you through to the next cut. We just had to improvise.

We'd have to make special cuts for Indonesia. Look here. For *On the Town* we had to delete the Ballantine's gesture—making a circle with your thumb and forefinger—because it had a dirty meaning. For South Africa we had to "eliminate scene showing negress dancing." For the Irish: "Eliminate Claire throwing up her skirts," in the girls' dance group. Here's *Northwest Passage:* "Eliminate scene of bayonet being stuck into Indian, and scene showing chopping off the head of Indian."

I don't think I was ever looking for appreciation. I was so satisfied with what I was doing, and I just tried to do it well.

September 1985
Westwood

Rudi Fehr in his heyday as one of Warner's top film editors.

RUDI FEHR

Film Editor

The son of a successful German banker, Rudi Fehr was born in Berlin in 1911. He began his career in 1931 when he joined a Berlin company that specialized in sound equipment and motion picture production.

He is a gracious, immensely good-natured man. After a few moments spent in his company, we know that he is a bon vivant, a talented raconteur, and a passionate music lover. Indeed, the walls of his study are lined floor to ceiling with shelves containing a perfectly organized record collection. Recalling the years at Warner Brothers, he speaks with the pride of someone who genuinely loved his work.

I left Berlin in 1936, for obvious reasons. Either Hitler had to go or I had to go. I am Jewish, and I would no longer be allowed to work in Germany.

As a young man I was so full of ideas. I had wanted to be a diplomat. My father was president of one of the biggest banks in Germany, and I could afford a diplomatic career. I really was gung ho because I thought diplomats do great things. Well, with the advent of Hitler, that was out of the question.

I arrived in New York on May 1, 1936, and stayed with a good friend, who put me up in his apartment. Initially I thought I would like to stay in New York. I had been in the picture business for five years by that time, and had edited fourteen films already.

But soon I thought, "This is not for me. I can't live in this. All these people living so close together. I'll go to Hollywood."

"You haven't got a chance," all my friends said. "Why waste your time?" (You know, a good German—slow-witted and heavy-handed. They all said there would be a hundred more qualified guys there than me.)

But I explained to them, "Look, I have enough money to last me six months." (That was all I could take out of Germany.) "If I don't succeed in six months, I come back and go to work at Macy's or Gimbel's."

So I took the train: three days, two nights—chug, chug, chug. I had several letters of introduction to various people all over town. I stayed at the Biltmore Hotel downtown and bought myself a two-year-old Ford convertible. Top down, I made my rounds. I had a letter to George Oppenheimer, one of the prominent writers at Metro. He took a liking to me and told me to come out and meet some of the executives.

At Metro then, I go to the little dining room, where about fourteen people are sitting around. I sit down, too, and on my left is Clark Gable, on my right is Spencer Tracy. I couldn't believe it. If my friends in Berlin could only see me now!

Out of that meeting grew a very nice relationship with Cedric Gibbons, the head of Metro's art department. Gibbons had a very good man who did their montages, but the guy became very arrogant, too expensive, and they were thinking about making a change.

I continued making all the rounds in Hollywood, and after exactly five weeks there I come home to my little apartment near the Ambassador Hotel, and there are three messages waiting for me: CALL MGM, CEDRIC GIBBONS. CALL FRITZ LANG AT COLUMBIA. CALL HENRY BLANKE AT WARNER BROTHERS. A miracle!

Of course, in those days everybody wanted to work at Metro. Metro was a giant. Gibbons said, "I've read your résumé. I'm very impressed, and I'd very much like you to do our next montage."

I said, "I'm very flattered. Can you give me an idea as to when that would be?"

He said, "Six to eight weeks, but don't worry, we'll call you."

I had met Fritz Lang in Berlin when I was starting out as an apprentice. On the phone he asked me if I was related to Professor Oscar Fehr. I told him he was my uncle. (Lang had been in the Austrian Army in World War I, and he had gotten shrapnel in his eye, which my uncle removed without hurting him in any way.) He said, "Out of gratitude to your uncle, I want to give you a job as assistant editor on *Fury*."

I asked him, "When would this start?"

"Oh, in about six weeks," he said. "I'll call you."

Henry Blanke said, "We have bought a film made in Vienna, and one made in Berlin. Can you take the German dialogue off and translate it into English?"

I said, "Of course I can do that."

"Fine. How much money do you want?"

I had heard about the fabulous salaries they paid in Hollywood, so I said, "I wouldn't work for less than one hundred dollars a week." I came on very strong.

He called me back and asked, "Would you do it for sixty dollars?"

Well, I did these two pictures in six weeks, and at the end I got a note thanking me and telling me I was through. In those days we used to work six days a week. That very Saturday morning Harold McCord, the head of the cutting department, comes to my office and says, "Rudi, a miracle has happened. One of my assistants has decided to leave. I have an opening for you on Monday." In those days every big studio made sixty movies a year—forty B-pictures and twenty A-pictures. They had about sixty actors and actresses under contract—twenty top stars and featured players and forty young actors and actresses who were coached. They had a coach on the lot. They took lessons and did little plays. It was wonderful, a little family affair. In the cutting department then, there were twenty-two editors and twenty-two assistants, and they never moved. It was very hard to get in.

I thought quickly to myself, "Well, it's better to be a working assistant editor than a nonworking editor." Since I had been a full-fledged editor in Europe, it was hard to step back again. So I asked him, "If I get an editor's job on the outside, can I leave?" He understood, and so I took the job with that understanding.

But I liked it at Warner's so much. Everybody was wonderful to me. Every year they had a drive for the United Jewish Welfare Fund. This was an anti-Nazi drive, and I felt very strongly about it, obviously. I gave a week's salary, which was a big sixty dollars. One day I get a letter from the president of the company, Harry Warner. It was a little pink memo—I still have it—with my check attached:

> Dear Rudi,
> I appreciate your generous donation to the
> Welfare Fund, but I also know how much you
> are making a week. Please tear up the check
> and give me one for $10.

That's just a small example of the kind of thing people don't know about the Warners. I was so touched by that gesture.

There were eight kids in the Warner family, three girls and five boys. One of the boys was somewhat retarded and didn't function very well. The other four were the Warner Brothers: Sam, Harry, Albert, and Jack. Jack was in charge of production, so I worked mostly with him. It was very fortunate that he took a liking to me; he helped me very much, shall we say, up the ladder of success. He was a real mentor. I knew his likes and dislikes. He hated it when people took advantage, when they were alone with him, asking him for a vacation or a raise, or a better office or something. Never, never, never did I ask him for anything—except once.

My wife pushed me. We have four daughters and we had rented a cabin in Arrowhead. I had to get permission. I was alone with him one day, and he was in a good mood, so instead of going through channels I said, "Mr. Warner, could I take two weeks off? My whole family wants to go to Arrowhead."

He looked at me and said, "Rudi, when I'm here, you're here. You'll take your vacation when I take my vacation."

So later, when he left on his vacation, I went to his right-hand man and asked for two weeks off. He said, "Are you crazy or something? We need you more than ever when he's gone. Do you want me to carry the ball for you, too?" Honestly, for seven years, from 1956 to 1963, I didn't have one day off. My wife almost divorced me. I met her at Warner's; she was under contract there. Her name was Maris Wrixon. She only worked from about 1938 to 1942; we got married in 1940.

For three years I worked as an assistant editor, and then one day somebody spoke up for me and I was promoted to editor again. I was an editor for twelve years, working on some wonderful pictures with some wonderful directors—Hitchcock (my favorite), Huston, Negulesco, Vidor, de Toth.

I worked exclusively at Warner's, editing thirty-six pictures, until one day in 1952 or 1953 I got a call from Warner's secretary. She said, "Rudi, tomorrow there'll be a story about you in the trade papers. The boss said, 'Don't sign with any agent.'"

I knew nothing more until the next day, when it appeared on the front page: JACK WARNER PROMOTES RUDI FEHR TO PRODUCER STATUS. He never asked me. That was the way he did things. I made an appointment to see him. I said, "Mr. Warner, thank you very much. I'm very appreciative of the confidence you have in me, but I must be very honest with you. I never dreamed of becoming a producer. Or a director. Or anything else."

So for a time I reluctantly became a producer. And I later realized why Mr. Warner had done it. By that time, television had come in and theaters were empty. Most of the producers were getting $1,200 to $1,500 a week. My regular editor's salary was $350 a week. I was young, I had good ideas for editing, I made good suggestions, all of which he appreciated.

Mr. Warner didn't like dry people; to work for him you had to have a sense of humor. He liked nothing better than to make people laugh. He told the corniest jokes. This was Mr. Warner's sense of humor: He once said, "Rudi, I stuck up for you last night."

Naturally, I had to say, "Oh, that's wonderful. What did you say?"

"Somebody said you weren't fit to sleep with pigs, and I said you were." That was his sense of humor.

I got even with him once. When I first started as an assistant there, I worked in a cutting room which he had to pass every day on his way to lunch. He called the editor out of the room and asked him, "Who's that kid working with you?"

The editor said, "Rudi Fehr."

"Oh, yes, Rudi Fehr." A week later he came by, and again, "What's this kid's name?"

"Rudi Fehr."

This went on for three weeks. The fourth week he came by and said, "Hello, Rudi, is everything Fehr?"

I said to myself, there's got to be an answer to that.

So a few weeks later, Jack Warner comes into the private dining room, spots me and says, "Rudi, is everything Fehr?"

My big chance. "Yes, sir," I said. "Fehr and Warner."

Anyway, I made one picture as a producer and it didn't work out too well. They knew I was into music, and so they looked for a musical for me. All of a sudden I get a call from the front office.

Mr. Turnick, Mr. Warner's right-hand man, said, "I have good news for you. This is a great assignment. You're going to make the third version of *The Desert Song.*"

I turned white. "Why *The Desert Song?*" I asked.

He answered, "Well, Metro just made *Showboat* for the third time, and it was a great success. We can do the same."

"Mr. Turnick, there's a big difference between *Showboat* and *The Desert Song. The Desert Song* is very dated. Nobody will buy it anymore unless we do it tongue-in-cheek."

"No, straight romantic," he insisted. Well, I'm a good soldier and I did it, though I wasn't happy with it. Soon after, they let every producer go and asked me if I would go back to editing, which I did happily. The money was the same.

Next, they sent me to Rome. It's funny how things happen. In 1954 Warner's had a lot of frozen liras in Italy. The only way to get it out was to make a movie there and then bring the negative out, print it here, and make money on it. So they decided to make two big epics. One was *Helen of Troy,* with Robert Wise as director. It was a big production.

The second came about while Jack Warner was in Paris, staying at the George V. One day he goes into the lobby and here is Howard Hawks with William Faulkner. Faulkner had had some troubles with his income tax and he's run away to Paris. So Warner sees them and says, "Hey, you guys, do you have an idea for a story? I could make a big picture in Italy."

"Oh, Mr. Warner, what a coincidence that you should say that. We have a great idea."

"Come on, let's sit down, and you tell me."

"Mr. Warner, could you have breakfast tomorrow morning?"

These two guys stayed up all night dreaming up *Land of the Pharaohs,* the building of the pyramids. Warner was so impressed he said, "Okay, you've got a deal."

Now Howard Hawks runs into Lewis Milestone. In the course of the conversation Milestone tells Hawks, "You really don't have to bring those high-priced editors over from Hollywood. There are very good editors in London. I just made a picture in Italy, and I had a wonderful guy from London."

Howard Hawks took down this guy's name and hired him and this is what happened. Hawks (who's about six-foot-six) sort of leans down and says to this guy (who's about five feet tall), "Now listen here. I want this picture cut differently from any other picture." Well, this is the most stupid thing anybody could say to an editor. There is only one way to cut a picture, and that's the right way. But this man was so in awe of Hawks he went along with him. After about a week Hawks sent for him and asked to see some of the film he'd put together.

When he saw it he fell out of his chair. He picked up the phone and said to Warner, "Send an editor, please!" It was his own fault, really, but that's how I got to Rome. Since I was familiar with the story, I was selected. I always said if Howard Hawks had kept his mouth shut, the guy would have done a good job and I would never have gone to Rome.

As an editor, you have to follow what you feel; you have to tell the story the best way possible with the material at hand. Editors don't have a style. Editors interpret the director's style. You're tied to the way he shoots the picture, and you can only use the film he gives you. I learned that early.

I was able to make Hawks happy, and after I put the film into shape I became the supervising editor (having asked that the original editor stay on).

Warner liked everybody who was good at his job, and he liked me in my job as an editor. When I went back, I went to Mr. Turnick and said, "I appreciate everything you've done for me, but I don't want to cut anymore." I wanted to take a break from being an editor. I had done it from 1931 to 1954.

When I got a call from Universal to come over there, Mr. Warner heard about it and he was furious. He said, "Rudi, don't accept any assignment. We have plans for you." (Again, he never told me what they were.)

At that time, we were making a wonderful film called *Giant*. Warner kind of wanted to know what was going on in the cutting process. For some reason, George Stevens was taking forever in the cutting and Warner wanted to know why. I didn't really spy, and I never volunteered any information. Warner had called Stevens and said, "I have a man here who is a very fine editor. We're preparing a new position for him. In the meantime, would you mind letting him sit in when you cut it, and he can give you some suggestions."

He had a projection room reserved to himself. He had a record player in the front of the room, and before we started working we played western music, to get in the mood. In the first row with Stevens was a secretary, then a writer, and George Stevens, Jr. Then came the head editor, and the other editor, and I sat with the assistant. Stevens had a funny routine. He would stop the film and turn to the writer and say, "There's a line of dialogue in the picture there. Do you think we really need that?"

The writer would say, "Well, I wrote it and I think it's important."

Stevens would turn to the editor and say, "Take it out." Just like that. Very arbitrary.

There was a scene in the film between Rock Hudson and Elizabeth Taylor; it was a two-shot, meaning they were both on the screen at the same time. Stevens stops the film and turns to the editor and says, "Don't you think it would be better in close-ups?"

And he said, "Yes, I think so. We can play it in close-ups."

Stevens then said, "Leave it alone."

In another scene, Jimmy Dean hits it rich and buys himself a little MG. He drives it up to a big hotel and, as he stops, he rear-ends somebody. It was a short scene. The guy gets out and says, "What did you do that for?" And Jimmy Dean hits him and knocks him down.

Well, I had just begun to like Jimmy Dean. He worked hard, he became wealthy. All of a sudden he hits a guy for no reason at all . . . and I don't like him anymore. Sure enough, we run by the scene and Stevens looks to me and asks, "Rudi, do you think we need that scene?"

I said, "I think we do. I really think we do, Mr. Stevens."

He said, "I think you're right."

My plan had backfired. It was the only time he agreed, and I really wanted that scene out. Later I said, "Mr. Stevens, knowing how you operate, I wonder why you need that scene."

He said, "Rudi, I want to throw the audience off balance in regard to Jimmy Dean's character. I really don't want them to like him all that much." It made sense because at the end Dean gets into a terrible fist fight with Rock Hudson, and they throw over every table in the bar.

Along about then Mr. McCord, the head of the department, had a heart attack. He wasn't functioning as well anymore, so he was retired. It was a big job to be in charge of all the editing. We gave him a farewell lunch, and all of us lined up at the end to wish him well and thank him for being so nice to us. I go up and shake his hand and he says, "Rudi, congratulations."

I said, "For what?"

"Don't you know? You're going to get my job." Again, nobody had told me. I knew so many other guys who wanted that job. I never asked for it, but I got it. And it was wonderful. Through that job I became very close to Jack Warner. Every day I would spend two or three hours alone with him in the projection room. For a long time I was in charge of both feature and television films. It was a real challenge, managing as many as 130 people. My title was postproduction executive.

So many interesting things happened with Warner. One of the last films I edited was *House of Wax*. In those days, with television on the scene, the studios wanted to come up with gimmick pictures to bring the audiences back to the theaters. Fox came out with Cinemascope, the elongated screen, and Warners latched onto 3-D. Jack Warner called me and said, "I want you to edit *House of Wax* because we are in terrible financial trouble." (We weren't, in fact, but he always talked that way.)

But he was right in saying, "Business has been lousy." It was. Theaters were empty. He said, "We're making this thing in 3-D and I want it in the theaters five weeks from the day we finish shooting."

It was an impossibility, in 3-D and all, so I asked him to tell me the schedule.

I said, "Mr. Warner, forget the five weeks unless you shoot in continuity. If you start shooting on page one you'll have your picture in the theaters in five weeks. I'll cut each reel, show it to the director, show it to the producer, show it to you. If you all approve it, we'll turn it right over to the composer and sound department."

That's exactly how the film was done, and it was in the theaters five weeks from the last day of shooting. I could only do that because I knew the story. I went to the set and I knew what was happening all along. I knew what to play up and emphasize.

Now, about what the film editor actually does. First of all, the editor is always given the script to read and make suggestions on how to improve it, what he thinks is superfluous, how it should be shot. The editor is usually on the set only with a new director. In those cases, the editor is very important because he keeps the director informed of what coverage he needs, when and how to move the camera for different effects. Once the director knows the routine he doesn't need the editor on the set.

Once in a while, even a seasoned director will call the editor in to ask what coverage is needed. Mostly it's a long shot, where you see the geography of the whole set. Then you break it up into over-the-shoulders, being careful not to get too close. You use close-ups sparingly, only to record reactions. When a character says, "I'm going to kill you," you want to see the face of the person he's threatening. Timing is the thing. The cameraman never makes that decision; he's told what to do, he lights it accordingly, he decides which lens to use, and he shoots it. That's his job. If the cameraman makes a mistake it's very expensive because the scene has to be reshot. That's why he gets more money than the editor. If an editor makes a mistake he orders a reprint or two and recuts it. That's much cheaper.

The next step is to get matte film. Some directors shoot very sparingly, others go crazy; one director shot a million and a half feet of film, to be covered from every angle. (The average footage shot in a film is around 200,000 to 250,000 feet. The average length of a picture is 10,000 feet.)

The editor's job is to run the film with the director the day after it's shot, and take notes. Some directors leave it entirely to the editor. The rule at Warner Brothers was only print one take of everything. If you had doubts, you held the negative. If you liked what you saw you ordered it printed up. But you didn't order two, three, or four prints of the same thing. You might not need them and they cost money.

In the cutting room there are different ways of editing. You can work with the moviola. The old-timers all worked with the moviola, which I still think is fastest. There is now the Kem (flatbed) table, where the film goes through and there is a larger screen you can watch. You can have two and three different scenes lined up. The problem with the Kem table is that it is cumbersome and time-consuming to thread the film and then wind it back.

Most of the time, the director is so busy on the set and working on the script that he doesn't look at anything edited until maybe halfway through shooting, when he'll say, "Let me see what you have." The gentlemen's agreement is that nobody looks at the cut film until after the director has seen it. The contract between the Directors Guild and the studio says that the director has the right to two sneak previews of his version. A few directors—and you can count them on two hands—like Richard Brooks, Mike Nichols, and Elia Kazan, have the right to the final cut, which the studios are very reluctant to give. But it isn't necessary. I think if you discuss things intelligently with the executives you can get things done.

Now, the editor is supposed to make suggestions. He has about three weeks from the day they finish shooting to finish his presentation, his cut. There are no musical effects in there at all; it's just the dialogue and the picture. Then the director looks at it without any comments.

They run it a reel at a time. Each reel runs an average of nine or ten minutes. They stop after each reel and discuss how it could be improved—what they could lose, where to add a close-up, where to trim, that sort of thing. Then the editor takes it back to the cutting room and does all the things they agreed on. Then he sees it again, and there may still be a few little trims out of that viewing.

Then they show it to the head of the studio, the producer. It's their version—the director's version. Then the head of the studio makes other suggestions. If the director likes them, he makes them; but if he doesn't, he suggests a preview.

If there isn't a good reaction at the preview, they go back and run it again and see how they can help it. This is what we did on *No Time for Sergeants,* but it was quite an experience. Mervyn LeRoy made the picture. When I read the script, I thought the first half played like a house on fire; the second half might have been written by somebody else. It was contrived, it was dreary, the jokes were dragged in. It just didn't flow. We took it to a preview out in Westwood, and I never heard so many laughs—for the first half. Comes the second half and people start walking out in droves. By that time, Mervyn LeRoy had been put on another assignment, so he's gone. I get a call from Jack Warner, who says, "Rudi, you have to work on *No Time for Sergeants*. Why don't you meet me in the projection room?"

We took about eighteen minutes out of the second half and we left the first part alone. The eighteen minutes amounted to almost two full reels. When we were through I said, "Mr. Warner, are you going to tell Mervyn about this?"

He said, "Rudi, don't worry about it."

Mervyn comes back from shooting on location in New York, and we are ready to preview it again. Mr. Warner calls and says, "I just told Mervyn that we're going to preview it again next week."

I asked, "Mr. Warner, did you tell him about the cuts?"

"Rudi, don't worry about it."

Comes the night of the preview. For some reason I'm invited to ride in Mr. Warner's limousine; there are five of us in the car, including Mervyn. All of a sudden I hear Mr. Warner say, "Oh, by the way, Mervyn, while you were gone we made a few little trims—nothing of importance—just to clean up the picture."

I thought to myself, "He's going to die when he sees this." And, sure enough, when Mervyn LeRoy saw the picture he was furious.

Warner gave him permission to work on it again, and he put about seven minutes back in, so we were still eleven minutes ahead, which helped the picture. He would never have taken out those eleven minutes.

Getting back to the editing process, the editor orders all the opticals—dissolves, fades, titles—and works with the special effects people. If there's a light background, he checks the titles, he times it, and works with the title people. Then he supervises the recording of the music. He also works with the sound editor, who cuts the sound effects. Many times the background is so noisy that they have to loop the lines (reread the dialogue without the background noise). Then he's in on the mix.

He goes to the preview and sits with the director and makes notes. Then they discuss it, and there will be some additional changes. Then the negative cutter and he look at the answer print. The answer print is the one the cameraman should look at, after the negative is cut and combined with the sound, because he is best qualified to see if these are the right tones, the right quality, the right density. Then, when they approve the answer print, that's the end of the editor's assignment. Most of his responsibility is to work well with the director and exchange ideas along the way.

In the old days, when we made sixty movies a year, the minute the director finished he was already handed another assignment, so he was busy. Nowadays, the directors have more time, so many of them go into the cutting room. If any director said to me, "Cut there," I would give him the scissors and say, "You do it." I was lucky enough never to have a director in my cutting room.

I guess my biggest challenge was in *Humoresque,* making John Garfield look like a violinist. We had two professional violinists, one kneeling underneath Garfield—we only showed him above the waist, with the bow—and another behind him doing the fingering. Garfield just stood there with his hands behind his back. That was all done on the set.

Very seldom can an editor save a movie. *High Noon* was an exception. The preview was terrible. They brought in Elmo Williams, who came up with the idea of periodically cutting to a clock in order to build suspense. That was a big contribution.

In the actual editing you shouldn't have any jarring cuts. That happened when all of a sudden they eliminated dissolves. There were straight cuts, and they were very confusing. Dissolves always gave you a time lapse, or a change of location, very smoothly.

I always liked working with directors whose work was stylized. As an editor, I always saw the script before they began shooting. Once in a while the producer would ask me if I would come to his office and talk with him about the script. I did that with Hal Wallis, who was a big producer. He had made *Casablanca,* then he made *Passage to Marseilles.* I was assigned to edit the third picture called *The Conspirators.* He sent me the script and he asked me to come over. One thing about me, I'm very honest. I cannot pretend. I said, "Mr. Wallis, I read the script and I'll be honest with you. It looks like you had things left over from *Casablanca,* a few things left over from *Passage to Marseilles,* you threw them all together, and here's *The Conspirators.*"

He was stunned when I said that. "You don't like it?"

I said, "Well, I'm not crazy about it, Mr. Wallis."

"Well, I like it."

I said, "Mr. Wallis, that's all that's necessary. If you like it . . ." Two weeks later he was fired off the lot and somebody else took over. We had two good-looking people in the picture, neither one great actors, the actress we called "Headache" Lamarr and Paul "Hemorrhoids."

Warner always had me sit next to him whenever he ran a film. We were in London, where he showed *My Fair Lady* to the VIPs; it was his proudest accomplishment. After the end of the invitational screening the audience rose in a body. Warner turned to me and said, "Rudi, what do I do now?"

I said, "Mr. Warner, stand up and take a bow."

He asked, "Do I have to?"

I said, "Yes, you have to." All this goes on while the people are waiting. He stands up and kind of sheepishly takes a bow. He sits down; they keep applauding.

He says to me, "Now what do I do?"

I said, "You have to get up once more, Mr. Warner."

He said, "You get up."

I said, "Mr. Warner, why me?"

He said, "Don't argue with me; that's an order."

So I stood up and bowed to fourteen hundred people who must have been saying, "Who is that guy?" But it felt good, it felt wonderful.

I have worked with directors who don't have a clear concept of what the film should be, and in cases like that the editor has to be the coach and persuade the director with logic, pointing out why something isn't working, why it would be better if done a different way. When Mr. Warner had a crazy idea to do something, I had a system. I would argue with him three times. After the third time, if he still felt the same, I would give up.

I had a very special relationship with Herman Shumlin, who actually lived here in my house while he did *Watch on the Rhine*. He had directed Hellman's stage play, but he knew nothing about making motion pictures, and I was assigned to work with him, which I enjoyed very much.

The first time I put a scene together he asked to see it, and I ran it for him in the projection room. He was so overwhelmed that he walked out in a daze, turned around, walked back in and said, "Rudi, I've got to see it again." He was so pleased with the way it flowed. I had also been responsible for the setting of the camera, movement and all. I worked very closely with Shumlin, night and day. Each day we would work out the next day's shooting. It's very important that the director have the authority and come to the set with it. He can't be wishy-washy; he must be positive, otherwise the crew does not respect him.

I always went to the previews. We made *The Wild Bunch*, a picture I was not particularly fond of. The director and producer decided to preview this picture in the heart of America—Kansas

City, Missouri. We stayed at the Muehlbach Hotel and, lo and behold, at the same time we preview our picture there's a convention of school teachers. Little old lady school teachers. They heard about the sneak preview. They wanted to lynch the director. They wanted to lynch him. The picture was long, and the gentleman who was the vice-president of Warner Brothers, Ben Kalmanson, wanted it shortened, so he called the producer, Phil Feldman, and said, "Feldman," and he used four-letter words all the time. "I want this damn picture shortened, and tell me what you're going to take out."

I get a call from Phil Feldman. (I wasn't there when this happened.) "Could you come up to my office?"

I said, "Yes, I'll be right over."

"You're the maven around here. You know everything," he said to me. "How can we shorten this picture?"

I said, "Mr. Feldman, there's a scene at the railroad station: there's a woman standing at the end of the train with a guitar and singing Mexican songs. All of a sudden people start shooting at each other. To this day I don't know who they are, I don't know why they shoot each other. I think that's a scene you can really lose."

He started to explain to me why they could not possibly cut that scene, why it was important. While he was doing all this talking—rhetoric—the phone rings and his secretary comes running in and says, "Kalmanson is on the phone. He wants to talk to you right away."

"Hello, Ben."

Ben says, "Have you cut the damn picture yet?"

"Ben, there's a scene at the railroad station . . ."

Later I found out that the director had an affair with the guitar-strumming singer. He promised her that the scene stays in the picture. Lo and behold, when it played in Mexico that scene was back in. But nowhere else. That's the old Hollywood.

It was the biggest fluke that I got the *Prizzi's Honor* assignment. This is how it came about. One night I was out with Paul Kohner, who is a very prominent agent. Driving home he told me that John Huston was very unhappy with his editor and wanted to make a change. We discussed the editor they were considering, and I told him how much I loved working with Huston on *Key Largo*.

The next day I get a call from Paul, who says, "You got yourself a job. I mentioned it to John Huston and he'd love to work with you again."

I said, "Paul, I haven't edited a film by myself for thirty years, not since *Land of the Pharaohs*."

His answer was, "How much money do you want?" And you know, it's funny, I mentioned a goodly amount and he said, "That's not enough for you. You deserve more." So he got me more than I asked for.

I was a little nervous working on *Prizzi's Honor*, but I took my daughter Kaja as my assistant. She cut several scenes very well and she got full credit with me. I had the first cut a week after they finished shooting, and I was eight months on the picture.

My daughter is going to go on with editing. We had a wonderful time working together. She said to me, "This is the nicest experience I ever had, working with you, Dad."

September 1985
Los Angeles

FILMOGRAPHY

1940   *My Love Came Back* (dir. Curtis Bernhardt, Warner Bros.)

           Honeymoon for Three (dir. Lloyd Bacon, Warner Bros.)

           Alice In Movieland (short)

1941   *Million Dollar Baby* (dir. Curtis Bernhardt, Warner Bros.)

           Navy Blues (dir. Lloyd Bacon, Warner Bros.)

           All Through the Night (dir. Vincent Sherman, Warner Bros.)

1942   *Desperate Journey* (dir. Raoul Walsh, Warner Bros.)

           Watch on the Rhine (dir. Herman Shumlin, Warner Bros.)

           Devotion (dir. Curtis Bernhardt, Warner Bros.)

1943   *In Our Time* (dir. Vincent Sherman, Warner Bros.)

           Between Two Worlds (dir. Edward Blatt, Warner Bros.)

1944   *The Conspirators* (dir. Jean Negulesco, Warner Bros.)

           Nobody Lives Forever (dir. Jean Negulesco, Warner Bros.)

1945   *A Stolen Life* (dir. Curtis Bernhardt, Warner Bros.)

1946   *Humoresque* (dir. Jean Negulesco, Warner Bros.)

           Possessed (dir. Curtis Bernhardt, Warner Bros.)

1947   *The Voice of the Turtle* (dir. Irving Rapper, Warner Bros.)

           Romance on the High Seas (dir. Michael Curtiz, Warner Bros.)

1948   *Key Largo* (dir. John Huston, Warner Bros.)

           The Girl from Jones Beach (dir. Peter Godfrey, Warner Bros.)

The Inspector General (dir. Henry Koster, Warner Bros.)

1949   *Beyond the Forest* (dir. King Vidor, Warner Bros.)

The Damned Don't Cry (dir. Vincent Sherman, Warner Bros.)

1950   *Rocky Mountain* (dir. William Keighley, Warner Bros.)

1951   *Goodbye My Fancy* (dir. Vincent Sherman, Warner Bros.)

1952   *I Confess* (dir. Alfred Hitchcock, Warner Bros.)

1953   *House of Wax* (dir. André de Toth, Warner Bros.)

Riding Shotgun (dir. André de Toth, Warner Bros.)

Dial M for Murder (dir. Alfred Hitchcock, Warner Bros.)

The Desert Song (producer, dir. H. Bruce Humberstone, Warner Bros.)

1954   *Land of the Pharaohs* (dir. Howard Hawks, Warner Bros.)

1982   *One from the Heart* (co-editor, dir. Francis Ford Coppola, Columbia)

1985   *Prizzi's Honor* (co-editor, dir. John Huston, Twentieth Century–Fox)

≡ COMING ATTRACTIONS ≡

HUBERT VOIGHT

Publicity Director

≡

Hubert Voight was born in 1902. From 1930, when he went to Holly-
wood, until World War II, he designed and launched publicity cam-
paigns that introduced Greta Garbo, Joan Crawford, Jimmy Cagney,
Mickey Rooney, Joan Blondell, Peter Lorre, and many other celebrities
to world audiences.

At the precise hour we are to meet, Hubert Voight is waiting on the
curb in front of the retirement home where he lives. He is extremely
personable, with a slightly offbeat sense of humor.

I was a poor kid from a little Wisconsin town called La Crosse.
My father was a laborer and an alcoholic, a wonderful man who
would have been great if he hadn't hit the booze. My mother died
when I was five or six, and I was taken in by my spinster aunts,
who lived in a home for old women and little kids off the streets,
most of them bastards. The name of the place, believe it or not,
was the Home for the Friendless.

As I got to high school age I knew I wanted a little more
education. So I went out to live with my older brother in
Minneapolis, where I got a job as a janitor in a garage. There I
saved enough money, in addition to supporting myself, to pay
my first year's tuition at Columbia University.

I had become a great devotee of journalism and of the theater.
I used to see every play that came to Minneapolis. I wanted to be
a drama critic, and I knew there was a famous professor at

Columbia who was an expert on English drama, so I decided that's where I wanted to go.

I met Corey Ford, later a great humorist, during my first few days and he got me pledged to a fraternity, which was a great boost to my morale. That gave me a great start, because my lonesomeness died. I learned about the theater and about the movies. I learned that MGM was the best studio. I still have a sheaf of notes that I made of my calls on the major film companies. MGM was *the* company, so it was the one for me.

By then, I wanted to be in the picture business, and I wanted to be in publicity. I hardly knew what it was while I was in school, but I soon learned when I did publicity on the varsity shows at Columbia. There I came in contact with men like Oscar Hammerstein, Richard Rodgers, and Larry Hart.

So, after a series of events I became the national publicity director of MGM, based in New York. When I started out in 1925, the letters *PR* were hardly in existence. We were simply publicity men. But our job at the studio level was to create the publicity, the stories, and also to supervise the taking of movie scene stills. The job was many faceted because we had to have a basic knowledge of publicity, promotion, and advertising, and we had to be reasonably good writers. But above all, we had to have a good sense of what makes news, what makes good publicity, good features.

The actual job of putting together the publicity was the province of the New York office, where they had access to the printers, the graphics, and so on. Our job was the basic creative work of getting together all the material—the publicity releases, the photos, the interesting feature stories—into a packet that would go out to the press, coinciding with the release of the picture itself.

The publicity director in Hollywood was responsible for all the contacts that could be handled right there. I remember visits by Henry Luce in the early days of *Time* and *Life,* and people from *Harper's Bazaar* and *Vogue.* I would occasionally get publicity in those magazines, which wasn't easy. We had to develop all those contacts, and I had to plant ideas when I could.

We would also give as much time as we could to the foreign press. They could be very important to us in those days. For example, Garbo's pictures brought in greater returns in the world market than they did in the American market, even though she was very popular in this country.

We would get involved from the time that a property was announced or acquired for production, in anything that was at all newsworthy pertaining to the film.

My entire experience was that of a publicity director. I never had to work for anyone, except those first four or five months at MGM. I started out as the flunky, doing all the odd jobs, like meeting the boats and the trains and doing the little annoying things that no one else wanted to do. That publicity department was in chaos at the time, because the man who had hired me was, within a matter of days, ousted because of his drinking.

Howard Dietz, who succeeded him as advertising manager of MGM, had come in with Goldwyn. When he left the department he left things to me. That was extraordinary because I was just a kid of twenty-two or twenty-three.

A lot of things would have to be done on the coast. I'd have to put them in a memo and get them started. I remember going down to the boat one day to meet an incoming Swedish girl, actually not to meet her so much as meet the director who was bringing her over. His name was Mauritz Stiller, a very outstanding director in Sweden.

Stiller had much the same status in Sweden as D. W. Griffith had in this country. He was the great dean of directors of the really classic films. Well, he discovered a very pretty girl whom he thought had possibilities. He first met her while observing how she did her job in a barber shop in Stockholm. She would lather the faces of the men. He was intrigued by her. I suppose there was a romance, too, but he was many years her senior.

In 1929 Warner's hired me away and brought me out to Hollywood. I had turned down a job at that time, of handling the publicity for Gloria Swanson, for a picture she was to make in Paris. But Charlie Einfeld, the head of publicity at Warner's, took a fancy to me and determined that he was going to get me away from MGM. And I was won over by the idea of going out to Hollywood.

MGM had Howard Strickling out there. Howard was my friend. We had corresponded because we had similar jobs. He would write me about my "girlfriend" (Greta Garbo) and about how, when she needed some time to rest she would say, "*Ay* tink *Ay* go home now." I thought that was a cute line, so I made a beeline for *Photoplay* magazine to see my friend Agnes Smith, who wrote the column called "Cal York." She led off her column that month with that gag, and it started a national fad of saying: "*Ay* tink *Ay* go home now."

At Warner's I had a staff of six that I inherited from the previous publicity director. I remember when I first came out I was a little incensed at the idea of giving Louella Parsons exclusive stories. I thought that was nonsense. We had a round table of publicists in those days. At my very first meeting I came up with the idea that we abolish that policy of giving Parsons exclusives. And, oh boy, what a reaction I got! I didn't realize what a kettle of fish I had jumped into. However, I was a persuasive kid, and they eventually voted it in. So I didn't exactly endear myself to Louella. In fact, she was pretty angry. But later on she and I made up and she had me over to her house and showed me how to fix martinis.

When I worked at Republic I had direct contact with a man named Herbert Yates, who was a vulgarian of the first order. I used to spit on the petunias in his patio behind his office. His damn petunias were always dying, and he wondered why.

Here's a story that illustrates how a publicity man works. Yates called me one day and said, "Autry is kicking over the traces and I'm going to have to show him that he's not the only cowboy that can sing in the saddle. I want you to announce a contest to find a new cowboy. Go ahead, and take your time, because we want to do this right."

I started making my plans, but before I had a chance to get very far he signed a young fellow. He didn't seriously want to replace him, because Autry was very big; but Autry wanted more dough, he wanted a private dressing room, he wanted this and that. So Yates signed a singer from the Sons of the Pioneers by the name of Leonard Slye, a kid who couldn't have been more than twenty-three or twenty-four. He came into my office one day and he said, "Mr. Voight, I'm your new western star."

I said, "My God, Len, you can't be. You can't even ride a horse."

He answered, "I can learn, can't I?"

I said, "Well, you've got to learn. I've got to have a picture of you on a horse. I can't photograph you sitting in a chair." So I called my friend Thad Jones. Thad was a good friend of mine who had a lot of very choice stock out in the Valley, not very far from the studio. I explained the problem and asked Jones to set him up. Well, when the first pictures came in from the still department, oh God, Len looked so scared.

So I called him in and said that he had to do a lot better than this. He was very ambitious and he agreed.

Finally, I got some pictures that really worked, with the horse rearing on his hind legs, and I said, "You look like you were born in the saddle. This is the picture." He just spent hours and hours riding every day until he learned how to do it. That was how Roy Rogers was born.

Then I started doing his official studio biography. It turned out he was from someplace in Ohio. I knew that would never do, so I said to him, "Let's pick out a town with some real western atmosphere." So he picked out Cheyenne. But after several months, word got around that he wasn't from Cheyenne at all and we went back to the Ohio town.

A publicity man always relied on his creative ability, his imagination. You had to think a little bit beyond the facts and embellish them.

Usually there were financial limits for our campaigns. There wasn't much that we'd have to spend money on, unless it was for trips. I was in charge of arranging personal appearances for the stars. They were called junkets in those days; we would take a whole group on a tour. We'd go into cities where a movie might have been set, for example.

There was one occasion when I wanted publicity for a girl named Laura Lee. She was a cute little blonde girl who was brought out from New York to play opposite Joe E. Brown in a film called *Top Speed.* Norman Krasna came up with the damnedest stunt. We were going to get Laura Lee lost off Malibu. She was attending a party at the home of Mervyn LeRoy, the director. In the course of the afternoon, somebody was to walk out on the beach and discover a boat tipped over. They would be looking for Laura because she had left the party, but they would find the empty boat. That would give rise to the terrible possibility that she was lost at sea. Oh, God, what a terrible thing!

This was the plot that we concocted. Unfortunately, Mervyn wouldn't go along with it. He said Warner would kill him if he ever did it. I said that we would have gotten national publicity, calling out the Coast Guard and God knows who else. We were going to spend a week looking for her; then we were going to find her over on one of the Channel Islands off Santa Monica. The navy planes would eventually find her. Her pretty little dress would be all torn from scrambling around, gathering berries and catching rabbits to eat. There she'd be: beautifully set up for pictures. We could have kept this alive for days.

I guess I was a little more controlled than most publicity men, but you had to be on the flamboyant side, and you had to show some color.

One of my most successful stunts involved the staging of a scientific experiment—"The Love Test," we called it. It was 1927 and Greta Garbo and John Gilbert had just made *Flesh and the Devil,* which we were premiering in New York. Down the street a few blocks Paramount was showing *Gentlemen Prefer Blondes*—the original version—at the Rialto Theater. That started the old bean working, and I began the ponder, "Why in hell should gentlemen prefer blondes?" At that time, being a normal young man of twenty-five, I liked them all—blondes, brunettes, and redheads. So I thought about how I might make something of this, since we were always in competition with Paramount anyway.

I went over to my alma mater, Columbia, to see my old psychology professor, Professor Poffenberger. I asked him to cooperate in an experiment with young women watching certain scenes on the screen. I visualized showing four or five minutes of the Garbo-Gilbert movie, culminating in a terrific kiss at the end. I figured any red-blooded American girl would be bound to show some emotion. I decided to do it in an unconventional way; I wouldn't send out any publicity. I literally stole some stationery from the psychology department at Columbia. Poffenberger turned me down and practically threw me out of his office, but he did suggest I enlist the help of a man called Marshton, who was supposed to be a bit nutty. So I went to him and he was very agreeable, except that I had to grease his palm with a hundred dollars.

I got Marshton to agree to meet me at a theater. I had arranged with the man who was the publicity director for Ziegfeld to pick out six of the most glamorous and exciting girls from the various shows that were playing at the time—three blondes and three brunettes.

One blonde and one brunette would be seated side by side while "Professor" Marshton's secretary took their pulse. I had my people tallying the results. A brunette named Beryl Hailey won the contest. She was the hottest of the girls watching the film. Well, it got publicity all over the world! It was a sensation. I counted twenty-two photographers, newsreel photographers, all kinds. Walter Winchell, Frank Sullivan, big names in that kind of column-writing ran it. The *New Yorker* carried about a page on it, which ended with the line that even the press agent—me—was a brunet.

The papers carried strip pictures of the whole series of Gilbert and Garbo clinches which went way across the page—eight-column stuff. I had all of the best love scene pictures in great quantity, so that as the press left the theater they could take some with them. That's what did it. They had art work—tremendous graphics right there. And they had the mimeographed rundown of the winning brunette and the losing blonde. That was creative publicity. Howard Dietz loved it so much that he took credit for it.

When I worked at Columbia Studios, Gower Street was called Poverty Row. That's where Columbia began, and that's where Harry Cohn reigned. He was the meanest, nastiest, dirtiest s.o.b. that you could ever imagine. If they had ever done a picture about him it would never have passed the censor. But he and I were pals; we got along. I was the only one who could talk back to him. He'd call me a son-of-a-bitch and I'd call him a son-of-a-bitch.

I remember Cohn once sent me down to Palm Springs one day with a can of film, still unreleased, called *Lady for a Day,*

Capra's last picture. I arranged for it to be shown to Constance Bennett, a bitch if there ever was one. After she saw it she said, "Well, Mr. Capra is certainly a good director for old ladies, but he wouldn't work for me." And she turned down the lead in *It Happened One Night!* This was the part that made Claudette Colbert a star. The picture won more Academy Awards than any picture up to that time.

The choice of Gable was made in desperation. Mayer decided we could have him since he wasn't so hot then, and he was available. Colbert came about through a search for every likely woman star; they had all turned down the part. I was on the set from the very first day. Then I'd sit in the dining room and listen to Bob Riskin, the writer, working with Capra.

I was so enchanted by that picture. I really was on the set every day. That wasn't customary because I had a lot of work to do; but I couldn't miss a scene, I was so delighted by it.

I would always have to battle at the end of a picture to get time to take advertising stills. I was very serious about this. I would have sketches made of the kind of poses I wanted. I would try to sex the picture up and get a lot of very choice love scenes, but I had to battle to get the actors' time. I was always left at the short end because they would always walk out on me. But this time I was determined to get them. So, one Saturday afternoon, after the picture *Twentieth Century* ended, Carole Lombard and John Barrymore came in looking haggard. It had been a pretty tough picture, but they had finished.

Barrymore yelled at me, "Voight, you son-of-a-bitch, we're tired. We're not going to waste any time around here. We'll give you half an hour."

I thought, "By God, we could hardly get warmed up in half an hour." I had Irving Lipman, then a very fine still man, on tap. I had spent the morning in the prop room getting a beautiful bear rug, a Victrola, and an incense burner. Everything was ready for hot scenes. We were set up in a little intimate gallery at Columbia. Finally, I got them into the room with some liquor nearby, where they would be sure to see it. Well, they went straight for the booze. After a while I heard the loudest shrieks, and Jack would say, "Carole, you have the most beautiful . . ." and she would laugh uproariously. They were having a hell of a time.

Within two or three hours the call came: "Voight, we need more refreshments." So I had to go out for another bottle of Pinch, and that went on all afternoon. Toward the end of the day I went over to see what was happening. When I finally got in, the place was a mess and they were both terribly drunk. I could see that we couldn't take any more pictures.

I could hardly sleep that night, worrying about the pictures. But when Irving spread out the proofs, I thought, "Oh, Irving, God bless you. These are the best pictures you've ever taken. These are going to sell this picture in a big way." I knew we'd get a great campaign out of them.

Then I noticed a strange thing. One tray of proofs looked like they had been shot through a gunny-sack filter. I asked Irving what happened. He said, "Hubert, I cannot tell a lie. That's when *I* got drunk."

March 1986
Palo Alto

Editors' Note: Hubert Voight died in October 1988.

CAREER HIGHLIGHTS

1925–1929   Publicity Manager, MGM, New York

1930–1932   Publicity Director, Warner Brothers/First National
Studios

1933–1944   Publicity Director, Columbia
Publicity Director, Universal
Publicity Director, Republic
Publicity Director, Wald-Krasna Productions

1944   Publicity Director, Fourth War Loan

1948   Publicity Director, Enterprise

FILMOGRAPHY (Top Promotion Campaigns)

1925   *The Big Parade* (with John Gilbert and Renée Adorée,
dir. King Vidor, MGM)

1926   *Flesh and the Devil* (with Greta Garbo and John
Gilbert, dir. Clarence Brown, MGM)

1929   *Broadway Melody* (with Bessie Love and Charles King,
dir. Harry Beaumont, MGM)

1930   *Little Caesar* (with Edward G. Robinson and Douglas
Fairbanks, Jr., dir. Mervyn Le Roy, Warner Bros.)

1931   *The Public Enemy* (with Jimmy Cagney and Jean Harlow, dir. William Wellman, Warner Bros.)

1934   *It Happened One Night* (with Clark Gable and Clau-
dette Colbert, dir. Frank Capra, Columbia)
Twentieth Century (with John Barrymore and Carole
Lombard, dir. Howard Hawks, Columbia)

1936 *Three Smart Girls* (with Deanna Durbin, dir. Henry Koster, Universal)

    My Man Godfrey (with Carole Lombard and William Powell, dir. Gregory La Cava, Universal)

1942 *The Pride of the Yankees* (with Gary Cooper and Teresa Wright, dir. Sam Wood, RKO)

1948 *Arch of Triumph* (with Ingrid Bergman and Charles Boyer, dir. Lewis Milestone, United Artists)

JULES GREEN

Booker

Jules Green cut his teeth on the movie business when he took tickets and ran the equipment at his father's theater. In his early twenties he became a theater manager and then a booker for theaters in the Pennsylvania area. Later, he moved to television, where he produced "The Steve Allen Show," the forerunner of "The Tonight Show."

He is now in his late seventies—slim, bearded, and full of nervous energy. Very much a "last angry man," he is passionate about his likes and dislikes. Several years ago he was forced to retire from his job as an executive producer of network television programming for a major New York advertising agency, and he is still mad as hell about it. He is married to Nancy Green.

I started way back, when my father had his first theater, and I was seven years old. I was around there all the time, weekends and after school, until my father died and my mother sold it. I did everything. I sold tickets, took tickets, all that kind of stuff.

My first actual job in the movies was as a utility manager of the Shumway Theater—owned by Warner Brothers—on the Pitt *[University of Pittsburgh]* campus. It had about twelve hundred seats and there, too, I did everything. I went to work at ten o'clock in the morning, took two hours off for dinner, came back and worked till midnight, six days a week. I was a doorman, a ticket-taker; I typed up the box office receipts; I ran the theater when the manager was off. I'd make up the schedules of when the

Jules Green, booker, in the 1940s.

pictures were supposed to play; I worked as an usher, swept up the theater, took chewing gum off the seats, painted the floors, cleaned the restrooms.

In 1939 I took a leave of absence and went out to Hollywood with letters of introduction from our zone manager in Pittsburgh to Jack Warner and Nat Blumberg, who was then head of Universal Pictures. I got the leave because they were about to give me a job as a booker.

The zone manager was very understanding and he liked me very much. I told him I wanted to be a producer, and I asked if he could help me. So when he gave me the leave he said, "I won't fill the booker job until you tell me that you're all set."

I went out to the Warner's studio and instead of seeing Jack Warner as I expected, I was sent to a guy by the name of Charles

Einfeld. He was in charge of all publicity and public relations for Warner Brothers. I walked into Einfeld's office cold.

We talked, and he said it was very difficult out there at that time. He would maybe try to get me a job as an usher in a Warner theater, the theater on Hollywood Boulevard. As he talked, I understood he didn't know what the hell I was there for. I guess I was about twenty-five years old at the time, and I was incensed that this guy was going to get me a job maybe as an usher or ticket-taker when I had a much better job on hold as a booker and buyer for forty-nine theaters. At which point I got very angry and swore at him and walked out.

The next thing I know, I hear these footsteps running after me and Einfeld grabs me and he says, "Come back into my office. You sit down. I've never run up against anybody like you. You got more guts than any young man I know. You're going to become my personal property. I am going to look after you; you're going to work for me." Charles Einfeld was considered really the fifth Warner brother—that's how high he was in the organization. He asked me, "Do you have any money?"

I said, "Sure, I have money. You don't come out here and plan to go to work if you don't have any money."

He said, "Well, then, why don't you take a vacation, because I'm going to New York for two weeks."

I said, "I don't want to take a vacation. I want to go to work. Get me on a set. Get me a pushbroom. I want to learn everybody's job, and the way to learn is to start on the set and clean up and see whatever's going on, and then, when I know everybody's job, I'll know I'm a producer."

"I don't think I can do that for you on account of all the union regulations, but you can call me back and I'll find out," he told me. "Here's my private home phone number. Call me when I get back."

And then he picks up the phone and calls a fellow by the name of Bob Taplinger, his assistant, and he says, "There's a young man up here by the name of Jules Green. I want you to pick him up and send him to the studio with a personal guide. I want you to take him into lunch at the Green Room and introduce him to everybody you can, and send him back to his apartment in a car."

Wowie, wow!

The following day I call Einfeld back and he says he can't get me on a set but not to worry about it, that I should go out and enjoy myself and call him again in two weeks. So, during that time I wrote letters to everybody I knew. But by the time Charlie Einfeld returned, Germany had gone into Poland, and that was the end of my chances. Since about 55 percent of all distribution monies came from abroad, the studios were firing everybody.

I stayed in California another few months, and everywhere I went everybody fell in love with me. I had the most sensational, wonderful interviews. I don't even think they were really con Hollywood interviews; I think I was really making an impression on people because they really understood where I came from. Theaters were really very, very important then. That's where the people put down their money and bought tickets.

I went to Universal and was treated extremely well. I had just sent letters off cold to people at MGM and Fox, and got to see them, based on my letters. But everybody I saw had the same problem. At the end of almost every conversation they would say, "You really should get Warner Brothers to give you the job. After all, you've worked for them. We don't have anything; we're firing people." So I had to go back home to Pittsburgh.

One day, several years later, out of the blue I get a phone call from Charles Einfeld. By then he had left Warner Brothers and formed his own company called Enterprise Pictures. He'd made a picture called *Body and Soul* with John Garfield—a tremendous success—and he was involved in making *Arc de Triomphe* with Ingrid Bergman and Charles Boyer. He asked, "Can you come out? Can you find any time?" I went straight out to the coast. At the studio he said, "I have a job for you."

"Great, when do I start producing?" I asked.

He said, "It's not as a producer. It's as a special representative for me." Because I knew distribution work, he wanted me to make sure that the deals were set properly in the motion picture houses.

I told him, "You know that's not what I want." But he offered me $550 a week, and since I was then making $75 I said, "I'll think about it." A couple of days later I went to the studio to tell him I would take the job. I figured, "If I take the job, maybe I could eventually wind up being a producer." If I could just get in. When I showed up for work, the gates were padlocked. They were bankrupt.

A booker's job is not that simple. The word itself means you book pictures into movie houses, but in order to do that you have to own the pictures, and then you have to make a deal for them. You have to agree with the distributor on when they're going to play. I was booking before and after divorcement, during the period that studios owned theaters and after, when they had to give them up. Once divorcement came in, anybody could bid for any picture.

I saw virtually every picture that was ever made. We played many pictures before they ever opened up in New York. I'd see a picture every day, and two on Tuesdays and Thursdays. So I developed instinct, and used it booking pictures from 1936 to 1947. A good booker needed that strong instinct.

Nobody booked pictures better than I did. I would book pictures the way you would draw a picture or a painting—creatively. I was very, very original. I wasn't interested in what other people did. I did things that no one else ever did, and they worked.

The first time I ever went in to see Harry Feinstein to get bookings, I gave him mine and he just looked at me. The second time I went in he did it again. After that he said to me, "As soon as I can I'm bringing you in to work for me."

You see, virtually everything then was double bill, and I just had a completely different approach to putting together combinations of pictures. Here's an example of a little thing that I did on "bank nights" (give-away nights). Most bookers would take the second-run movie, which was an A or B, then put in a slough picture—a small, nothing kind of picture, not even a B or C—or a western. I wouldn't do that. Instead, I always put in an old movie. I would even repeat some of the old favorites, and eventually I would put together two old movies. This practice was soon picked up all through the territory because it did so well. My feeling was that people would have more interest in seeing two good old movies than two pieces of junk. Of course I would then have to trade it off with the distributor, because you'd have a contract to play off his product.

I'd pair a comedy with a drama, or a comedy with an action picture, and accumulate a lot of names, maybe half a dozen. Because I was putting together strong combinations, I went downtown one day and announced to my boss, "I'm going to raise my prices Saturday and Sunday by a nickel." This caused an uproar because nobody had ever charged twenty-five cents before.

The trick was to give them lots for their money. When I became a booker and a buyer I broke all our agreements for second- and third-run newsreels and for short subjects. I got rid of most of them. The guys at Film Row all wanted to kill me. But I convinced everybody we didn't need them, that I'd only put in a seven- or eight-minute short subject if I needed to fill out the time, or if the manager needed to make a schedule. Because of the union agreements, you opened up at a certain time and you closed at a certain time, and if you went overtime you paid for it. Who needed second- and third-run newsreels? They were absolutely meaningless, like two-week-old newspapers. Only in the first-run situations were they hot.

I just went ahead about my own business day after day. I did everybody's job, to learn the business. I did it in the theater; I did it in the booking and buying department, with newsreels, short subjects, working as Harry Feinstein's secretary when I didn't have other things to do, when somebody would come in from New York to clear up product which hadn't been played off.

A word about clearing up the product. As a booker, you have a commitment to play a certain number of pictures, depending on the deals. If you bought, say, fifteen or twenty pictures, and time goes on and you haven't played them off, the managers want to clear them up and get them off the books. So when the managers came you'd make trades, reduce prices, anything to get rid of them and get your quota played.

Division managers in distribution would come east from California. They didn't bother me; in fact I was so strong-willed I would often refuse to book Warner Brothers pictures. So when the Eastern Division manager of distribution for Warner Brothers came to New York to get product placed, my boss would make me take the day off. I thought many of Warner's pictures were no good at all, and I had already bought superior pictures for less money. I was a terror.

In those days, there was always a flagship house. The A-house in Pittsburgh was the Stanley, which Harry Feinstein always booked. We had a pooling agreement with Loew's (which was part of MGM) and the Loew's Penn played the slough picture, but with a presentation. There was live entertainment—a stage show—and so it was called a presentation house.

We found the stage shows all over, but they were mostly booked out of New York. I would book stuff on my own, out of Pittsburgh, from an agent there. The shows would go to Greensburgh and Johnstown, but they never played at the Stanley

Theater. That was the cream; that was the best. Thirty-seven hundred seats.

We would hold over pictures every now and then. That was almost academic downtown, whether to hold them over or not. When I put pictures together I used to call them "bouquets." The funny thing was, whenever business was bad the zone managers would blame the bookers, as though they made the pictures.

At one point, a very bright man by the name of Moe Silver was our zone manager. A real bulldog. Very hard-working; very, very good zone manager. I'll never forget the day Silver and the four district managers came in. We were all sitting and talking, and all of a sudden Moe Silver said to me, "Let me have your books."

I asked, "Why, business bad on account of my work?"

"Let me have your books. I want to look at your bookings," he said.

I said, "Mr. Silver, please, do me a favor. Don't take my books. You mustn't touch my bookings, because if you pull one picture out of any one of these situations the whole thing is going to fall apart."

At this point my boss looks over at me and says, "Jules, give him the books, will you please?" So I did. He looked, he worked, he must have spent thirty minutes going over those books.

Once more I repeated, "Don't touch it, Mr. Silver."

That book came flying across the room at me, and Silver says, "You little son-of-a-bitch, you know, you're right."

The Stanley had all the Warner product, all the MGM product, and some Paramount. Other houses had Columbia, Universal, Fox, RKO. In the neighborhoods, the product from all the companies, regardless of where they had played downtown, were fed into all the neighborhood houses. I had houses all the way from Pittsburgh up to State College. There'd be towns like Johnstown and Greensburgh which would all have their first-, second-, and third-run houses. We also had houses in West Virginia. I had half the territory.

Deciding how long the pictures had to play wasn't too hard. In the theaters that were out in the territory, a picture could maybe play five days to a week, so you'd usually open it up on Friday. It would be Friday, Saturday, Sunday, Monday, with a hold on it. You would hold the print. The receipts were called in every night, and so you would tell them to hold it or pull it. You just called the exchange and made sure that the print of the next picture was up there, that was all.

It was also a question of how much product you had. You'd make sure you had your prints both ways so you could hold a picture over a day or let it go a day early. We were fairly flexible.

We had all this in a sort of big ledger. There would be so many theaters on this sheet, with all the deals: which pictures you bought and for how much, the A's, the B's, certain percentages. Some were on percentages, some were flat buys.

If it was a 40 percent picture, you got 40 percent of every dollar that came into the box office. Before divorcement you bought a studio's output, whatever it was. Afterwards there was no longer booking in blocks, so you were able to buy as you saw fit. But before, you either bought it all or you bought a part and shared it with somebody.

If you saw something you hated you'd slough it off—you'd put it in bad playing time, especially if it was on a percentage basis. You'd play it Monday and Tuesday and Wednesday. Your biggest business was Saturday and Sunday, so you wanted to get your best pictures into that best playing time.

On the other hand, the trick was being able to manipulate when you showed which pictures. If you could take a percentage picture and keep it out of A playing time, substitute a good picture which you'd maybe paid only a flat $150 for, you could play it over the weekend and do $1,000 worth of business, and you were only out that $150. Whereas if you had a picture that cost 40 percent, you'd be paying $400 in film rentals.

I was an agent with Jimmy Saphier for about five years, but I was always more interested in the creative end. When I got Steve Allen and got into television, I was finally producing. I tried to do it in the movies, got properties like André Gide's *Les Caves du Vatican*—which I'm still working on—and Howard Fast's *Citizen Tom Paine,* and had I don't know how many other of my own ideas. But I've always been accused of one thing, the most terrible accusation in the world—and that is, my taste is too good!

January 1984
New York

BIBLIOGRAPHY

Anger, Kenneth. *Hollywood Babylon.* New York: Dell Publishing Co., 1981.

Baker, Fred, and Ross Firestone, eds. *Movie People: At Work in the Business of Film.* New York: Douglas Book Corporation, 1972.

Balio, Tino, ed. *The American Film Industry.* Madison: University of Wisconsin Press, 1977.

Behlmer, Rudy, ed. *Memo from David O. Selznick.* New York: Grove Press, 1981.

Brooks, Louise. *Lulu in Hollywood.* New York: Alfred A. Knopf, 1982.

Brosnan, John. *Movie Magic: The Story of Special Effects in the Cinema.* New York: New American Library, 1976.

Brownlow, Kevin. *Hollywood: The Pioneers.* New York: Alfred A. Knopf, 1979.

———. *The Parade's Gone By.* New York: Ballantine Books, 1969.

Cahn, Sammy. *I Should Care: The Sammy Cahn Story.* New York: Arbor House, 1974.

Cole, Lester. *Hollywood Red: The Autobiography of Lester Cole.* Palo Alto: Ramparts Press, 1981.

Dunn, Linwood C., and George E. Turner, eds. *The ASC Treasury of Visual Effects.* Hollywood: American Society of Cinematographers, 1983.

Edwards, Anne. *Shadow of a Lion.* New York: Coward, McCann, Geoghegan, 1971.

Farber, Stephen, and Marc Green. *Hollywood Dynasties.* New York: Delilah Communications, 1984.

Friedrich, Otto. *City of Nets: A Portrait of Hollywood in the 1940's.* New York: Harper and Row, 1986.

Green, Stanley. *Encyclopedia of the Musical Film.* New York: Oxford University Press, 1981.

Griffith, Richard, and Arthur Mayer. *The Movies.* New York: Simon and Schuster, 1970.

Halliwell, Leslie, ed. *Halliwell's Filmgoer's Companion.* 8th ed. New York: Charles Scribner's Sons, 1984.

———. *Halliwell's Film Guide.* 3d ed. New York: Charles Scribner's Sons, 1984.

International Motion Picture Almanac. New York: Quigley Publishing Co., 1978.

Katz, Ephraim. *The Film Encyclopedia.* New York: Thomas Crowell Publishers, 1979.

Kauffmann, Stanley. *A World on Film.* New York: Harper and Row, 1966.

Kindern, Gorham. *The American Movie Industry.* Carbondale, Ill.: Southern Illinois University Press, 1982.

Klotman, Phyllis Rauch. *Frame by Frame: A Black Filmography.* Bloomington: Indiana University Press, 1979.

Kobal, John. *People Will Talk.* New York: Alfred A. Knopf, 1986.

Koury, Phil A. *Yes, Mr. deMille.* New York: G. P. Putnam's Sons, 1959.

Langman, Larry. *A Guide to American Screenwriters: The Sound Era, 1929–82.* Vol. 1. New York: Garland Publishing, 1984.

Leese, Elizabeth. *Costume Design in the Movies.* New York: Frederick Ungar Publishing Co., 1978.

LeRoy, Mervyn. *Take One.* New York: Hawthorne Books, 1974.

Leyda, Jay, ed. *Filmmakers Speak: Voices of Film Experience.* New York: Da Capo Press, 1977.

Macgowan, Kenneth. *Behind the Screen: The History and Techniques of the Motion Picture.* New York: Dell Publishing Co., 1965.

Maltin, Leonard. *Behind the Camera: The Cinematographer's Art.* New York: New American Library, 1971.

McBride, Joseph, ed. *Filmmakers on Filmmaking.* 2 vols. Los Angeles: J. P. Tarcher, 1983.

McGilligan, Pat, ed. *Backstory: Interviews with Screenwriters of Hollywood's Golden Age.* Berkeley and Los Angeles: University of California Press, 1986.

Mordden, Ethan. *The Hollywood Musical.* New York: St. Martin's Press, 1981.

Navasky, Victor. *Naming Names.* New York: Viking Press, 1980.

Powdermaker, Hortense. *Hollywood, the Dream Factory.* Boston: Little, Brown and Co., 1950.

Rosenblum, Ralph, and Robert Karen. *When the Shooting Stops: The Cutting Begins.* New York: Viking Press, 1979.

Schatz, Thomas. *The Genius of the System.* New York: Pantheon Books, 1988.

Schulberg, Budd. *Moving Pictures: Memories of a Hollywood Prince.* New York: Stein and Day, 1981.

Schwartz, Nancy Lynn, and Sheila Schwartz. *The Hollywood Writers' Wars.* New York: Alfred A. Knopf, 1982.

Selznick, Irene Mayer. *A Private View.* New York: Alfred A. Knopf, 1983.

Shale, Richard. *Academy Awards.* New York: Frederick Ungar Publishing Co., 1982.

Smith, John M., and Tim Cawkwell, eds. *The World Encyclopedia of the Film.* New York: Galahad Books, 1972.

Spoto, Donald. *The Dark Side of Genius: The Life of Alfred Hitchcock.* New York: Ballantine Books, 1983.

Stenn, David. *Clara Bow: Runnin' Wild.* New York: Doubleday, 1988.

Taylor, Deems, Marcelene Peterson, and Bryant Hale. *A Pictorial History of the Movies.* New York: Simon and Schuster, 1943.

Taylor, John Russell, and Arthur Jackson. *The Hollywood Musical.* New York: McGraw Hill Book Co., 1971.

Walker, Joseph, and Juanita Walker. *The Light on Her Face.* Hollywood: American Society of Cinematographers, 1984.

Withers, Robert S. *Introduction to Film.* New York: Barnes and Noble Books, 1983.

Who's Who in America. 43d ed. Chicago: Marquis Who's Who, 1984.

Woll, Allen L. *Songs from Hollywood Musical Comedies, 1927 to the Present: A Dictionary.* New York: Garland Publishing, 1976.

GLOSSARY

Answer Print The first print combining sound and picture; used to make any necessary adjustments before striking final release prints.

Arc Light High-intensity lamp.

Backlight Light source behind object to be filmed.

Best Boy Assists the key grip in assigning tasks and managing the work of other grips.

Bipack Printing A method for making a composite print by melding images from two separate color negatives.

Blue Screen Literally a blue-screen background that is filtered out so that only the image of a person or object placed in the foreground is recorded on film, to be superimposed onto a different background.

Boom A maneuverable metal arm on which a microphone or camera is mounted.

Boom Mike Microphone suspended from a boom above the area included in the frame.

Broad Light that illuminates a large or "broad" area.

B-movie A feature-length movie produced in the 1930s, 1940s, and 1950s to fill the second spot on a double bill. They were made quickly and inexpensively. Today "B-movie" refers to a low-budget exploitation film.

Call Sheet A schedule of the day's shooting, advising actors and crew where and when to report for work.

Call Steward Takes calls for jobs for union members.

Changing Bag A lightproof bag used for loading and unloading film magazines in daylight. The film-loader inserts his hands and arms into the bag through tight, elasticized sleeves.

Chroma-key A method for filtering out a single color during printing. Often used to eliminate the color blue in blue-screen compositing.

Crab Dolly A platform on wheels, with mounts for a camera and other equipment, capable of being moved in any direction.

Cutter Cuts and splices prints or negatives, often an assistant editor.

C-movie Even quicker and cheaper than a B-movie.

Divorcement Consequence of a landmark federal court decision reached in 1948 that prohibited studios from owning movie theaters. By the early 1950s the separation had been completed and block booking, the practice of studios forcing exhibitors to take their mediocre low-budget films—sight unseen—in order to get prestige movies, came to an end.

Dolly Track Track laid on uneven surface to permit smooth movement of the dolly on which the camera is mounted.

Extra An actor who has no lines to speak, often part of a crowd scene.

Film Noir A genre named by French movie critics, referring to a film of dark visual and emotional character, often cynical and always pessimistic.

Flag A small black square mounted on a stand, used to keep direct light out of the lens.

f-stop A number derived from the ratio of the diameter of the aperture to the focal length of the lens. The lower the f-stop, the greater the amount of light that will pass through the aperture at any given shutter speed.

Gaffer Sets up and aims lights at the instruction of the lighting director or cinematographer.

Gobo   A large opaque screen used to keep direct light out of the camera lens.

Grille   A piece of wood used to cast shadows or reduce light (sometimes called a "kook").

Grip   Sets up and pushes the dolly for the camera operator, and does much of the unskilled work on the set.

Internegative and Interpositive
An internegative is a negative made directly from color reversal film. An interpositive made from the internegative is then used to produce duplicate negatives.

Key Light   The dominant light used in a scene, often determining its mood.

Lap Dissolve   A technique that melds one scene into another, used to indicate a change of time or place.

Loop   A postproduction rerecording of dialogue without background noise. Lip movements must match original film.

Matte   An opaque device used in a camera or printing gate to obscure a selected area of a scene during exposure; used in trick photography.

Night Penalty   Overtime pay for working at night.

Optical Printer   A machine containing a camera that photographs sections of a projected film, used to create special effects.

Page-turn   A special effect in which a scene is changed as if it were a page turning; an alternative to the lap dissolve.

Pan   The lateral motion of a stationary camera pivoting on its axis.

Per Diem   Pay for daily expenses (when on location, for example).

Process (Background) Shot
Filming an actor or object in front of a rear-screen projection.

Screen Roll-up   An optical effect in which one scene rolls up, revealing the next.

Scrim   A translucent screen used to diffuse or soften light.

Second Unit   A separate and self-contained production unit assigned to film scenes that do not require the presence of the director or main members of the cast.

Second Unit Director   Often the assistant director, who is especially skilled at shooting in the same style as the director, so his scenes blend effortlessly into those shot by the director.

Shooting Script   The final version of a screenplay, containing both dialogue and camera instructions for the director's use.

Slate   A small, hinged blackboard with a clacker, used to mark the scene and take numbers, and to mark the start of sound; usually used at the beginning of each take.

Snoot   An opaque, cone-shaped device attached to a lamp to narrowly direct the light.

Source Light   Place from which dominant light originates.

Story Editor   Person in charge of finding new properties for a studio. Employs readers, who write synopses and evaluations of material that might be suitable for a film.

Studio System   The old repertory system for making films, from concept to completion, in which studio managers assigned all the necessary personnel from a pool of permanent employees. The system died out when divorcement came in, and was dealt the final blow with the advent of television.

Wipe   A special effect in which one scene appears to wipe away the scene that came before it.